Bigger than Me

By

Peter Henderson

For JJ, Jess, Tom and Rex

The Rory Peck Trust

The RPT does incredible work for courageous freelance journalists who bring us stories from some of the world's most challenging places. I am honoured to be able to donate all proceeds from this book to support their safety and wellbeing through the Trust. I've been lucky to survive my years of international news gathering, and in my small way I would like to give something back to help my colleagues who are less fortunate.

Copyright © 2020 Peter Henderson

All rights reserved. This book or any portion thereof may not be reproduced or used in any manner whatsoever without the express written permission of the publisher except for the use of brief quotations in a book review.

First Printing, 2020

Contents

Prologue 1

Chapter One 13

Chapter Two 25

Chapter Three 37

Chapter Four 48

Chapter Five 55

Chapter Six 75

Chapter Seven 92

Chapter Eight 104

Chapter Nine 119

Chapter Ten 135

Chapter Eleven 147

Chapter Twelve 165

Chapter Thirteen 174

Chapter Fourteen 194

Chapter Fifteen 212

Chapter Sixteen 229

Chapter Seventeen 249

Chapter Eighteen 266

Chapter Nineteen..286

Chapter Twenty..307

Chapter Twenty-One 320

Chapter Twenty-Two 344

Chapter Twenty-Three...355

Chapter Twenty-Four 367

Chapter Twenty-Five 377

Prologue

MY PATERNAL GRANDMOTHER once told me I have a powerful Guardian Angel. He is an Irishman, she said, and always stands behind me. If I looked carefully over my shoulder, I could see him.

I never did see him, but what was stranger to me as a ten-year-old was that he is an Irishman. My grandmother was a thoroughbred Scot, with a Celtic accent sharp enough to slice haggis. Living in Africa had not dulled her "ochs" and "ayes". So why would I have an Irishman on watch?

This anomaly was never fully explained, but I suppose it had something to do with the fact that my great-grandfather came from Armagh in Northern Ireland. Be that as it may, I was just happy to bask in the knowledge that I had a solid sentinel somewhere up there watching my back.

But on Sunday 8 May, 1983, on the stroke of four p.m., I could have been forgiven for thinking that my Guardian Angel was a myth. Or at the very least, sleeping on the job.

I was a budding TV cameraman, just twenty-one years old and had recently left the South African army after an enforced stint on the increasingly hostile battlefield bordering Namibia and Angola. To get some rest and recreation, I decided to take up an army friend's offer of filming a just-born litter of lion cubs on his family's game ranch.

This was a great opportunity, not just to go roaming in the bush, but with the added bonus of getting some vivid wildlife footage to sell to the TV networks.

The ranch is close on five-hours drive north of Johannesburg and a premier Big Five reserve. As we arrived we were greeted by some scimitar-horned rhino, ungainly yet graceful giraffe, and herds of antelope. It was a spectacular day and I was getting fabulous video footage.

The highlight was to be later that afternoon filming the lion cubs. With my girlfriend at the time and Willie, a hefty South African game ranger, we jumped into an open Land Rover and drove off to the big cats' enclosure.

There were three cubs, cuddly, cute, and seemingly as harmless as fluffy toys. I started filming, careful not to get too close. These cubs may be as playful as kittens, but they were still wild animals, even though to some extent habituated to humans.

As anyone who has shot video footage will know, looking through a camera lens induces tunnel vision. The focus is all-consuming. I was concentrating solely on getting the best pictures possible, oblivious of all else around me.

Suddenly I heard a noise, something between a bang and a crunch, and felt this extraordinarily powerful force seize my right hand. Then my arm was yanked to one side like a chicken bone and the camera went flying.

With the camera gone, I could now see clearly. I reeled back in horror. There, just two feet away, was a fully-grown, extremely angry lioness chewing the end of my right arm. Her canine teeth, the size of yellow daggers, had pierced through my wrist, while the front incisors had bitten off my index finger. I could feel my knuckles crunching. My bones were cracking like matchwood. The pain was excruciating.

I heard loud screaming and wondered where all the commotion was coming from. To my astonishment, I realised it was me. I was yelling at the top of my lungs but was so suspended in shock and dread that I couldn't grasp that this nightmare was actually happening.

My girlfriend had my left arm and Willie, the brawny game ranger, grabbed me around my waist trying to pull me away from the monster cat. This was a tug of war we could not win. A human, even one as powerful as Willie, is a baby compared to the strength of a lion. And this one was yanking me with her teeth, shaking her head violently from side to side while dragging me away.

We strained hopelessly against this unimaginable force of nature for several seconds. It seemed much longer, of course, but all I could grasp at the time was that I was being eaten alive.

Then there was this fantastic release — a whoosh of euphoria. The lioness suddenly let go and all three of us tumbled in a heap.

To this day, I don't know why the lioness released me. Maybe she was like a cat playing with a mouse and wanted to get a better grip. Maybe she'd had enough. She certainly didn't see me as dinner. She had not attacked because she was hungry. She had done so because she felt her cubs were threatened. She was doing her job as a mother.

We scrambled off the ground, retreating rapidly. I looked at my friends who had fought to free me. To their eternal credit, neither had run. They had come to my aid with extreme courage.

But now that the lioness had released me, they weren't being very helpful. In fact, the exact opposite. Both were retching noisily on the ground. I couldn't blame them as my mangled hand looked as though it had been through a meat grinder.

My finger was hanging from my hand connected by long white tendons. I pushed the finger back into the hole in my hand and wrapped the tendons around it making a tight fist. I was still in a daze, thinking these things don't happen to me.

Then reality hit me, sharp and brutal. It *was* happening to me. My survival instinct, honed after spending most of the past 12 months in a war zone, kicked in. I knew from experience that the power of positive thinking and determination is absolutely vital in any life-or-death situation. Positive thinking may be a lifestyle guru's cliché, but a key rule of survival is that if you don't believe you are going to be OK, it's highly likely that you won't.

Even so, things looked pretty bleak. I needed to get help fast. There was a huge risk of bleeding to death and I was kilometres away from medical facilities.

We drove back to the homestead. By now everyone knew what had happened and a well-intentioned lady ran out with a tumbler of brandy for 'medicinal purposes'.

I shook my head, saying that if I had any brandy I would almost certainly bleed to death as the alcohol would thin my blood. And if I needed an operation, which I quite clearly did, a doctor wouldn't be able to put me under anaesthetic.

The nearest medical facility, which was more of a basic clinic than a hospital, was a good four hours' drive away. So we got into an old Mercedes Benz and headed out at speed through the Bushveld.[1] I was in the back seat, hyperventilating, woozy and weak, with every bump jarring my crushed hand.

Eventually we arrived at the clinic where a sympathetic nurse bandaged me up and put my severed finger in ice. Even though I was still in shock, the pain was unbearable. I needed some industrial strength painkillers to endure it.

Regretfully, the nurse shook her head. Only a doctor could dispense drugs, and there weren't any on duty at the clinic that Sunday. All she could give me was a couple of aspirin. Hugely disappointed, but with a new bandage and an over-the-counter headache pill, we set off for another three-hour drive to a hospital in Pretoria.

My friends assured me that when we got to Pretoria everything would be fine. I would soon have the best doctors and the finest medical care in the country. That thought kept me going.

Through a haze of agony and terror, I watched the road signs counting down the kilometres to Pretoria; from eighty

---

[1] Vast woodland in southern Africa, populated with acacia and baobab trees, thorn bushes, and tall grasses. Not the ideal place for a medical emergency.

to sixty to thirty until we finally arrived at the outskirts of the country's administrative capital.

As we pulled into the Accident and Emergency entrance, my relief was absolute. Help at last.

I was rushed into theatre, given a pre-med and the anaesthetist inserted a drip in my arm as the surgeon walked in.

He started taking off the bandage. However, he did so without using saline solution or ointment. He just ripped it off, exposing the nerve ends. Red-hot coals of pain shot up my arm.

"Hey, cool it chappie. That's really sore," I said through gritted teeth.

He stopped and looked at me. I could see he was angry.

"Who's your 'chappie'? I'm a doctor!"

Yikes, we're in trouble here.

He got the bandage off, studied my mangled hand, then said he was going to amputate it.

I was stunned. "I beg your pardon?"

"I'm going to amputate your hand two inches above the wrist."

This was the worst possible news imaginable. I had not for a moment thought I was going to lose my hand. As a 21-year-old cameraman the idea of having no hand — something I obviously needed for my job — was devastating.

"Do you think that's necessary?" I asked.

He shrugged impatiently. "I have been a doctor for twenty-six years. I know what I'm talking about. You have a multiple crush injury with infection. Gangrene has already set it. In order to save the rest of your arm, amputation is absolutely necessary."

He was adamant: my hand had to go.

"Is there anyone else I can talk to? Get a second opinion? Amputation is a pretty drastic solution."

"I know what I'm talking about. I'm a doctor. I'm going to cut your hand off. But don't worry. You can go home in two or three days."

I stressed again that I wanted a second opinion. He said he was the only available surgeon in the building and his opinion was the right one. I could take it or leave it.

"In that case," I said, "I'm leaving."

I pulled the drip out of my arm, got off the table and left the operating theatre with my bare bottom hanging out of my theatre gown. I walked down the corridor to the nurse at reception and asked if I could phone my parents in Johannesburg.

To my dismay, she refused point blank. There was no way she would allow me to use the hospital phone.

I was stunned. First they wanted to chop of my hand — now they wouldn't even let me make a call.

I continued walking down the corridor, dripping blood along the floor in my efforts to try and find a public phone box.

I soon found one, but the problem was I had no money to dial out. I stood there, stupefied, when out of the blue, a true Florence Nightingale arrived and quietly slid a few coins into the slot. I don't think she will ever know how much that simple gesture meant to me.

I dialled my parents, and luckily my elder brother Stewart happened to be home and answered. At the sound of his voice, I burst into tears. At last, someone whom I could relate to and who would understand what I was going through.

"Stewart, I've been eaten by a lion," I half-spoke, half-sobbed.

He was fantastic. Within an hour he had dispatched a private ambulance while his girlfriend, a nurse, said she would have the best doctors in the city ready when I arrived at the Johannesburg General Hospital.

However, I had been promised the best doctors when I arrived at Pretoria earlier that night, so was sceptical.

This time it could not have been more different. There were actually seventeen doctors waiting.

I didn't know it at the time but the reason for this VIP treatment was due to the rare nature of my injury, which Stewart's girlfriend had stressed when phoning her contacts.

The Johannesburg General is also a training hospital and the professor of microsurgery summoned his entire fifth-year medical class late on a Sunday to come and witness surgery on a lion bite. It was something most of them would probably never experience again. Perhaps if I had been in a motorbike accident I wouldn't have had the same amount of attention.

I was first X-rayed, which seems a pretty obvious thing to do, but one that eluded the staff at the Pretoria hospital. Then orderlies whisked me into the operating theatre. As I was wheeled in, I looked at the clock. It was a quarter past midnight and I had been mauled at four p.m. So it was eight hours and fifteen minutes from attack to anaesthetic.

When I woke eight hours later, I looked down and got a huge shock. Where was my hand? It wasn't at the end of my arm where I expected it.

Instead it had been stitched into my groin like a glove. There was so much flesh ripped off and the swelling and trauma meant that the hand was dying. The only way to keep the hand alive was by sewing it into living tissue where it would hopefully regenerate.

In effect, it was as though my hand had been put into a trouser pocket — in this case an incision in my groin — and the elbow turned outwards in a most uncomfortable position, but vital for everything to grow back straight. They then put a bandage around my waist and chest so I looked like an Egyptian mummy.

After three-and-a-half weeks my hand came out of the living 'glove'. It was pretty useless. In fact, it was little more than a claw.

For the next eight months I painstakingly re-learnt how to use my hand from scratch. The crushed bones were intricately re-set and reconnected through a series of eight operations. My middle finger that had been bitten off was pinned to the ring finger, then sewn together for several months to keep the severed digit alive.

After almost a year of surgery and therapy, I could make a fist and open my middle finger with the help of my index finger. However, to this day, I cannot bend the first two knuckles.

While recovering, I had no option but to use my other hand exclusively. I played table tennis, shaved, and even wrote thank-you letters to all who helped me during the awful ordeal with my left hand. Eventually, I became left-handed.

Then a strange thing happened. One weekend I was playing football with some friends and instinctively started kicking the ball left-footed. It had somehow organically defaulted to being the stronger leg, without any practise whatsoever.

So not only was I now left-handed, I was also left-footed.

Then something even stranger occurred. I discovered my brain's dominant side had shifted as well. I was suddenly more creative, more understanding and more considerate. My family and friends all noticed the change. So it seems that even the 'gravity' in my brain had altered as a result of the attack.

Things happen in life that are unexpected and can cause serious setbacks but take us in unexpected directions. This we all know.

But the infinitely more important lesson is that we all have the power of choice. If I had merely accepted the first doctor's opinion, I would be living a vastly different life today. Even worse, I would only have one hand and in fact I might not have met my wife, JJ.

Luckily, I made the right decision.

However, perhaps it wasn't just luck. Perhaps my grandmother had been right. That mysterious Irishman she said was my Guardian Angel had not been missing in action on that fateful day after all.

I think he was with me all the time.

Chapter One

In the blood

AS A BOY growing up in apartheid South Africa, I was blissfully unaware that I lived in an oppressive society.

I had even less idea that I was one of the privileged few; that close on 90 per cent of South Africans were discriminated against by ethnicity.

All I knew was that in the affluent Johannesburg suburb of Saxonwold, staff were black and my parents' friends were white.

Reality came fast and furious. I was about eight when I heard a loud commotion in the street. There was shouting and screaming, people stampeding and general panic and mayhem. I ran out with Tony Wendy — an American friend — and saw policemen chasing groups of black people, slashing them with long whips made from raw animal hide called *sjamboks*. It was total pandemonium. Anyone caught would be flogged and ordered to produce his or her *dompas* — the colloquial word for a permit allowing blacks into segregated white areas.

Those without permits were jailed or fined an amount they often couldn't pay. It was classic Catch-22. Black South Africans could only apply for a *dompas* if they had work, but couldn't enter white areas without one. For many urban blacks, menial labour in white towns and cities was the only work available.

When Tony and I arrived, the police were sprinting down the street after another batch of fleeing domestic staff. In front of us was a prison van with an assembly line of hands sticking out of the iron bars. About fifteen people were locked inside.

The keys were still in the lock. Tony and I looked at each other and nodded. We quickly unlocked the cage and there was a rush of desperate bodies scrambling out of the van. Within seconds, the *dompas* detainees had disappeared.

It was probably the first time I grasped the chasm of inequality in the country and something stirred in my youthful conscience. I was seeing first-hand the reality of social injustice. People whipped like dogs and put into a cage was simply barbaric. There is no other word for it.

I'm immensely proud of that act of juvenile defiance. But before I get too virtuous, I have to admit something else was stirring within me. The spirit of audacity ... of adventure.

Fate deals each of us a unique hand, and like it or not, I come from a family of adventurers. Call it a blessing, call it a curse; it indisputably lurks in Henderson DNA. So for me to unlock a police van — and believe me, in those apartheid days you didn't mess with the South African Police — had as much to do with being a mischievous kid as it did with a sense of moral outrage.

The original Henderson swashbuckler in my immediate lineage was my great-grandfather Robert Hugh. He was an Irishman from Kildarton in County Armagh and the first of our bloodline to step on African soil. That was in 1884, and he was not only an archetypal Victorian pioneer, but also a canny entrepreneur. He arrived in Kimberly, South Africa at the height of the world's largest diamond stampede and instead of prospecting, made a fortune selling spades and tents. He saw there was as much money to be made from people's dreams as there was digging in the dirt.

In those rough-and-ready days, Kimberley rivalled any Wild West frontier town and Great-Granddad Henderson soon made a name for himself. Among his friends were Cecil Rhodes and Barney Barnato, the biggest mining magnates of their time. RH, as he became known, was elected mayor of

Kimberly and was in office during the famous siege of the city during the Boer War.[2]

He later wrote a book about his adventures called 'An Ulsterman in Africa'. I read it many years after his death and instantly empathised — he was a kindred spirit. We were born on the same day, 25 March, exactly one hundred years apart. I wish I'd had a chance to talk to him and discuss his approach to life, arriving penniless in a foreign country and creating amazing opportunities out of nothing.

Robert's son, my grandfather Ernest Henderson, went into politics and supported Jan Smuts during the bitter parliamentary clash on whether South Africa should join the Allies fighting the Nazis. Thanks to principled people like him, the country declared war on Germany in September 1939, winning the debate by a wafer-thin margin. In so doing, he was acutely aware that his own son would be sent to the front. It was my grandfather who had the casting vote. He was the chief whip and a minister without a portfolio. So when the ballot was tied and one vote would swing the decision, he crossed the floor taking South Africa into the Second World War.

---

[2] The Boer War (October 1899 - May 1902), also known as the Second Boer War, or Anglo-Boer War, was fought, between Great Britain and the two Boer (Afrikaner) republics — the South African Republic (Transvaal) and the Orange Free State.

My father Eric was a Lieutenant in the Second Transvaal Scottish Battalion and saw intense action in North Africa against Rommel, arguably Germany's greatest general. He was, with most of his men, captured at Tobruk and force-marched to a prisoner of war camp in Italy.

He soon escaped and headed north, hoping to cross into neutral Spain via France. He was captured by the Germans and spent several months in solitary confinement, cooped in a cage little larger than a dog kennel. If he attempted to flee again, the camp commander told him he would be shot.

But my father was an officer. It was his sworn duty to escape and no death threat would thwart him. He escaped again and this time he got away.

For most of that year —1943 — he was on the run, and no one, least of all the Germans, knew where he was. After many months of anguished waiting, my grandmother received a telegram from the Red Cross stating, "We regret to inform you Second Lieutenant Eric Henderson is missing, believed killed in action."

The family was devastated and feared the worst. Except my grandmother. She shook her head and said, "I can feel in my bones that he's alive."

Her faith that her son Eric was still out there dodging bullets and running for his life never wavered. Nothing could shake her steely belief that no Nazi would ever catch her boy.

They didn't. Nine months later he arrived in France, having walked most of the length of Italy through mountains, forests and even crowded towns and cities festooned with Axis soldiers[3]. He lived entirely by his wits, helped by the fact that he was a linguist and spoke fluent French, Italian and German. Fortuitously, he was also a talented artist and could forge food ration and identity documents, some of which we have to this day.

He wanted to get back into action, but the War Office decided he'd had enough death-defying escapades for one lifetime, not to mention the Germans would execute him on sight if captured. He spent the rest of the war as an interpreter.

On returning to civilian life, he joined the family business in Johannesburg manufacturing air filters for the gold mines — South Africa's largest industry. Sadly, he did this more out of duty to his father than his own wishes. He was never truly happy as a number-crunching businessman. Instead, he would have been a brilliant doctor.

However, he and my mother, who was a nurse, made up for this restlessness and had an extremely active social life. Johannesburg was a vibrant, almost hedonistic city and there

---

[3] The three principal partners in the Axis alliance were Germany, Italy, and Japan. The Axis was opposed by the Allied Powers, led by Great Britain, the United States, the Soviet Union, and China.

were plenty of parties, dancing on tables at the Johannesburg country club, and round-the-clock fun and hilarity. The Hendersons were also mad-keen sportsmen. My dad's brother, Chick Henderson, played rugby for Scotland and later became one of South Africa's best-known sport commentators.

Then tragedy struck. Dad contracted lung cancer, almost certainly triggered by chain-smoking cheap and nasty hand-rolled Red Cross cigarettes to while away the monotony of prisoner of war life.

He started fading in front of me. I was ten-years-old and watched in torment as my strong hero became a frail, bedridden, emaciated husk of his former self.

He died soon after his fiftieth birthday, courageously battling the killer disease for eight years. Mum was forty-two and it was a harrowing time for our family, both emotionally and financially. My father had no life insurance and cancer treatment was ruinously expensive.

We'd had it all. Now we'd lost it all.

As with all bereavement, my first reaction was anger. I felt I had been short-changed as I had no Dad to play in the father's cricket match at school. Then I became inconsolable.

My wise Scottish grandmother put her arms around me and said, although the loss was terrible, I had to move forward. She advised me that Henderson men were sometimes authoritarian and dictatorial, which could be restrictive, but I would never be suffocated by such constraints.

At the time I didn't fully grasp what she meant. But somehow I understood this was an oblique reference to my father who had never pursued his own dream of being a doctor. He had dutifully joined the family business at the insistence of his father, then spent the rest of his life regretting it.

In essence, what my grandmother was saying was never to allow anyone to stifle goals and ambitions, no matter how well intentioned. I cannot stress how valuable those words, spoken in a time of dire sorrow, were to me. I am eternally grateful that my grandmother, who died at the age of 104, lived long enough to see it was advice I heeded.

The first inkling that life had changed irrevocably was when my newly widowed mum took a job at The Ridge, the private prep school I attended. We could no longer afford the fees and it was the only way she could get a bursary. We no longer had money for football boots, cricket bats or toys, and we moved to a smaller house in Parktown, a less expensive neighbourhood.

My father's side of the family did not get on well with my mother, who came from Dutch Royal descent. As a result, after Dad's death she had to fend for herself, but she was an independent, free-thinking and extremely optimistic person, and could handle it. She always saw the bright side of life and had an ironclad belief in the power of optimism.

Another seminal lesson I learned in those bleak days came from the family of my best friend Kevin Fleischer. We first met as babies in cots.

The Fleischers invited me for dinner one night and at the table were black guests. I had never seen that before, certainly not in my household, so it was an invigorating experience. The adults were discussing politics and Kevin's mum, Dolores, turned to me and asked, "Pete, what do you think?"

I was completely taken aback. No one asked my opinion at home. Yet here was an adult enquiring what I thought during a grown-up discussion, and genuinely interested in my reply.

Unfortunately, I don't remember my answer. But that fleeting moment, when I realised someone might be curious in what a ten-year-old had to say, is seared indelibly on my memory. Thanks to that simple and considerate gesture all those years ago, I have never been afraid or reluctant to voice an opinion when I felt I had something to contribute.

We weren't exactly poor, but finances were tight. A big event in Johannesburg was the Rand Show, which still remains the largest consumer exhibition in southern Africa to this day. It was a fun three-day event over the Easter holiday weekend, attracting hundreds of thousands of visitors, but I also saw it as an opportunity. Despite being underage, there were plenty of casual jobs available and I planned to take advantage of that.

On the first day I left a note on the front door telling my mother "I'm big now" (I was eleven), and had gone to the show.

It was still dark when I caught a bus to the other side of Johannesburg and joined a queue of youthful job seekers.

I was dressed in shorts and shirt, but noticed many of the other kids didn't wear shoes. That could possibly earn them sympathy points with the people hiring, so not to be outdone, I took mine off and hid them near a bus stop.

Eventually my turn came and a man asked if I was sixteen. I nodded, and he gave me a bright yellow Simba chips jacket and a large tray of crisps and peanuts that would be refilled when sold. My payment would be one rand per tray.

I spent the rest of the day walking around barefoot hawking my wares. It went well until lunchtime when some thug ran up, grabbed a packet of crisps, and sprinted away.

I was furious. I stormed off to the mobile police station at the show and said I wanted to report a theft.

"What was stolen?" a cop asked.

"Packet of chips."

"Just one?"

"Yes."

A packet of chips cost five cents.

"Is that all?"

I nodded indignantly. "But I'll have to pay for it."

The cop laughed and called over a few colleagues.

"Don't worry, we'll buy all your chips."

Which they did. I sold my entire stock.

The show closed and I hitchhiked home, having earned twelve rand that day. It was a huge amount in my eyes. I was getting twenty-five cents a week pocket money, so in one outing I'd made enough to last the entire summer holiday.

However, what was more important was the exhilarating sense of achievement. Walking into a shop and buying presents with money I had earned with my own sweat was an adrenaline rush like no other. The fact I had independently come up with the plan, successfully executed it, survived, and also had some fun along the way was, in my eyes, an absolute triumph. It's a sensation I have never forgotten — and one that never fades.

My mother couldn't believe what I had done. I hadn't even asked for a lift. However, I knew that if I had told her beforehand, she would have stopped me as I was underage. But she was still immensely proud of me.

Soon afterwards, Mum said that if I behaved she would allow me to attend St. Andrew's College — a boarding school in Grahamstown and one of the best schools in the country where my grandfather and brother had attended.

Although it was six hundred miles away in the Eastern Cape, I was beside myself with excitement. It was something I was desperate to do.

My High School days were about to begin. But I soon discovered that the most important lessons were not necessarily in the classroom.

Chapter Two

Saturday Night Fever

MY MOST MEMORABLE report from St Andrew's College was this: "Henderson totally disregards all school rules when it suits him and if it wasn't for having girls in class, I don't think he would still be here."

It was true that I was not an academic. Or even a normal schoolboy, as I was dyslexic.

But it was not true that I was there solely for the girls. I loved my schooldays as I was surrounded by great friends, thrived at sport and enjoyed the stability and stimulating environment St. Andrew's provided. Having girls at our sister school DSG (Diocesan School for Girls) next door was merely a bonus.

But the fact I was not a normal schoolboy was mainly due to a chance discussion with my sports teacher. Of particular interest to me was his gaudy truck with psychedelic 'Trax Disco' logos and a turntable, speakers, mixer, strobe lights, microphones and amplifiers stashed in the back. I asked what all the kit was for, and he replied it was a music system he rented out for parties, weddings or other festive occasions.

"You would call it a disco," he said. "I call it a cash machine. Just imagine opening your pockets and — ka-ching! — money gushes in. Even better, with a disco, people pay *you* to have fun."

I liked the sound of that. I was always on the lookout for ways of making extra pocket money, particularly after my initial foray into the commercial world as a barefoot crisps and peanuts seller. I asked how I could get my hands on one.

Simple, he said. I could buy his for six hundred and fifty rand.

"That's a huge amount of money," I replied.

It was in those days. It was the equivalent of a term's fees at St. Andrew's.

"Get the cash and the disco is yours," he said.

Undaunted, I went to Barclays Bank and asked if I could borrow the money. The bank manager looked at the 16-year-old before him with surprise. He then asked the crucial question.

"What for?"

"A disco."

I could see he was taken aback. It was clearly not the right answer. A disco wasn't exactly a solid business plan in a risk-averse, number-crunching mind-set.

"What collateral do you have?" he asked

I didn't even know what the word meant.

"OK," said the manager. "Tell me how you are going to pay the money back?"

Simple, I replied. I would open my pocket and — ka-ching! — cash would pour in. Just ask my sports teacher.

Again, wrong answer.

Luckily for me — and the entire family — my mum had remarried and Peter Carr, my stepfather, was a tremendous guy. He had been a fighter pilot in the war so was no stranger to risk. He said he would stand surety. The bank agreed to the loan.

I gave the money to my teacher, then asked, "Where are the keys?"

"Keys?"

"For the pick-up truck."

"Hang on, I only sold you the disco equipment."

I shook my head. "What's the good of that? How am I going to get all this stuff around without a truck?"

"No, the vehicle's not included."

"Come on, Sir. It's of no use to you. It's got Trax Disco painted all over it. You can't take it anywhere except to parties."

He laughed and we shook hands. So I now had a vehicle and a disco, but was too young to drive. That was a problem, which at first seemed insurmountable. There was no point in having a mobile music system without being mobile.

I weighed up my options and came up with a solution. Rather than moving around to multiple locations, as my teacher had done, why not find a fixed regular venue? Somewhere I would be guaranteed of money 'ka-ching-ing' into my pocket, as Sir had promised.

Grahamstown is a university town. Rhodes is one of the best-known campuses in Africa, and during term-time there are thousands of students out looking for fun. But as it's a small town, there are only a few bars where they can let rip on weekends. Three, to be precise.

I got permission to go into town and, dressed in school blazer and straw boater, knocked on the door of the Victoria Hotel. The manager was intrigued by the idea of having a freelance disco on the premises, but when I said it was going to cost him fifty rand a session, he baulked.

"You're crazy! How do I know I'm going to sell an extra fifty bucks in booze just by playing music?"

I mulled that over. "OK, let's do a deal. Whatever extra you make on bar sales, we split. If you don't make anything, you don't pay me anything."

He agreed. I said I would rig up the sound system in the pub on Friday and Saturday nights, and come and see him on Monday.

The next hurdle was to get someone to work the disco. I obviously couldn't sneak out from school at night. Even if I did, as a 16-year-old I was prohibited by law from entering pubs.

I phoned Alan Hird, a friend and student at Rhodes University, and asked if he wanted a job. It must have been one of the shortest employment interviews in history. I simply told him all he had to do was play music, drink beer and get paid for it. Besides, all the girls would love him as a hip DJ.

Friday night was moderately successful. But on Saturday all hell broke loose — in the best sense possible. The Vic, as the students called it, almost burst at the seams. I snuck out of school to have a look and it was my first ever taste of a wildly successful product launch. People were dancing in the street as there was not a square inch of spare space inside. Pink Floyd had just released the 'Brick in the Wall' album — vinyl in those days — which Alan was playing over and over, despite my orders to have as much variation as possible.

People everywhere were chanting, "Hey teachers, leave them kids alone."

On Monday I went to see the hotel manager. This time the reception was vastly different. He asked if we could go back to the original proposal of fifty rand a night. No doubt he considered profit sharing would result in paying me too much, by a long way.

I said OK, but only if he hired me for three nights a week.

"No, just Friday and Saturday," he said.

I shook my head. "You need to have Wednesday as well. I recommend you call it "ladies night" and let them in for free. This will fill up your bar on a week night."

He reluctantly agreed.

But on Wednesday night when the pub was again crammed to capacity, his tune changed dramatically — pun intended.

I was now running my own business from behind school walls, hiring the disco out for three nights a week and employing students as DJs. As this happened at the beginning of the school term, I had three months of 'ka-ching' to go before packing up for the holidays. From nowhere I was earning a hundred and fifty rand a week, or six hundred a month. I paid off my bank loan in little over two months.

I didn't have a bank account, so had to place my profits with the housemaster. He was used to handing out thirty cents pocket money to schoolboys, so imagine the shock on his face when I was instead giving him money each week.

"Where are you getting it from?" he asked.

"I'm running a disco in town."

"You're doing that yourself?"

I looked at him with a feigned pained expression. That would be highly illegal, involving slipping out from the dormitory at night and going into bars. Even if I was doing that, I would never admit it.

"I've got a student running it for me."

At the end of the term I was wallowing in cash. So much so that my mother suggested I settle the school fees. She would reimburse me back in Johannesburg.

This was extremely unusual and to my embarrassment the headmaster called me and another pupil, Grant Fowlds, up on stage during assembly to congratulate us on paying our own way. Grant was the son of an Eastern Cape farmer, running his own goat herd. Today he is an internationally acclaimed conservationist and we still keep in touch.

Soon Trax was the most popular disco in town. I also ran gigs at school, which endeared me to the girls as I'd copied all the hipster DJ moves. "Put a rocket in your pocket and zoom around the room," I would yell as I flipped another disc.

Soon afterwards I ran into another problem: I didn't have enough records. Such was the demand that my music was fast getting stale.

I phoned the music company EMI explaining my predicament and stressing that I had a solid client base of rowdy Rhodes students, entertainment-starved conscripts at Grahamstown's army camp, and six schools in town.

Thankfully, EMI were impressed and said they donated records to people in the music industry like me. I could collect whatever I needed.

"For free?" I asked.

"Yes. But you have to come in personally."

That posed two potential problems. EMI's offices were in the district capital Port Elizabeth, eighty miles away from Grahamstown and I would have to get special permission from the school to go there. Fortunately, I managed to book a dentist appointment in Port Elizabeth which would allow me the opportunity to visit EMI as well. So I caught a bus to the city.

The second problem was that I couldn't very well go into a cutting edge record company posing as a trendy DJ dressed in school uniform. I stopped at the first men's shop and bought an awful brown jacket and yellow tie. Looking like a complete idiot rather than a hipster, I sauntered into the EMI offices pretending I was twenty, not sixteen. I was shown a box of records and told to select what I wanted.

"I'll take the lot," I said.

"Aren't you going to look at them?" the EMI man asked.

"I'm sure they'll be perfect."

Back at school I sifted through the box and reckoned I only needed a third of the discs. There was some great stuff — Supertramp, Elton John's 'Yellow Brick Road' — but a lot was geared for the vibrant black jive scene rather than disco.

This provided another opportunity. I strapped the box onto my bicycle carrier, rode into the township and sold the surplus records for ten cents each.

Sadly, school days were nearing an end. After our final exams we headed for a holiday at a beach resort south of Grahamstown called Kenton-on-Sea. It's a tourist town, but it also has a fair-sized municipal hall. An idea popped into my head: why not hire that for a disco night?

The council was not keen, saying it was expensive — thirty-six rand a night — and way out of reach for a youngster like me.

To the town clerk's astonishment, I booked for seven nights, including New Year's Eve, paying cash up front.

I put up posters advertising the "event of the year" in the seaside town, and dragooned my mother into doing door duty. Entrance fee was one rand.

I was on stage spinning discs when I noticed my mum waving frantically.

"Come quickly," she mouthed.

I put on the Santa Esmeralda song 'Don't let me be Misunderstood' as it's five-minutes long, and ran to the door.

My mother pointed to the Tupperware container we used as a cash box. It was spilling over with one rand coins. And there were still people queuing outside.

"I don't know where to put the money," she said.

"Put it in your handbag."

"I can't — that's full too."

We rushed outside, opened the boot of the car, and tipped the money in. Then we ran back just as Santa Esmeralda stopped being misunderstood and Mum started filling up the Tupperware again.

That night we made almost a thousand rand. I had never seen so much money. It was worth more than the entire disco system and the vehicle combined.

Without knowing, I had tapped into the zeitgeist of the decade. The disco era was in full swing with movies such as 'Grease' and 'Saturday Night Fever'. Everyone was not only dancing, but wanting to look trendy doing so. I was simply monetising a craze by being at the right place at the right time. Just as my great-grandfather had sold shovels to miners with dreams of wealth and adventure, I was peddling an outlet for those aspiring to be supercool.

I left school, somehow scraping through my exams, and the army beckoned. Hostilities on the Namibian-Angolan border were heating up. Ostensibly, it was a civil war between two Angolan liberation movements that had previously fought the Portuguese colonists: the pro-West UNITA and the communist MPLA.[4] In reality, however, it was a superpower proxy conflict with South Africa, backed by America, assisting UNITA and Cuba, armed by the Soviet Union, fighting alongside the MPLA.

Military conscription, or "the draft", was compulsory for all white youths, but I was not yet ready for the army. I wanted the fun to continue, so enrolled at Rhodes University.

That didn't last long. After two months I was kicked off campus for "being disruptive". It happened after I threw a girl into the swimming pool, 'rescued' her, and then gave mouth-to-mouth resuscitation in front of the entire class — all consensual, of course. But the academic suits didn't see it that way and sent me packing.

I had a fair amount of money banked from my disco days, and as the army thought I was still at university, I decided to go travelling.

---

[4] UNITA: National Union for the Total Independence of Angola. MPLA: The Popular Movement for the Liberation of Angola

I booked a plane ticket to Greece. As I paid, the wonderful, warm feeling that I'd first experienced after the Rand Show, cloaked me — a sensation of immense achievement; the satisfaction of buying something earned with my own sweat.

Only this time it was doubly intense.

Chapter Three

Marching to different drums

THE TRAVEL BUG sunk its infectious fangs into me the moment I boarded the plane. I have never recovered from the virus.

I recently tallied up my voyages and discovered I have been lucky enough to visit one hundred and twenty-five different countries around the world, witnessing history unfolding in front of me.

However, back in 1980, I had never set foot outside South Africa and arriving in Athens as an eighteen-year-old was a culture shock like none other.

Much of it was just lifestyle. In South Africa, I drank water straight from a tap, which I had taken for granted. Not so in much of Europe where potable water in those days had to be bought in shops. A pineapple, for which South Africans paid a few cents, or even picked for free, set me back the equivalent of twenty-five rand in an Athens grocery store. I even had to pay to go onto the beach.

However, the flipside of the coin was the total fascination of new experiences. People speaking different languages, wearing different clothes, eating different food — for the first time I realised what a magnificent adventure life could be.

I island-hopped around the Ionian Sea for a couple of months, ending up in Corfu just before my money ran out. To pay for basics, I washed dishes and mopped floors in restaurants, which was boredom personified.

One morning, while scrubbing grease off plates, I looked out of a kitchen window to see a guy windsurfing in the azure sea. That seemed a far more civilized way to spend the day, so I rushed down to the beach and asked the windsurfer to teach me how to do it; which he kindly did. Thanks to some insane good luck on my behalf, he was desperate for more instructors as this was the height of the holiday season.

After a few more lessons, I had a new job, which was almost as much fun as being a disco DJ. My office was the beach; my work clothes a suntan, dark glasses and pair of Hawaiian baggies. It was also a great way to meet girls.

But fun jobs are not necessarily the most lucrative. I still wasn't earning enough cash to get home, so needed to come up with a more profitable money-making scheme quickly.

I caught a ferry back to Athens, and purely by chance picked up a discarded guidebook on the steps of the Acropolis chronicling the history of Greece's most iconic monument. It was fascinating stuff. It also gave me an idea.

I starting approaching tourists, usually German, asking if they would like a guided tour of the ancient citadel. As few spoke Greek but almost all understood English, I soon had a captive audience. I walked them up the famous stone steps to the top of the rocky outcrop, regurgitating information I had gleaned from the guidebook with the gorgeous pillars of the Parthenon as a backdrop. Finally, I would suggest going to a restaurant where the owner gave me free food for bringing in clients. It was a win-win. Not only was I earning money, I was eating for free.

This worked brilliantly until I was accosted by the Greek tourist police demanding to see my guide's licence. Fortunately, we were at the top of the Acropolis hill so I apologised, saying my papers were in my car on the street below.

The policeman sent me down to fetch them. As soon as I reached the bottom, I ran for it.

This meant I had to leave Greece somewhat rapidly. But by now I had enough money to board a ferry to Brindisi, hitchhike through Italy to Venice, then take a train to Holland and catch a plane back home from Amsterdam.

Perhaps the most important lesson I took from my travels was that it was not only possible, but invigorating, living hand-to-mouth in a foreign country. I discovered I didn't have to flee back to the safety net of home simply because I had run out of money. Being stone-broke without a return ticket was not shocking or scary. It was part of the adventure. I could survive by thinking on my feet and living by my wits.

However, once home I couldn't hide from the army any longer. My call-up papers arrived and I was off for two years of enforced order and discipline, a galaxy removed from my chaotically carefree months as a traveller in the Mediterranean.

My hair was shaved to the scalp and suddenly I was living cheek by jowl with people from all walks of South African life. The army is the harshest, most unemotional leveller imaginable. Corporals shouting at us did not care if we were rich or poor, clever or stupid, handsome or ugly. A good number of recruits had never used a flushing lavatory before, while others, like me, had attended private schools. It meant nothing. To the impersonal military apparatus, we were all the same — insignificant bodies to be forged into tough fighting machines.

The predominant language in the army was Afrikaans. I was far from fluent as the rudimentary Afrikaans taught in

English-speaking schools was vastly different to the expletive-riddled orders constantly barked at us. I learned fast.

For the next year I was going to be a serf of the state, and it was pointless denying it. So I decided to make the most of the situation and volunteered for an officers' course. I had a decent education and could run as fast as everyone else, so was accepted.

The course was basically a gruelling elimination contest with far more losers than victors. One thousand two hundred recruits applied, of which a mere hundred and twenty were selected. Only four who passed were English-speakers.

I must have impressed someone as I was asked to remain at the base in Oudtshoorn to train future officers. I declined, as I wanted to return to Grahamstown to be close to my girlfriend and friends at Rhodes University.

In other words, I wanted to see out my army days with as cushy a lifestyle as possible.

I was soon disabused of that. As we arrived in Grahamstown, the commanding officer walked into the mess and told everybody to sit "except Lt. Henderson and Lt. Pearce."

We soon discovered why. "You two are off to the Angolan border," he said.

My plans for the quiet life blew up in smoke. Not only that, the army was short of officers and wanted me to take over the role of company commander, normally a captain's position.

I arrived at the camp in Ondangwa, Namibia to find I was in charge of 120 troops. I was nineteen and had no experience of a frontline command. In fact, I had no experience of commanding anyone. I was somewhat apprehensive, to put it politely.

The troopies, some of them hard-bitten lifers, were keen to suss out their new *rooinek* (English-speaking) leader. I called the company together and had to stand on an ammunition crate in the centre of the parade ground so the people at the back could see.

I introduced myself and said my job was to get them home safely to their families and loved ones. I wasn't sure what to say next, but remembered a story my father told when asked if he had been scared during the war. He replied that if a bullet has your name on it, there's nothing you can do.

But, he added that there are thousands of bullets that instead simply had "plain bloody fool" on them, and you can certainly do something about those. If you got taken out by such a bullet it was your own fault — or your officer's, in the event of a stupid command.

"I am not going to send any bloody fools back in body bags," I told my troops. "You're all going home with me at the end of this tour."

I kept that pledge. I didn't lose anyone, despite being in a volatile area with enemy activity all around.

However, I had a very conflicted tour of duty. Despite my country's flaws I was a patriotic South African, and we were fighting a well-equipped foe intent on killing us. That was the reality, and something I had to cope with. I was proud of being an officer, but there were some nagging concerns. There was no denying that this wasn't the life for me. All I really wanted was to be back in Grahamstown, running my disco, having parties or being on the beach with friends. Like most nineteen-year-olds, I guess.

One incident I remember clearly was capturing a guerrilla. He wasn't an Angolan or Cuban, but a Namibian fighting for the South West African People's Organisation (SWAPO), the liberation movement that eventually won independence for that country from South Africa.

He didn't co-operate during interrogation, so was tortured. I didn't like that one bit and quoted the Geneva Convention on POW treatment to my commanding officer.

His response was hostile. In fact, it was raging fury. He shouted that I would be court-martialled if I continued complaining about the prisoner's treatment.

The guerrilla escaped that night and I was called in by my superior officer angrily demanding to know if I had anything to do with it.

I hadn't ... unlike the time I unlocked the police van during a pass raid in Johannesburg.

My border tour ended and I returned home. It had been a great eye-opening adventure; I made some amazing friends and experienced things I would never have encountered in civilian life. I had my own helicopter to fly me around and went on long patrols deep in the Angolan bush. We slept in trenches called fox holes and on occasions had shrapnel exploding around us. Once we were lost and had to walk over a hundred kilometres back to base with no water. It taught me that if you truly set your mind to do something, you can do anything.

Once home, the next decision facing me was possibly the most crucial; what did I plan to do with my life?

The answer came totally out of the blue.

My stepsister Carol Carr was an advertising producer for a company called Screen Machine, and during a TV shoot taking place just up the road from our house, she borrowed our sitting-room curtains for a set backdrop. For some reason this — and the fact that our living room windows were now bare — intrigued me and I wandered over to the location to watch Carol in action.

I was instantly captivated by the bustling activity ... crews pushing cameras on dollies, setting up lights, rigging sound systems while technicians — or grips as they are known —

checked the dolly tracks. It was an intensely vibrant buzz. Not to mention the beautiful models lounging around the set.

I stood around gawping until Carol called me over and told me to do something useful, like making tea or coffee for everybody.

The next day I was invited back and this time I was paid for serving refreshments. It was my first formal job. A tea boy.

On the third day, I was busy in the kitchen when I noticed a youth playing marbles as part of the video script for a TV commercial. I watched fascinated as the cameraman, focus puller and sound technicians operated in total synchronicity.

But something was wrong. Like most kids, I had played marbles at school. And this youth wasn't doing it right.

I walked up to the director, Jeff Corey, to give him what I thought would be sage advice.

"That guy's not shooting marbles properly. You don't do it like that."

I then attempted to show Jeff the correct way.

He signalled the crew to stop. Then turned to me.

"Who are you?"

"Umm ... I'm Pete, the tea boy."

"You're fired. Get off my set. Now."

I was shattered. I rushed off to the production manager asking her to talk to Jeff, to tell him I was sorry and plead for me to get my job back.

She shook her head. "You're the lowest person on the set. You simply can't tell the director what to do in the middle of a shoot."

I refused to accept I had been fired. In my youthful arrogance, that only happened to other people. I went home and paced around the house for a while, absolutely distraught. Then I thought, to hell with this, and went back to the studio to look for Jeff.

Fortunately, he was still there, working in the editing room. He glanced up as I walked in.

"You again! I thought I'd told you to get lost!"

I apologised profusely. Then asked what he was doing.

"I'm editing," he harrumphed, not wanting to waste time or energy on some brat asking dumb questions.

"How do you do that?"

"By splicing rushes together," he said, staring intently at footage on the monitor as he fed film into the splicing machine. "Hold that, will you."

I eagerly assisted. We worked until four a.m.

Just before leaving I asked, "Am I still fired?"

Jeff looked at his watch.

"Work starts in two hours. You had better not be late."

It wasn't the most auspicious start, but for me there was no going back.

This was where I belonged.

Chapter Four

Forged in fire

I LOVED THE job. The sheer energy involved in TV work was intoxicating. Fast moving, creative and dynamic, it was just what I needed at the time.

Also, thanks to Jeff Corey, I can truly say I started at the bottom, and am forever grateful for that. From kicking off as a tea boy at Screen Machine, I 'graduated' to runner, and then started working for several other production companies.

Promotion came quickly as TV was in its infancy in South Africa, and booming. As a result, the advertising industry was rocketing at an exponential rate. Before long I was a production manager.

Then my finger was bitten by off a lioness at a game reserve while filming her cubs— as told as in the prologue. I spent almost a year unable to work with skin grafts and operations on my hand.

But I was determined to fight my way back, and as soon as I could work again I moved to Cape Town, where my girlfriend lived. The city was considered a creative hotspot.

Or so I thought. I came down to earth with a crash. Cape Town may be one of the most beautiful cities in the world, but in those days it was also the most 'cliquey'. Not only did you have to be born within sight of the iconic Table Mountain, you also needed a generation or two of Cape DNA in your veins to be considered a blueblood. Old money firmly ruled the roost.

This was particularly true for upstarts like me from crass Jo'burg. Even with a résumé from top agencies, I couldn't get work. As soon as prospective employers saw I was from 'somewhere else', I was shown the door. That's if I managed to get through the door.

I decided the only alternative, apart from scampering home tail between legs, was to set up my own company. One studio had an empty office, and the owner with magnanimity seldom found in the Cape at the time, graciously let me move in. The Cape Connection film production company was born.

But I needed some local big hitters to get up and running. Otherwise I would be vainly banging on the same closed doors as before.

There was no point in thinking small so I hired the best freelance producer and cameraman in the city. I didn't have funds to pay their exorbitant fees, so instead offered them partnerships promising that they would still be charging clients top rates. The key difference was that they would be company directors instead of hired guns.

It worked beyond my wildest dreams. Cape Town was a key location on the international film market due to its beauty and unbeatable summer weather. We had big name German, French, British and Italian production companies queuing up for commercial shoots.

Soon I was driving a snazzy MGA sports car, and to my pleasant surprise, discovered we had three million rand in the bank.

Then it went dead. Virtually overnight.

It happened during in August 1985 when Chase Manhattan Bank announced it would not roll over its loans to the apartheid government. Within days' other international banks followed Chase Manhattan's lead. The consequences were instant and devastating — a total fiscal massacre. The economy reeled drunkenly as foreign exchange markets dried up and even the Johannesburg Stock Exchange temporarily shut down.

Suddenly nobody wanted anything to do with South Africa. No one would touch products tainted with toxic apartheid. Production companies that had previously been banging on our door closed their accounts with immediate effect.

We watched helplessly as business evaporated faster than dawn dew in the desert. It still is quite shocking when I think back how suddenly the world can change. We went from six-figure salaries to zero in one gut-wrenching swoop.

At the same time the township riots that first detonated in Soweto during the winter of 1976 flared again. Violence and mayhem erupted with an intensity the country had never seen before. We all knew there was no going back.

However, not only the townships were on fire. Mass protests started at white universities, and a friend tipped me off that there was going to be a student demonstration at the University of Cape Town. I grabbed my camera and went to see what was going on.

I arrived during a standoff in the street between students and cops. The situation was as volatile as gelignite.

Suddenly it took off with a vengeance. Police stormed the campus, whipping students with *sjamboks*. Hundreds fled in all directions as police on loudhailers yelled at full volume that the rally was an "illegal gathering".

It was the first time South Africans saw police lashing into white kids, highlighting the extent of civil unrest. Most township turbulence was censored by the government-owned

South African Broadcasting Corporation (SABC), but this punch-up wasn't in some scrap-iron shanty town. It was happening on the steps of the main entrance of a world-rated university. Thousands saw it just by driving past.

However, they weren't seeing it on their TV screens. I had great exclusive footage, but wasn't sure what to do with it. I knew the SABC wouldn't use it, so hopped on a plane and flew to the BBC offices in Johannesburg.

The bureau chief, Michael Buerk, was impressed when he saw what I had in the can. In fact, he said it was amazing footage.

"How much will you pay for it?" I asked.

He looked at me quizzically. "We don't pay. We have our own crews."

Talk about a letdown. Even more galling was that the BBC treated my exclusive film as a tip-off, realising everything was now kicking-off in Cape Town. A camera crew caught the next flight out to be where it thought the action was.

I remained behind, wondering what to do as I had wasted rapidly depleting funds on a dead-end trip.

Then I got another tip-off that students at the University of the Witwatersrand — Wits as it is better known — were about to stage a demonstration in Johannesburg.

I grabbed my camera.

It was even more dramatic than the Cape Town rally with police again charging the campus and whipping terrified students running for cover. Wits is South Africa's largest university and slap-bang in the commercial heart of the country. As the BBC crew was in the Cape, I once again had exclusivity.

I returned to the BBC offices.

"This time will you pay me?" I asked.

Michael Buerk threw up his hands in mock defeat. "You had better come and work for us," he said.

Thus started perhaps the most hectic period of my working life. I was appointed sound recordist for cameraman Francois Marais, one of the most legendary and fearless frontline photographers at the time. My job was to work the audio system and carry the heavy tripod as I ran behind him, more often than not into precariously dangerous situations. The scenes we were witnessing and filming were extraordinary, and the footage was being screened around the world.

The international media, grasping that this was the story of the decade, arrived in droves. But guys like Francois and I had a distinct home advantage. We were South Africans. We knew the country, the people, the history and the situation on the ground.

We filmed mass rallies and uprisings in all of the major townships, as well as highly charged funerals of riot victims that attracted hundreds of thousands of angry protesters screaming for justice.

We were teargassed, pelted with stones and sometimes even petrol-bombed. We were targeted by township vigilantes, repeatedly harassed by the police, and constantly stonewalled by the authorities.

Welcome to an adrenaline junkie's world.

Yet despite the horror, I found myself in danger of becoming addicted.

Chapter Five

Cry the beloved country

ALMOST OVERNIGHT, I had a ringside seat to highly combustible history in the making. To report on it was not pleasant, but it was exhilarating. White South Africa lived in a cocoon, a bubble surrounded by a seething mass of resentment, of which most were blissfully unaware.

As part of the international media, I had a foot in both worlds. This was fascinating, but also potentially dangerous and I soon realised just how hazardous when the two worlds almost collided with me in the middle.

It happened when I was assigned as a cameraman to accompany veteran CBS correspondent Bill Mutschmann on a trip into Angola. However, I wasn't told our destination, or anything else for that matter. My instructions were just to pitch up at the airport with my equipment and passport.

I only discovered where we were when we landed at a top-secret South West African People's Organisation (SWAPO) base deep in the Angolan bush. I was horrified. Technically, I was an officer in the South African army and we were at war with SWAPO, who were fighting for the liberation of Namibia. At the time, South Africa ruled Namibia as a colony.

As SWAPO fighters escorted me into a structure smothered with camouflage nets, I couldn't help reflecting with considerable trepidation that not long ago I had been leopard-crawling through the same bush, possibly not far from this base, with a rifle. Our marching chant was, "Who we're gonna shoot? Joe Slovo! Who we're gonna kill? Sam Nujoma!"

(Joe Slovo was a white South African communist and high-ranking member of the Soviet-era KGB secret police; Sam Nujoma was the SWAPO leader).

Now, barely two years later, I was sitting in an officers' mess breaking bread and drinking tea with sworn enemies, about to film an interview with the guy the South African military had been trying to kill for decades. It redefined the word surreal.

Listening to these men the government labelled "terrorists" was a huge surprise for me. As the camera rolled, they eloquently explained what they were fighting for, why they wanted independence, and how they felt about the South African invaders. They said exactly what I would have if a foreign power occupied my country.

I kept quiet, not just because I was interested in what the SWAPO soldiers were saying, but I knew with cold certainty that my accent would give me away. If they discovered I was South African, they would also know I had been in the army as all white males my age were conscripted. I would have been killed on the spot.

The big moment arrived and I set up the camera for the Nujoma interview. To my dismay, Bill Mutschmann turned towards me and asked a question. I don't remember what it was — probably something innocuously technical. What I do remember is the astonished look on Bill's face when I replied in possibly the most over-the-top, pseudo-American accent invented. It was pure Candid Camera spoof. Fortunately, he had the presence of mind not to reply, and to say I dodged a bullet — one with "fool" written all over it — is an understatement.

My life was on the trajectory of a rocket. Each morning I woke up thinking how exciting it was. I was part of a fast-breaking news story that was simultaneously fascinating, thought provoking and frightening. Every day delivered a jolt of adrenaline.

One of my most traumatic assignments was covering the deadly turmoil in a township called Crossroads, a densely populated squatter camp near Cape Town's airport. In 1986, Crossroads was a snapshot of human misery at its bleakest. Most shacks were constructed from tin and garbage, there was no electricity or running water, the roads were trash-strewn tracks with raw sewage oozing down clogged, open drains.

This particular assignment concerned youths organised by the ANC-affiliated United Democratic Front who were boycotting schools, burning books, destroying their classrooms as well as setting alight public buildings. They called themselves "comrades".

Bizarrely, in this case their chief opponents were not the police, but their parents. Conservative groups of adults, believing they had lost control of their youth, started to mobilise, and Crossroads was at the bitter coalface.

It was a tragedy of Shakespearean proportions; father against son, mother against daughter. Rumours that police were assisting the parents added kerosene to the wildfire.

To identify themselves, the adults wore white headbands and were consequently known as *witdoeke*, an Afrikaans word meaning "white cloth". They gathered in groups of up to fifty and armed themselves with machetes, spears called *assegais,* and knobkerries, a stick with a rounded 'knuckle' considerably stouter and harder than a cricket ball at the end. They then stormed into the comrades' conflict zones and start banging heads, or worse. The rioting kids, who were busy throwing stones at police and burning buildings would retaliate, fighting their own parents.

The situation was getting uglier by the day and the BBC flew me and a sound engineer to Cape Town. In true BBC fashion, we booked into the five-star Cape Sun and rented a BMW to venture into the raging violence.

But not just any BMW. It had to be a bright red, open-roof convertible. This was for two reasons. Firstly, we could stand on the seat and film over the windscreen while driving, but most importantly, the bright colour starkly differentiated us from the ubiquitous yellow police cars. We also stuck large "Press" banners on the windows as we drove into what could only be called hell.

There was anarchy and mayhem wherever you looked. Police were shooting rubber bullets and teargas at the comrades from one side, while the *witdoeke* came at them from another. Consequently, panic-stricken youths were scurrying in and out of the tin shanties, scattering like shrapnel in all directions. They knew if caught by the vigilantes, they would most likely be killed.

We followed the *witdoeke* chasing the bolting youngsters on foot and as I ran around a corner, I saw one kid, about twelve years old, trapped on a dusty dead-end track. He was like a rabbit in a spotlight, hypnotised with terror as twenty or thirty *witdoeke* charged him.

What happened next still haunts me. As the kid went down, the adults started hacking him with machetes. He was barely ten yards from me.

I had been busy filming the chase, and couldn't truly grasp what I was seeing. Looking through a camera lens has the effect of detaching reality. But right next to me my sound engineer was freaking out, his voice gargling in horror. I lifted my head and saw exactly why. It's one thing looking at something panning out in black and white through a viewfinder, but completely different watching the terror in real life while holding a mic amplifying the sickening sounds of slashing machetes.

We were in a terrible dilemma. The savagery of the group's bloodlust and rage was palpable. You could smell it, feel it — even taste it. As human beings, we desperately wanted to save the kid, but the murderous crowd would have killed us in a blink if we had intervened. Any doubts about that were later dispelled when a colleague, George De'Ath, was chopped to death by *witdoeke* that same weekend, although we were unaware at the time.

Knowing our lives were in mortal danger, we sprinted to our hire car and sped out of the township.

Back at the office we started editing our material. It was one of the most shocking rolls of film I have taken. Stark and gruesome, the footage was as horrific as actually being there, dragging viewers down into the darkest pit of barbarity.

One part of me wanted to release the footage and try to stop the horror by mobilising international outrage. But I couldn't square that with the fact that we would be reducing the last moments of a human's life to a ghoulish frame. Not to mention the incalculable anguish it would cause his family.

I shook my head. There was no way we were going to screen this on international television. I decided that as witnesses, we would have to be the ones coming to terms with what savagery we had seen. We would have to deal with that evil knowledge alone.

I selected a series of wide, distant shots that told the story without graphic or gory images, while the correspondent explained that viewers were watching the murder of a twelve-year-old filmed in real time.

I sent the footage to the BBC and when I arrived back at the Cape Sun there was already a 'hero-gram' from the news desk in London congratulating us. We had beaten the opposition who had nothing compared with what we had filmed.

I had a shower, scrubbing myself vigorously, and went downstairs to dinner. All the foreign press was staying at the luxurious Cape Sun and the mood was festive. Everyone was tucking into five-star food, and booze was flowing like rivers in flood. There were also plenty of gorgeous women, attracted by the adrenaline-fuelled aura of the international press corps. Many of the guys who thrived on frontline action were fun, exciting and interesting to be around. It may be an indictment on the profession to say this, but in those harrowing times, TV cameramen were the rock stars of journalism.

I sat at a table groaning with rows of silver domes covering platters of prawns, caviar and crayfish, while champagne corks popped like firecrackers.

It was bizarre. I felt as though I was living in some weird dream. I had just had one of the worst days of my life, and here I was surrounded by obscene opulence.

At about eleven p.m. I went up to my room accompanied by a young woman who worked for a car-rental company. It was a beautiful suite with a majestic view of Table Mountain. There were flowers on the windowsill and chocolates on the pillows of the king-size bed. The perfect setting for a romantic encounter.

My 'date' ran herself a bubble bath and I sat by the window, reflecting on the past twelve hours. I was living a life that I could never afford as a normal person — exclusive hotels, hired BMWs, cuisine served in silver domes, magnums of champagne and beautiful women. I should have felt on top of the world.

But I felt terrible. I couldn't stop seeing the dreadful images of the attack.

I had just watched a child being murdered barely yards in front of me. That, not five-star abundance, was the reality of the country.

I stared out of the window overlooking Table Mountain and started crying uncontrollably. At that moment, my date walked out of the bathroom in a skimpy towel, glistening from an aromatic foam bath. She asked what was wrong.

"I have no idea," I replied. "I've had such a bad day. I just don't know what reality is anymore. I have no idea what normal is."

She frowned. This was definitely not what she expected. She was ready for an evening of fun.

She left, probably to find some more convivial company. A journalist shedding tears over a bad day was not her idea of fun.

I lay in bed crying throughout the night. The next morning, I phoned Michael Buerk, the BBC bureau chief in Johannesburg.

"I think I've had a bit too much of this stuff, Mike," I said.

It was the first warning bell for me that the trauma we saw on a daily basis could take a terrible toll. For us at the frontline, there was no reset button. The extremes were too high.

Mike asked if I was OK. I said I had been working solidly for forty-five days and needed a break. I didn't mention that I'd had a bit of a meltdown. One didn't in those days.

He told me to take a couple of days off. There was no talk of therapy or counselling. There was no support or even recognition of post-traumatic stress disorder at the time. We were expected to suck it up and get on with it. Not just our bosses; we expected it of ourselves.

That's what I did. Despite that brief blip, in many ways I was better equipped to cope with lingering PTSD issues than my colleagues. For a start, I had already spent time in a combat zone while in the army, and I am blessed — thanks to my mother — with a positive attitude. That, I realised, was my reset button.

It was then that we heard of the murder of George De'Ath. The press corps was shocked to its core. George, a South African freelance TV cameraman had been filming in the townships at the same time as us when he and his soundman Andile Fosi were attacked by *witdoeke*. George was repeatedly slashed with machetes while Andile, a black man, courageously tried to save his life. George was admitted to hospital in a coma. He died a few days later. Miraculously, Andile was not seriously injured.

This was a turning point for the international media. We previously thought we were untouchable and warring factions would allow us to do our jobs. Obviously that was not the case anymore. Anyone of us could be next.

And I very almost was.

May Day, or International Workers' Day, was not an official holiday in apartheid South Africa as it is in much of the rest of the world. Instead, it was a conflict day. Without fail, on the first of May each year, township protestors gathered in force, preventing people from going to work or buying goods from white-owned shops and supermarkets.

This often turned violent, with people viciously kicked off buses if they defied the boycott, or if they were carrying shopping bags, they were forced to eat or drink whatever was in the bag. This sometimes included washing detergent or drain cleaner, resulting in excruciating internal injuries.

On 1 May 1986, the BBC were very excited as they had recently got their first mobile car phone. This was for us a logistical miracle, as now a single call could get us speeding off to a riot or demonstration rather than having to hang around in the office waiting for tip-offs.

I was given the car with the phone in it and didn't have to wait long before the new-fangled device rang loudly. It was

Michael Buerk saying there was a riot in Daveyton, a township southeast of Johannesburg, and police were shooting. We needed to get there as soon as possible to get the exclusive.

With Zed Manona, my Xhosa sound engineer, fixer and close friend, I drove at speed into Daveyton, a township neither of us had visited before. It seemed we were too late. Teargas smoke lingered in the air, spent rubber bullets littered the ground, and people sat on pavements nursing injuries. But the main crowd had dispersed.

I wound down my window and asked one guy with a bloodied head what had happened.

"The police broke us up," he said.

"Where is everybody?"

"In the hall," he said, pointing down the road.

Township town halls were all built the same, looking like American small town chapels with twin-doors at the front and a stage and a side door at the back. We parked outside and immediately saw the building was packed to capacity. Throngs of people were peering through windows as there was no room inside.

Knowing the layout of these halls, Zed and I eased our way in through the side door and onto the stage.

The agitated crowd suddenly noticed us. Then a cry went up, *"Chesa umhlungu!"* Burn the white man.

It turned into a chant. *"Chesa umhlungu! Chesa umhlungu!"*

The hairs stood on the back of my neck. We had unwittingly walked slap-bang into an Azanian People's Organisation gathering. AZAPO was easily the most hostile of the liberation movements. Their slogan was "one settler one bullet" and they meant exactly that.

Zed grabbed my arm. "Pete, we have to get out of here. Now!" I could see the dread on his face, no doubt also reflected in my own.

But I knew there was no way we could turn and flee. It would be impossible to outrun the baying mob. There would be at least five hundred people chasing us. If they caught me, a foregone conclusion, they would wire my hands behind my back, force petrol down my throat, put a car tyre around my neck and set me alight. In other words, the awful township "necklace", made infamous by Winnie Mandela when she said, "with our matches and our necklaces, we shall liberate this country".

"Necklacing" would have been quite normal for AZAPO militants. It was their preferred method of eliminating anyone deemed to be an enemy.

I looked around the stage and saw a woman in a nun's veil speaking into a microphone at a lectern. Sister Bernard Ncube, a Catholic nun as well as courageous anti-apartheid activist, was also a town councillor. She turned to see what the chanting was about and saw me, just a few yards behind. Her eyes flew wide with horror. She knew exactly what was going to happen next. A necklace.

I had two choices: to run, as Zed was urging, or seize the initiative. My life depended on it.

I strode up to the lectern, grabbed the mic from Sister Bernard. and bellowed:

"Amandla!" Power — the liberation movement's rallying call.

"Awethu!" It is ours, the crowd responded.

I then shouted *"Hlala phansi."* Sit down.

I knew I had to act with confidence and the next few words could be the most important in my life. Or else they would be the last.

"I am from the BBC," I said. "I know I may not be welcome here but I have done more for the struggle than many of you will do in your entire lives. So please sit down and behave yourselves."

There was silence. It lasted a few seconds, but seemed like an eon.

Then a remarkable thing happened. At great personal risk — both physical and to her reputation — Sister Bernard hugged me. By putting her arms around a strange white man in the middle of a red-hot, emotionally charged rally, she saved my life. There is no doubt about it.

Also showing incredible courage, the other twelve councillors formed a human shield and escorted me off the stage. Once out of the door, they advised me in no uncertain terms to get the hell out of the area, as this tiny window of relative calm would not last. Advice Zed and I heeded with alacrity.

I drove back, hands still shaking, and reflected again on the incredible power of personal choice and opportunity. If I had made the decision to flee, I would not be writing these words.

Or perhaps, as my grandmother would argue, the Irish guardian angel watching my back had once again done his job.

The next day I drove back into Daveyton to thank Sister Bernard. I went in without a camera, feeling extremely vulnerable, stopping and asking people where she lived. I got a glut of instructions — straight, right, left, U-turn — going deeper and deeper into the township until I finally found her tiny home.

She answered my knock, looking at me quizzically. No doubt she was as surprised as she had been when I stumbled onto the stage.

"I want to thank you for saving my life."

She invited me in. All township houses were like matchboxes, small, square and architecturally dreary. Hers was no different, even though she was a town councillor. It was clear material possessions were not high on her priorities.

We sat in her miniscule living room. She offered me tea and said, "You were very brave."

I shook my head. "I was stupid."

"No. You were brave. We need people like you in this world."

I replied that on the contrary, we needed more people like her. A conviction I still firmly hold.

I then asked if there was anything I could do to help her. Could I make a donation to her charities, pay for food or children's schooling?

"You don't need to do anything," she replied. "I helped you and I'm sure you will help someone else one day."

I vowed that I would.

Although I was flattered that Sister Bernard thought I was brave, I think my own assessment of stupidity is possibly more accurate. After the murder of George De'Ath, we never again took it for granted that we would be welcome in the townships. Yet I had broken that rule by barging into a rally and could have paid dearly for it.

It was true that most of the anti-apartheid political movements — with the obvious exception of AZAPO or vigilante groups such as the *witdoeke* — did trust the foreign press to get their side of the story out to the rest of the world.

But even so, many situations were as volatile as nitroglycerine, so wherever possible we followed a semi-formal procedure or protocol rather than barging in and starting filming.

For example, at a mass funeral in Uitenhage in the Eastern Cape where twenty-two people killed by police were being buried, Zed and I drove to the houses of the victims' families several hours beforehand to gauge the situation.

We offered condolences, paid our respects to the soldiers of *Umkhonto we Sizwe* (armed wing of the ANC), had tea with the families, and then asked permission to film the funeral. It was done with quiet dignity and something the grieving families seemed to appreciate.

If permission was granted, and it usually was, we had incredible access. We drove with the families to the cemetery and filmed mothers, fathers, brothers and sisters saying heartrending goodbyes at the edge of newly dug graves.

It was always extremely emotional, and the anthem *Nkosi Sikelel iAfrika* sung by tens of thousands of harmonious voices could be heard for miles. Everyone would stand in the dust, raised fists clenched in salutes.

Sadly, these funerals often ended in violence when the police arrived. It would start with a commotion on the fringes of the cemetery, the crowd stirring angrily as yellow Casspir[5] armoured troop carriers appeared. The ugly but highly effective riot vehicles would be parked in the surrounding fields as cops emerged with automatic weapons and tear gas, ostensibly to keep the peace.

Invariably, the opposite happened. All it took was one hothead to throw a rock and all hell broke loose with teargas canisters hissing into the sky and round after round of rubber bullets fired into the crowds. Sometimes police used live ammunition if they deemed the situation was getting out of hand.

It was a vicious circle with both sides looking for confrontation.

The end result was always another funeral.

Unlike many other international crews, I was a South African; this country was my home. There was nowhere else. Consequently, part of my inner struggle was that after a day of intense emotion, I would go back to the white suburbs, drinking cold beers and mingling with sometimes angry friends who thought I was either a bleeding-heart liberal or a raving communist. Both, in the eyes of the white minority, were equally bad. They accused me of deliberately showing the worst aspects of the country to the rest of the world merely to generate sensational headlines.

---

[5] The Casspir is a mine-resistant infantry mobility vehicle that has been in use in South Africa since the 1980s.

I tried to explain they were shooting the messenger. The world I lived in each day was vastly different to theirs. And it was the real world for the majority of South Africans.

Many couldn't — or wouldn't — believe what I was telling them. So I decided to give them a dose of reality and compiled an hour-long documentary of live footage I'd filmed in the townships.

I phoned twenty of my closest friends and invited them over to see it.

"Bring Pimms and pizza," I said, hoping it would be an interesting, informative and enlightening evening.

However, as the documentary finished, there was dead silence. I expected there to be a lively discussion as these were highly intelligent people. I was showing the reality of what South Africa was going through. This was what was happening outside the white bubble.

There was no reaction. None whatsoever. With a few mumbled goodbyes, my house emptied.

I was devastated. If my closest friends, all educated achievers, couldn't understand what was happening, then who could? I don't think I have ever felt so alone.

Sometime later, a friend who had been at the screening told me what had really happened. No one had said anything for the simple reason they had not known what to say. They were all too shocked. They didn't know how to respond, so they left in silence.

This resentment towards what I was doing also occurred in my own family. My only uncle, a hugely successful businessman, decided in his wisdom that the real reason for international boycotts was not apartheid. It was instead the "distorted" portrayal by the international media. In other words, it was my fault.

I was summoned to a family meeting and told in no uncertain terms that my father was turning in his grave. I was a "left-wing commie" and would be ostracised from the Henderson family.

It was laughable. To blame me for the consequences of the apartheid regime was ridiculous. Threating to disown me was derisory.

Thankfully, my always-positive and bubbly mother sided with me. She told me to ignore them. I was doing the right thing.

I did just that. The next day I was back at work, camera on my shoulder, determined to continue showing the world what was happening around me.

Chapter Six

Going my own way

ALTHOUGH BASED IN Johannesburg, much of my time was spent jetting elsewhere around the country, covering breaking stories at huge cost to the BBC.

Jo'burg was at the epicentre of the troubled times, but it was increasingly clear that a disproportionate amount of township unrest was starting to erupt in the Eastern Cape, homeland of the Xhosa tribe and Nelson Mandela. This was also the historical flashpoint where white settlers and migrating Xhosa warriors first clashed in 1779, resulting in what historians call the Cape Frontier Wars. It lasted a hundred years and is the longest running military action in the continent's troubled colonial history

Despite being a hotspot, there were no international TV teams based there. This got me thinking. Why don't I set up the first permanent international Eastern Cape bureau? I would be the news responder saving the big Johannesburg-based networks time and money, and I would basically have a monopoly on fast-breaking news.

I approached the BBC, Visnews (now Reuters) and NBC, informing them I was moving to Port Elizabeth as a freelancer, and asked if they would be interested in hiring me. All three liked my idea and guaranteed a monthly retainer of ten days each.

This meant I had work for every day of the month — and I hadn't even relocated yet. Things were looking good.

However, there was a problem. I didn't own a broadcast camera, an essential requirement for a freelancer. As a camera cost more than a house in a middleclass Johannesburg suburb, this was a serious stumbling block.

In those days, an international network cameraman earned two hundred and fifty dollars a shift. It was good money, but if he or she had their own camera, they could charge another five hundred and fifty dollars. So a camera earned more than double what the person operating it did.

To me, that was a business no-brainer. I had to get a camera. That was where the money was.

The next morning, I knocked on the manager's door at Barclays Bank and said I needed fifty thousand dollars — the equivalent of about half a million rand at the time — to buy a TV camera.

The manager in his immaculate suit eyed this twenty-something guy in front of him, dressed in jeans and a smart shirt, and asked what I would be using the camera for.

"News coverage," I said.

"In the townships?"

"Especially the townships."

I got the same astonished look as I had when applying for a loan to buy a disco. To take gear worth close on half a million rand into some of the most dangerous places in the world was not a business plan some suit in an air-conditioned office was likely to get excited about.

Once again, the word "collateral" cropped up. I said I would pay back the loan with the top rates the camera earned. Five hundred and fifty U.S. dollars a day, I stressed. Unconvinced, he pointed out that no sane insurance company would cover me without crippling premiums.

Unfortunately, he was right. All other banks said the same thing. No one would finance me. I was dead in the water. I went back to the bureau chief at NBC, a remarkable woman called Heather Allen, and said sadly I would not be moving to the Eastern Cape after all. I could not take up her offer of a retainer.

"Why?" she asked.

I told her. No camera.

"Have you got a valid passport?"

I nodded.

"What are you doing tonight?"

I shrugged. I didn't know.

"Well, I do. You're getting on a plane and flying to London and going to NBC in Tottenham Court Road. You then ask for Vivian. She will write out a cheque.

"Then you're going to catch a train to Basingstoke and meet Peter who runs Sony's Europe office. There you will get yourself a broadcast-quality camera and catch the next flight back to South Africa.

"Then you'll be covering a funeral for us next weekend in Port Elizabeth."

I looked at her, stunned. I didn't know what to say.

"Go — before I change my mind," she ordered.

Everything happened exactly as she said. A few days later I returned to South Africa with a brand new camera and covered the funeral for NBC. For that I earned eight hundred dollars — the highest day's pay I'd ever received.

As I had hoped, basing myself in Port Elizabeth was a strategically sound move and also resulted in getting assignments in Cape Town and Durban. Money started pouring in. So much so that, nine months later, I arrived at Heather's office in Johannesburg brandishing a cheque.

"What's this?" she asked when she saw the amount.

"Fifty grand plus interest."

She laughed. "I don't want the interest. All I want is that you do the same in helping someone else out one day."

That was exactly what Sister Bernard had said after saving my life in Daveyton. Once again, I pledged to do so.

Soon I could afford a tripod, top of the range lighting systems, and was one of the best-equipped freelancers in the business.

But the manager at Barclays bank was right about one thing: insuring this expensive kit was costly — and with good reason, as I discovered during a riot in East London some months later.

The government had just repealed the infamous Mixed Marriages Act, which prohibited people of different races marrying each other. From now on South Africans could tie the knot with whom they chose, a fundamental human right in the rest of the world, but a big deal in apartheid South Africa.

However, the Group Areas Act that stipulated different racial groups had to live in ethnically segregated areas was still in force. So while whites, blacks, Indians and coloureds (the official word for mixed-race people) could now marry, they could not live together as man and wife.

I realised straight away that, stripped of all legalese and verbiage, this bizarrely quirky story brilliantly captured the essence of those strange days. Distilled to its core, it was an intrinsic illustration of the craziness of apartheid.

But how to tell it?

I decided the best way would be to photograph the surreal contrasts of black and white residential areas. The backdrop would be that legally wedded bi-racial couples could not legally live as husband and wife in either.

Together, the supremely talented cameraman Willie Khubeka and I, filmed the leafy suburb of Selbourne in East London, a city about a hundred and seventy-five miles from Port Elizabeth. From there we drove to a dusty township called Duncan Village.

At first, everything seemed normal with people going about their business and kids playing in the street. We shot some footage contrasting shacks with villas, then drove into a valley.

It was going well. Willie was doing great camera work and I was deep in thought contemplating how to tell this uniquely South African story.

Then, faster than a mamba strike, the situation changed. We rounded a corner and almost ploughed into a barricade of planks and poles nailed to forty-four-gallon drums strewn across the road. We had inadvertently driven into a no-go zone.

I slammed the car into reverse, about to do the quickest U-turn of my life. But as I glanced in the rear-view mirror, I saw about a hundred people sprinting down the road towards us. The cry went up: "Target! Target!"

This was most definitely not a welcoming committee. Willie and I looked at each other, horrified. There was no way out.

Then a volley of rocks and stones struck the car, thundering like a giant hailstorm.

Willie jumped out to remonstrate with the stone-throwers, yelling above the clattering missiles that we were journalists wanting to tell their story. He was black, so they were more likely to listen to him than me.

But the enraged crowd was in no mood to listen to anyone. As they streamed down the hill, another barrage of rocks battered the car.

I grabbed Willie's arm. "Get in. We have to go."

The only way out was forward, which meant smashing through the blockade. To reverse into the stampeding mass of humanity was not an option.

I rammed my foot flat on the accelerator. Metal screeched as drums and planks and poles went flying.

Unfortunately, whoever set up the barricade had also scattered thousands of sharp little metal tacks on the road. All four tyres instantly punctured.

This slowed us down to little more than a crawl, no matter how hard I gunned the gas. By now even more youths had joined our pursuers, banging dustbin lids, repeating the refrain, "Target! Target!"

Neither Willie nor I had been to Duncan Village before. We had no idea where we were, or which street to take. I had no option but to keep the crippled car hobbling forward as fast as I could.

Then a kid, barely a teenager, ran in front of us. He was holding a rock the size of a football.

I could have driven at him to force him out of the way. But I knew if the car hit him, we would be dead — killed by the baying, rock-hurling mob. I slammed on brakes.

For a moment, the youth and I looked straight into each other's eyes: his blazing with rage; mine begging him not to throw.

With sinewy strength far beyond his juvenile years, he tossed the rock onto the hood of the car. It bounced off the metal and hurtled through the windscreen directly between me and Willie, ripping the rear-view mirror off and smashing into the expensive camera tripod on the back seat. I could visualise my bank manager nodding sagely. This was why he didn't give people like me loans.

I couldn't see where I was driving as the windscreen was a smashed spider web of shatterproof glass. In desperation, I punched a hole through the shards, slicing my hand in the process. I still have the scar.

Rocks hurtled down from all sides. Squinting through the gap I had punched in the windscreen, I somehow coaxed the flat-wheeled car past the barricade and down the road.

As we crested the hill, an apparition greeted us. At first I thought it was a mirage.

Instead, it was a *Buffel*— an armoured troop carrier used extensively by the South African Defence Force. It had stopped in the road directly in front of us, unsure of what was happening. Soldiers grasped their weapons as they watched two guys in a car mangled beyond recognition limp towards them.

The driver wound down his window.

"You guys look like you need some help."

The look on our faces gave the answer. No shit Sherlock. "OK, we'll get you out of here," he said, and barked orders to his men. Soldiers jumped out of the back, hooked a steel cable onto the dented car and towed us back the way we had come.

As we went past the crowd that minutes earlier had been hurling rocks, they cheered, waving and shouting, giving victory salutes. They may have won that round, but I reckon we were the real winners. We had escaped with our lives. My guardian angel had been working overtime.

The soldiers pulled us to the outskirts of the township and unhitched the car. I went into a café and called the rental company saying our vehicle had broken down. They apologised for the inconvenience. A replacement was on its way.

I suspect they regretted apologising when they saw the state of the vehicle we were returning.

One thing about being the only international cameraman in the Eastern Cape was that I had personal contact with the region's liberation movement leaders. This was particularly true of the United Democratic Front (UDF) and COSATU, the mass-membership Congress of South African Trade Unions. I was almost always first on the scene with breaking stories, and although I represented three international networks, I was known simply as "Pete the BBC guy".

However, this got somewhat scary at times. I once took a call from a guy claiming to be from the UDF saying they were going to execute a businessman who was an "enemy of the people". The public execution was scheduled to happen at a football stadium deep in the township. I should come along and film it, he said.

Talk about landing in a Catch 22 situation. The more I thought about it, the more devious it became. For if I went along and filmed a public execution, I could be charged as an accessory to murder. But if I alerted the police, the UDF would consider me an *impimpi* — informer — and my life would be in grave danger. I would have to leave Port Elizabeth.

But what if it wasn't the UDF after all? What if it was the security police setting me up?

We all knew cops loathed the international media with as much hatred as they did the township rioters. If they phoned with information of a crime, true or otherwise, and I didn't report it, they could arrest me for withholding potential evidence and throw away the key. For them, this would have the benefit of getting a pesky journalist permanently out of the way.

I was becoming paranoid as this was potentially a Machiavellian maze with no way out. I phoned the BBC head office and they told me to inform the police immediately. This was a fine idea in sedate London six thousand miles away, but here at the frontline it was another world. To be labelled an *impimpi* was by far the most lethal of all accusations. The end result was probably a necklacing.

I certainly didn't trust the police, but fortunately there was one person in Military Intelligence that I did trust. We had been to school together, and he was my last hope of coming out of this nightmare with any shred of credibility intact.

I phoned and asked him to record our conversation. I then repeated verbatim the 'execution' tip-off I had supposedly got from the UDF.

"If anything happens as a result of this, I want it recorded that I called Military Intelligence," I told my friend. "If for some reason I don't return from the football stadium, then you should submit this report and say it was all above board."

There was silence. This was not normal protocol. However, he finally agreed.

"But if nothing happens, then we never had this conversation," I said.

He agreed again.

I drove to the stadium. It was completely deserted — not a soul in sight. There was no businessman about to be executed.

It seemed I was being tested. They wanted to see if I had alerted the police. If so, at best I would no longer be trusted by the UDF. At worst, I would have been executed.

It wasn't just the liberation movements testing me. The security police did so as well.

I was once phoned by an officer who gave his name as Rademann, asking me to meet him at the Walmer Hotel in Port Elizabeth. I initially declined, saying I didn't have the time.

"Well, we can make this more formal if you want," he said, implying I would otherwise be subpoenaed. Reluctantly I went.

"Pete, we know a lot about you," Rademann said. "We know you went to Rhodes University. We know you were an officer in the army. We even know you ran your own disco."

He let that sink in. They had done their homework on me.

"But we can help you if you help us. If you give us information about your contacts in the UDF and ANC, we'll give you exclusive stuff on what's really happening behind the scenes. You'll get the best of both worlds. You'll be a media superstar."

"Are you asking me to work for you? For the South African security forces?" I asked.

He nodded.

"Well ... I'm very pleased I'm recording this conversation," I said, tapping my pocket. "I'm going to send it to the BBC the minute I get home. I want it to be on the record that there is no way I'm doing anything else but my job as a professional journalist. I'm not working for the ANC or any other political group. I'm not working for the South African

Government. I'm a journalist accredited by the Ministry of Foreign Affairs, so if you have a problem with that, I suggest you contact them and get my accreditation revoked."

I had been half-expecting this sly proposal, so was not taken completely by surprise. However, I could see the shock on Rademann's face when I said I had a tape recorder.

"This is a completely unacceptable meeting," I continued. "In fact, if any of these hotel waiters see me talking to you, a security policeman, my life could be in jeopardy. You have put me at serious risk. So goodbye."

I walked out, got into my car, and sped off.

The truth was that I hadn't been recording the meeting. I made that up on the spur of the moment. Even so, there was no way they dared call my bluff.

More importantly, they never tried to recruit me again.

That meeting showed what a difficult, not to mention bizarre, time it was for guys like me. We considered ourselves patriotic South Africans. We had done our stint in the army. We had fought what our government called the communist onslaught — *die rooi gevaar*, or red peril. We loved our country.

But that did not involve betraying professional ethics and spying for a dubious regime.

Despite this, I was privileged beyond belief to learn my craft in such an intensely turbulent crucible of conflict. Yet it wasn't all riots and mayhem, and we interviewed scores of fascinating people such as Bishop Desmond Tutu, Alan Paton, author of 'Cry the Beloved Country', and Helen Suzman, the sole anti-apartheid member of parliament for thirteen years. They were passionate about the future of the country. The story of the birth of democratic South Africa was not just bloodshed, but equally of courage, commitment, and unconquerable will.

I have mentioned how we toned down graphic images of township murders, but I was also determined that we, the international media, did not became part of the story. This was not about us. As I kept telling my friends, we were the messengers. So don't shoot us. The moment we became part of the story we were no longer go-betweens.

However, one time I did intervene was in KwaZulu-Natal, another volatile province on South Africa's east coast that I regularly covered from my base in Port Elizabeth.

We had chartered a helicopter and were circling KwaMashu, a township in flames just north of Durban, when we noticed a plume of oily black smoke spewing into the sky. The pilot flew us over to have a closer look.

Thank God he did. Below, huddled on the roof of a burning shop, was a family of eight. They had fled there when machete-wielding rioters started looting and setting fire to the premises.

The shop was on the top of a hill, surrounded by township shanties. The shopkeeper was Indian; the arsonists were Zulus. Indians were equally targeted by apartheid laws, but in the enraged centrifuge of a riot, that didn't matter. There was no doubt this entire family would burn to death.

Seeing us hovering above, they screamed pitifully for help. The abject terror on their faces, a father, mother and their young children, is still vivid in my mind. It was heartbreaking.

I asked the pilot to go lower so we could lift the family off with the landing skids, but he shook his head. With four of us and our heavy camera equipment, we would not be able to carry eight extra people. If we attempted that, we would all die, either in a crash or slaughtered by the savage mob below.

"We have to do something," I shouted into the pilot's earphones. "Can you call the police?"

"Well, we can tune into the police frequency and see what happens."

"Do so," I yelled. "Otherwise these people are going to die."

The pilot fiddled with the radio knobs as we held our collective breath. Then — absolute relief. Amid crackling static, a cop answered our call.

The pilot gave our position, stressing the critical urgency of the situation.

A few minutes later, several Casspir armoured vehicles charged up the hill. The cavalry had arrived, literally with seconds to spare. People were scurrying around, fleeing in all directions or throwing stones as police fired teargas and rubber bullets to clear a way to the shop. By now the building was an inferno, but police managed to get ladders onto the roof and grab the petrified family, hauling them to safety.

It was unbelievably dramatic footage. It would have headlined any news bulletin.

Yet I didn't film a second of it. And I have no regrets. The rescue was an incident that we, the media, had called in. We were an integral part of that story, something I didn't want on the news.

We had no footage, but that night I went to bed happy. It was a tremendous feeling — something thin on the ground in those bleak days.

We had saved a family from certain death.

Chapter Seven

Start the revolution without me

With the escalating number of hire cars trashed in the townships, the rental companies started cracking down on us.

Tired of seeing brand new vehicles needing bumper-to-bumper facelifts, or being completely written-off, they now stipulated that riot damages would be footed by the TV networks.

As a result, our bosses decided in their collective wisdom that one way to circumvent this was to teach us how to drive in crisis situations. That way we stood a better chance of getting a bright red BMW convertible out of a full-blown uprising more or less intact.

These advanced driving clinics were great fun, and soon we all considered ourselves potential Formula One candidates. We were taught how to reverse at top speed, double de-clutching for low gear power, or squeezing though gaps the size of a snake's hips. But the best was the high-speed turn, which involved yanking up the handbrake to lock the back wheels and whirling out of a ninety or hundred and eighty-degree spin. Doing it in reverse was even more fun, enabling an impossibly tight U-turn in seconds if you're a skilled rally driver — which we all thought we were. Mistakenly so, as my soundman Mike Mathews and I discovered.

After a bottle or two of robust wine, we decided to further perfect our Grand Prix skills and executed at least thirty of these stunts in our rented BMW on a street in Douglasdale, an upmarket Johannesburg suburb.

The next morning, we had to return the car and discovered it would no longer go forward. Yet it went perfectly backwards. We had shattered the forward gears during our Ayton Senna antics the previous night, but somehow the reverse gear was unscathed.

No problem. We decided to drive to the office in reverse. This entailed travelling backwards down Johannesburg's two busiest highways into the city centre, to the shock of fellow motorists. We didn't consider it particularly dangerous at the time. We even managed to overtake a slow-moving car, much to the driver's astonishment and to our amusement. The way we looked at it was that unlike many other occasions, no one was going to hurl rocks at us for going backwards.

We arrived, facing the wrong way, at the BBC office in Auckland Park and phoned Avis to fetch its car. Their driver was not happy that he had to reverse all the way back to his office.

On the plus side, as explained to the network number-crunchers, the fact we had not driven the vehicle into a riot meant we were not liable for damages.

I'm being flippant, as obviously the bigger picture of escalating violence was far more serious than a few dented cars. The runaway ferocity affected everything — community relations, livelihoods, businesses, properties, and of course, human lives.

TV cameramen were in an equally precarious predicament as to some extent the authorities regarded us as perpetrators. They accused us of igniting highly flammable situations simply by being there. They claimed people played up to the camera, and as a result turned peaceful protests into war zones.

I don't deny that a TV presence can alter the gravity of a situation. But does that mean every demonstration should only be allowed to happen in a vacuum?

The reality is that protest rallies, whether morphing into violence or not, are news. To ignore that is to negate the most crucial function of the media. Few disagree that a free, unbiased press is vital to democracy.

We all know the alternative, as at the time we had a blindingly obvious example: the USSR. The Soviets had a single communist-controlled news service called TASS (Telegraph Agency of the Soviet Union) serving an area the size of the North American continent. They also had two newspapers called Pravda (Truth) and Izvestia (News). The joke among those living under the yoke of Soviet tyranny was that there was no truth in Pravda, and no news in Izvestia.

Even the apartheid government realised that, and despite ham-handed censorship, the South African regime never matched the USSR in sheer paranoia.

So yes, the presence of the press could embolden people. But to say that is the key reason for mass discontent is being wilfully obtuse. Awful as it was, there is no doubt that the township violence we were filming was a catalyst for fundamental political change. As such, it was a hugely relevant story.

The police detested us not only because our presence could fan a fiery situation, it could also restrict their retaliation. So in one convoluted algorithm, we were simultaneously considered instigators and constraints in vicious confrontations watched around the world. To grasp that is to understand the ironies of South Africa in those days of fear and loathing.

The biggest laugh I got out of this was when an English cricket team defied the sports boycott to play a rebel test series in 1989. The team was captained by Mike Gatting, and its arrival sparked a large protest outside the British Embassy in the middle of Johannesburg.

I was filming the highly agitated crowd when the police, using a loudhailer, ordered us to put away our cameras. We ignored them, of course, and protesters were then given two minutes to disperse.

About two seconds later, the commanding officer yelled, *"Vat hulle!"* Grab them.

As the police charged with whips and batons, I felt a massive 'whack' on my back and sprawled on the ground. A hefty policeman towered over me.

"You *bleddy* BBC," he shouted. "You're the reason we have all these problems. No more photocopying, you hear?"

I stood and solemnly swore that I would not do anymore "photocopying".

The police were not alone in their apparent dislike for the BBC. The most militant far-right group in those tumultuous times was the Afrikaner Weerstandsbeweging (Afrikaner Resistance Movement), known as the AWB. Its leader was a neo-Nazi called Eugene Terre'Blanche, who considered the apartheid government to be dangerously liberal.

Despite his extremist views, he was a charismatic leader and his meetings were always lively, fuelled by high-octane brandy and spittle-flecked oratory.

We covered an AWB rally in Humansdorp, a town about ten miles inland from Jeffrey's Bay, one of the holiest of surfing's Holy Grails. But the inhabitants of Humansdorp were galaxies removed from the free-wheeling, endless summer wave riders, despite being neighbours. Instead of bright Hawaiian baggies, the moustachioed-men uniformly dressed in khaki shirts, shorts and *veldskoen*, or bush shoes, while the women would not be seen dead in a beach thong.

Arriving at the hall with Terre'Blanche already in full cry, I first took a wide-angle shot from the back showing the number of people attending. It was packed. Next, I got onto the stage, capturing the AWB leader in profile as he ranted and finger-wagged at the rapt audience. Then I moved behind him to show the adoring crowd stamping its feet in repeated standing ovations.

Suddenly I felt a powerful hand grab my shoulder. With a mighty heave, I was flung off the stage.

It was Terre'Blanche.

"Hey BBC," he shouted in Afrikaans. "What the hell can you see behind me that you can't see in front?"

The crowd burst out laughing, cheering and clapping as I picked myself up.

Afterwards, I asked Terre'Blanche why he had thrown me off stage.

"You *bleddy* BBC always do everything upside down and back to front, so I wanted you where I could see you. Not behind me."

Appalling as he was, he was tailor-made for lively TV and a brilliant rabble-rouser, even though his oratory was racist and ugly. However, I told him he was missing a trick by only speaking in Afrikaans. International viewers wouldn't understand a word, even if the primal thrust of his fire and brimstone was clear.

Like most politicians, he had a massive ego and wanted to reach a wider audience, although I don't think he grasped that most overseas viewers would be appalled at his racist rhetoric. From then on, whenever he was about to say something in English, he forewarned us by elaborately taking out a handkerchief and wiping his brow. We would then focus directly on him as he spoke to an international audience for all of thirty seconds. It was long enough, as the AWB message was not exactly intellectually taxing.

Another colourful politician at the time was Roelof "Pik" Botha, the Foreign Minister.[6] Unlike most apartheid

---

[6] "Pik" is the shortened Afrikaans word for "penguin" and was used as

proponents, Pik had a sense of humour and was easily the most popular cabinet minister, both in South Africa and abroad.

Along with other members of the media, I was invited to a *potjiekos* party, with Pik not only being our affable host, but also the chef.

Potjiekos — literally "small pot food" — is a meal cooked slowly over a log or coal fire in a three-legged, cast-iron pot, consisting of chunks of meat and various vegetables such as pumpkin and potato. Among many South African men, it is a ritual as well as a feast, and recipes — usually involving copious quantities of strong alcohol and Coca-Cola — are guarded tighter than Fort Knox gold.

Pik was such a man. He proudly served up his offerings, and one bite was enough to make me gag.

"*Dis kak*," I said to an Afrikaans journalist. It's crap.

Unfortunately, Pik overheard me.

"What do you mean it's *kak*?" he demanded.

I realised by the intense look in his eyes that I could argue politics, rugby — another Afrikaner religion — and even the questionable merits of apartheid with Pik. But not *potjiekos* recipes. That was sacrosanct.

---

the affectionate nickname for Roelof Botha due to his apparent likeness to the bird, particularly when wearing a suit.

I quickly retracted, saying it was *lekker* (delicious). I'm glad I did. Affable as he was, insulting his three-legged-pot skills was something he could not forgive and probably would never have spoken to me again.

It was also about this time that I decided to study for a pilot's licence. The Eastern Cape is the country's second largest province and I was covering an area more than twice the size of Scotland. Driving to reach fast-breaking stories with tight deadlines was often impossible. Instead, I had to charter small planes, which was hugely expensive.

The solution, to me, was simple. Get a flying licence. I would reach hotspots far quicker without having to hire pilots, and I could practise by taking an instructor with me on the TV networks' expense.

On one occasion, while doing pre-flight checks, my soundman Zed Monana watched as I tested the stall alarm, a vital piece of safety kit. This involved pulling myself up on the wing and sucking through a hole in the warning system, setting off an ominous 'bzzzt' sound.

"What's that noise?" asked Zed.

"If you ever hear that," I told him, "it means we're in big trouble."

"You mean about to crash?"

"Probably." That wasn't strictly true, as a stall is relatively easy to pull out of. But I didn't tell Zed that.

Overhearing us, the instructor remarked that we hadn't practised any stalls for some time. I said no problem, let's do some on the return trip.

He reminded me of this when flying back. Unfortunately for Zed, we were speaking through headphones. He couldn't hear us above the engine noise.

I eased back on the power, and as the plane's nose lifted there was a menacing 'bzzzt' as it stalled.

Zed started shouting, "Pete, we're going to crash!"

To add to his panic, the aircraft started buffeting as I worked the tail-stabilisers to pull the front down. This immediately increases speed, restoring power and forcing the aircraft out of the stall. It's a routine procedure, and usually only dangerous if you are too close to the ground.

We all laughed, Zed more from sheer relief than humour. He was risking his life regularly enough without his cameraman practising stalls in mid-air. He never flew with me again.

However, that was just how we were. It was probably embedded in our DNA, as one rather spooky, albeit highly unscientific, revelation confirmed. There were nine of us, all cameramen, at a party after a particularly volatile assignment, when one remarked it was his birthday.

Mine was also due in a couple of days. So I asked, "Who else has a birthday this month?"

Incredibly, eight of the nine guys put their hands up. It was astonishing. All but one was born under the Aries star sign.

Whether you believe in horoscopes or not, it's a remarkable coincidence. Even more so, as according to astrologers, Aries is the first constellation in the Zodiac and those born under the sign of the ram are most likely to barge into unknown situations with blind faith and fingers-crossed. That's pretty much a prerequisite for a frontline cameraman.

Without a doubt, one of the most momentous events in South Africa's history was the release of Nelson Mandela in 1990. Few believe that the country would not have been sucked into one of the bloodiest civil wars imaginable if it hadn't been for this extraordinary man.

I interviewed him after he had been elected president and asked what, in his incredible life, had been his biggest regret. I expected him to say the twenty-seven years he had spent behind bars, or the breakdown of his marriage to his second wife Winnie, a liberation struggle icon in her own right.

It was nothing like that. Instead he said his main concern was that his days were now so full that he no longer had time to "just sit and think".

"In fact, I've now told whoever's organising my diary to give me an hour a day of pure thinking time," he said. "Every man and woman should do that, whether it's under a tree in the garden, in the shower, or driving to work. If you don't think, you don't appreciate where you come from, where are you going, or what the situation is. As a result, you end up making mistakes."

I thought it unusual that someone who had lived such an eventful life could come up with something so simple, almost bland. It was only later I realised how wise those words were — that what he was saying was a profound antidote to much of the chaos in today's world.

It also made me question my own life. For the past three years I had been living on my nerves. I loved the adrenaline, but it was taking its toll. Perhaps it was time to explore other horizons. Just as the great Nelson Mandela advised, I needed some reflection time. To just sit and think.

But first I had another major story to cover. It involved walking in a minefield.

Literally.

Chapter Eight

Guerrillas in the mist

PART OF THE fun of journalism is that you often wake up having no idea how your day is going to pan out.

A last-minute phone call could result in jetting off to film some celebrity in a plush hotel, or conversely, disappearing into the steaming Angolan bush to meet an enigmatic guerrilla leader regarded as either a freedom fighter or running-dog imperialist stooge. Take your pick.

That's what happened one morning when I got a call from a woman in Washington D.C. suggesting an intriguing assignment.

"I'm Riva Levinson," she said. "I was given your name by Heather Allen at NBC. Would you be interested in doing an interview with Jonas Savimbi?"

Dr Jonas Savimbi was leader of the UNITA guerrilla army in Angola and considered one of the most accomplished bush fighters in Africa. He had originally waged war against the Portuguese colonialists. But when the Marxist MPLA movement seized power in 1975 after Portugal abandoned its overseas territories, he went back to the bush. His guerrilla army, consisting mainly of Ovimbundu tribesmen in southern Angola, controlled about a third of the country, albeit in sparsely populated regions. However, the most serious threat to the government was UNITA's highly effective sabotage of the Benguela Railway line, the country's economic artery.

Apart from being a skilled strategist, Savimbi spoke seven languages including Portuguese, French, and English. In short, he was a charismatic leader, and love him or hate him — and believe me, many did — he was very much part of the African story. I certainly was interested.

"Who do you represent?" I asked Riva. The fact Heather Allen recommended me was encouraging. Heather — who had financed my first broadcast quality camera — was one of the most respected people in journalism.

Riva said she worked for a public affairs company. Not only would she get me a face-to-face interview with Savimbi, there was a possibility of accompanying him on an attack at a strategic town straddling the Benguela railway line.

"Sounds good. Are you hiring me as a freelancer, or will I be working directly for you?"

"What do you mean?"

"If I'm going as a freelance journalist, I will have full editorial control. You won't pay me and you won't tell me what to film. I will be able to sell whatever footage I get to whoever I want."

"That's fine. We'll get you access; the rest is up to you. Just be at Wonderboom Airport tomorrow at six a.m."

"So I have total editorial control?"

"You do."

I called my brother Stewart. As a former army warrant officer, this assignment was right up his street. He also loved the wild outdoors so it would be a real adventure; a military mission deep in the bush.

"Hey Stew, do you want to come to Angola to interview Savimbi? You can be a freelance photographer."

He agreed instantly. There was only one hiccup. It was December 15, and his baby son's first Christmas was looming, he didn't want to miss it.

Rather naively, when one considers the logistics of assignments in the African bush, I assured him we would be back within a week.

We arrived at Wonderboom, a small airport outside Pretoria, and were taken to a dark, rather dilapidated hangar.

Looks certainly could deceive, as inside was a shiny, brand new, multi-million dollar Learjet with an American registration. It was then that I realised perhaps this assignment was considerably more substantial than I first thought.

The pilot filed a false flight plan, stating we were going to the Namibian capital of Windhoek. Instead, we landed at Katima Mulilo, a town on a thin ribbon of Namibia known as the Caprivi Strip that juts like a gut-hook knife into three other countries: Angola, Zambia and Botswana.

From there we boarded a Cessna 172 for the almost one hundred kilometre flight to Savimbi's base. We loaded bag after bag of equipment into the tiny plane, but a problem arose when Stewart insisted on bringing a case of beer.

The pilot shook his head. "We're too heavy. We won't get off the ground," he said.

"I'm not going without my beers," Stewart replied, holding the case firmly on his lap.

The pilot shrugged. We accelerated down the dirt runway, and as I feared, he couldn't muster enough speed for take-off. The beers would have to be ditched, even if it meant prising them from Stewart's iron grip with a crowbar.

The pilot turned the plane around and taxied back to the start.

"OK, we'll try one more time. See that steam roller?" he said pointing to a road-levelling machine halfway down the runway, "That's our marker. If we haven't reached take-off velocity by then, we're going to have to dump stuff. Including the beers."

Stewart watched the speedometer with mounting concern until we somehow lurched off the ground. He smiled triumphantly. At least he was not going to go thirsty in the bush.

We landed on a dusty strip near UNITA's headquarters at Jamba, a village that Savimbi had converted into a military base. This was where he and his fighters had been taking on the Angolan government for more than a decade.

We offloaded our equipment and the pilot returned to Namibia. As the plane disappeared, there was silence on the deserted runway, but we knew we were being scrutinised. We could sense human presence, eyes watching us through the dense bush.

Finally, a group of soldiers dressed in smart green uniforms emerged. They marched up and gathered our equipment, giving us the trademark UNITA handshakes — a slap of the hand followed by a bump of fists, symbolic of "the power to go forward".

We climbed aboard a GAZ truck and were driven to Jamba. It was an elaborate guerrilla encampment, heavily camouflaged against air attacks and equipped with sophisticated radars and anti-aircraft weapons, courtesy of the USA. Angola was very much at the forefront of the Cold War. The GAZ stopped outside a grass hut, which was to be our living quarters, and UNITA staff served a meal of goat meat.

The next morning Jonas Savimbi was waiting for us. He was an imposing figure, dressed in combat fatigues, pistol on his belt and black beret. With his thick bushy beard and burly features, he looked every inch a hardened guerrilla leader, which belied the fact that he apparently had a Swiss doctorate in political science.

He agreed to an interview right away, the first of several incredible conversations. We got footage of him claiming the Cubans and Russians were dropping chemical bombs on his fighters, which was a global news exclusive.

He also revealed that UNITA was planning to attack the town of Munhango, his birthplace, in a few days and we were welcome to film it.

Stewart and I couldn't believe our luck. That evening, we climbed onto a GAZ with mattresses on the floor and a platoon of soldiers at each end. Then the cry went up, *"Vamos lá!"* Let's go.

The large convoy could only move under cover of darkness as dust billowing off the bush tracks would otherwise be seen from horizon to horizon, alerting government forces. We would also be sitting-ducks in daylight for the Angolan Air Force, a formidable foe with Russian-trained Cuban pilots.

I was not sure how long the journey would take, but an indication was the flock of chickens in a wire coop on the truck. These steadily depleted as the trip progressed as every meal consisted of fowl. Our cook's name was — appropriately — Yum-Yum, and I think he knew more bird recipes than any chef alive.

Eventually we arrived at Munhango and the attack was scheduled at first light. Officers escorted us into a rudimentary 'ops room' where General Altino Sapalalo, who was in charge of the attack, was standing over a detailed model of the town moulded from sand.

Sapalalo, a UNITA legend better known by his *nom de guerre* 'General Bock', had lost an arm in combat. The other he wielded like a stick to point out how the battle would unfold, and where each company would be at any given time.

UNITA soldiers then dug two large foxholes, where Stewart and I spent the night. We slept fitfully, not knowing what the next day would bring. We would either have a world scoop if UNITA won, or be thrown into some hellhole of an Angolan jail if they didn't. Or worse.

At first light there was an almighty racket, a distinctive howling sound, as Katyusha 'Stalin Organ' rocket launchers started bombarding the town.

We scrambled out of our foxhole. Then, after hundreds of rockets had wrought total havoc, UNITA charged, overwhelming the Angolan forces. Once Munhango had been taken, we climbed aboard another GAZ truck and drove into the town centre as government soldiers fled in all directions, many hastily ripping off their uniforms.

Most buildings were aflame after the saturated Stalin Organ bombardment, thanks largely to a direct hit on a massive ammunition dump which exploded like a volcano. As Stewart and I waded through the wreckage, we came across a burnt-out Hind helicopter gunship with two charred Russian corpses in the cockpit. This gruesome scene proved direct Russian involvement — that the war was not solely being waged by Cuban surrogates.

However, the flip side of the coin was that the Hind, basically a flying tank, had been shot down by a UNITA-fired, state-of-the-art Stinger missile. This could only have been supplied by the Americans, underlining how important both sides considered the Angolan conflict.

For me, it was a worldwide scoop with undisputable evidence of Soviet helicopters and American missiles synchronously in a single graphic photograph.

We then went to the Benguela railway station, or what remained of it. It basically consisted of a destroyed siding and a sign displaying the station's name.

I asked UNITA soldiers to stand next to the sign, providing irrefutable proof that they had captured Munhango, the town where Savimbi had been born. General Bock and a bunch of battle-soiled soldiers stood bristling with rifles and ammo belts. For a dramatic introductory shot to the powerful footage I was filming, this was almost too good to be true.

It was.

Without thinking, I hopped off the siding platform and ran about 30 yards to get my wide-angle shot. As I did, I heard a cacophony of alarmed shouts.

I stopped and looked up. "What's the problem?"

"You've just run into a minefield," yelled Stewart. "The guys tell me that the whole area is full of landmines, especially on the side of the railway line. And they're unmarked."

I looked up and down the track. Then back to the concrete platform where Stewart and the soldiers were standing.

"How do I get back?"

Stewart looked at the soldiers. The soldiers shrugged.

I mentally computed the problem. We were several days away by truck from any form of civilization. There was strict radio silence. No helicopters were available. No ambulances, no hospitals. And here I was in the middle of a minefield on the most sabotaged railway line in the world. Even worse, everyone looking at me was shrugging.

Evidence of the staggering amount of landmines in Angola was everywhere. People crippled with missing limbs were, sadly, wherever you looked. Was there a landmine here with my name and "fool" written on it?

I looked at the ground. This was summer in the Southern Hemisphere and the soil was baked hard as rock. There were no footprints I could retrace.

In short, there was nothing I could do to alleviate my plight. I could not stand here for the rest of my life, waiting for better days. There was no way out except by trying to retrace invisible steps and hoping for the best.

I thought of my grandmother and looked over my shoulder, muttering to my guardian angel: "You've got to work hard to get me out of this one, mate."

There was silence as I started walking back. Everyone watched as I made one tentative step after another. Some of the UNITA soldiers didn't help by putting their hands over their ears.

It was the longest thirty yards of my life. Nothing will surpass that. The relief when I reached the station was inexpressible. I clambered up it faster than a Barbary ape.

But I had got my opening shot of UNITA soldiers next to Savimbi's hometown sign on the Benguela Railway. It was great; one of the best I have captured. Yet I still go cold when I think about it.

After that we toured the town. It was distressing in the extreme. Medical facilities were basic at best and so people shot in the stomach or other vital organs died in agony, exacerbated by the heat nudging forty degrees Celsius.

The only saving grace, and I use those words loosely, was that no civilians were killed for the simple reason that there weren't any. They had all fled the town some time ago. This was purely an attack on an army base.

It was also a clear indication of how feared Savimbi was. Wherever we looked, there were deserted posts, empty bully-beef cans and discarded army uniforms as government soldiers realised that was the only way to melt into rural populations.

Now we had to get home. Once again, we could only drive at night to avoid Cuban-led retribution, and it was slow going. When we arrived at Jamba it was Christmas Eve.

I called our pilot in Caprivi. Unfortunately, he had been celebrating the festive season with interest and was too drunk to fly and fetch us.

I told Stewart. This meant he was going to miss his son's first Christmas. The look in his eyes showed his keen disappointment. I also felt bad as I had promised him we would be back in time.

We couldn't even let our families know as there was no phone network in Jamba. Only radio.

However, I knew one person I could contact by radio. Riva, who had instigated this assignment.

It was a long shot, but I got hold of her on Christmas morning and asked her to sort something out. She told me to stand-by.

Less than an hour later, Riva got back to me. At that moment I realised exactly how resourceful and well-connected this amazing woman was. A plane would fetch us in Jamba, with a sober pilot, and fly us to Windhoek. From there, we could catch a commercial flight to Johannesburg.

We were home for lunch. Stewart's son celebrated his first Christmas with his dad and the rest of the family.

I later sold my footage at top rates to various networks and it was screened around the world. Riva called me a few days later to say she had even seen it on a mid-air CNN bulletin while flying out of Washington D.C.

Stewart got a front-page photo and a spread in the Johannesburg Sunday Times, so, apart from the adventure, he also made some money.

From Johannesburg, I flew back to Port Elizabeth where I was living in a mansion with my girlfriend. As a kid, my favourite place had always been my grandparents' large, palatial home. But this house, which I had just bought, was even bigger and better.

I first saw it advertised as a show house, arriving in my kombi with a windsurfer strapped on the roof and my dogs in the back for a viewing

I knocked on the door and a snotty old lady appeared. I said I wanted to have a look around.

"You're in the wrong place." Her disdain was palpable.

"This is a show house, right?"

I saw her looking at my kombi.

"Yes. But it's very expensive," she said. "Close on a million rand."

Perhaps I bought it just to spite her. More pertinently, it was because I could — thanks to the money I had made from TV journalism.

My girlfriend Sue and I were living the dream. We had a villa with an immaculate garden, a top of the range Mercedes, a kombi for the beach, windsurfers and a high-speed inflatable boat.

I was only twenty-two. Life was grand.

However, something nagged. I wasn't sure what until I woke one morning and in the insomnia-induced clarity of the darkness before dawn, it became clear. I had grown up too fast over the past few years. I had too many possessions.

There was excessive clutter in my life, much of it meaningless.

It was all too much. It was all too soon.

Also, I decided I was tired of being whipped, stoned and petrol bombed. Instead, I wanted to go exploring again. I wanted to bum around Europe like I had before being called up to the army. I wanted new adventures.

In the back of my head was another voice. A more ominous one. It whispered that so far I hadn't been killed or hurt. But how long would my luck hold?

I woke Sue.

"Let's sell the house and go to Europe," I said. "Let's hike around the continent, living free and easy. Let's go and have some fun."

She rubbed sleep from her eyes, instantly awake.

"Are you mad?"

"No. Let's go and do something new. Something crazy."

She flung her arms in the air. "What are you talking about? You've got everything you dreamed of here. You've worked so hard for it. And you want to throw it all away and go travelling?"

My silence was the answer. Not one she wanted to hear.

"This is insane," she said.

Later that day, I broached the subject again. I wanted new adventures. I also wanted her to come with me.

"I'm not doing that," she said. "You do it. Go and get it out of your system. Then come back to me."

A few days later I packed my bags. I had a ticket to London, which would be my initial destination.

I didn't know it then, but the question was not where I was going.

It was whether I would be coming back.

Chapter Nine

Seoul Olympics

TO MY SURPRISE, it was a relief leaving South Africa. There was some sadness, of course, but I told myself this was temporary. I would be back soon.

But overall, it was as though a ton of lead had melted off my shoulders. I realised in my heart of hearts I had made the right choice to get out while the going was OK, if not exactly 'good'. That perhaps I had sometimes been chancing my luck a little too far.

Arriving in London, I met up with Mike Mathews, an Irish/South African friend with whom I had worked extensively in South Africa. Among other escapades, Mike had been my partner in crime in stunt driving with hired

BMWs, resulting in returning the car in reverse gear. We bought a campervan and went bumming around Europe.

It was great fun, totally de-stressing after the hectic time in townships for both Mike, one of the best soundmen and TV editors around, and myself. I found that for the first time in three years, I didn't have a constant dull ache in my stomach. I had been living on nerves for so long that I barely noticed the discomfit. I only realised once my stomach pangs had vanished that the cause was unrelenting stress.

We were having such a good time that I phoned my girlfriend, Sue, in Port Elizabeth, asking her to meet up in France. She reluctantly hopped onto a plane and spent five days with us in the kombi.

For her, that was more than long enough. Cooped up in a tiny campervan, sleeping on a flimsy mattress in a stale sleeping bag, using Motorway Services as bathrooms, was light-years removed from our luxurious home with comfy double beds and sofas as soft as silk. Her bewilderment was not only attempting to understand why I was doing this, but why was I enjoying it so much.

"This is not for me," she said, as she caught a plane home. "Come back when you're done."

However, it was more complicated than that. The previous year, I had secretly moved into a flat with her in Cape Town, and when her father found out, he was furious as this was the last thing he envisaged for his little girl. To pacify him, I said my intentions were honourable and I planned to marry her. It was not a lie. I had even bought a glittering diamond engagement ring to seal the deal, but we hadn't set the date.

What we hadn't bargained for was my sudden bout of restlessness. Nor the fact that my trip meant we were in different hemispheres, let alone different continents.

However, as far as she was concerned, nothing else had changed. She was still my fiancée, albeit living in a mansion in South Africa while I was sharing a beat-up kombi with a mad Irishman in France. We were still going to get married when I got back home.

The key question, although neither of us knew it at the time, was whether I would go home.

I returned to London with finances running low, so needed to find a job quickly. First stop was the BBC as I had done extensive work for the 'Beeb' in South Africa. I called up old contacts, but due to stringent trade union regulations, they couldn't hire me. Even though I had previously risked life and limb getting stories for them, there was no skirting around the fact that I was not a member of the union and an application could take years.

I then went to NBC, the American news network. There I met up with Vivian, who had signed the loan for my first TV camera three years' previously.

"Have you got work for me?"

"Not as a cameraman. We've got loads of those," she said. "But I need a freelance editor. It pays the same, a hundred and eighty pounds a shift. If you want, you can come in tonight."

This was great news — except for one flaw. I had no real experience as an editor. I had to learn quickly. Very quickly.

"Sorry Vivian, I'm busy tonight," I fibbed. "Do you have anything for next week?"

She looked at her diary.

"There's a shift available next Thursday. Also Friday."

"I'll take both."

That evening I met up with Shane Macdonald, an Australian working as a freelance cameraman and editor. London was full of Aussies — it still is — and they are valued employees as they work as hard as they play. They are also usually great TV operators as they get superb training in their homeland without having their heads stuffed with crippling union regulations. Give them a crate of beer and a few hundred pounds and they will go anywhere without harping on about nanny state regulations.

I asked if he could teach me how to edit.

"Sure can, mate." And with those three words, not only a lifelong friendship was formed, but it also gave me an introduction to the adventurous, boisterous and utterly irreverent Aussie media brotherhood that I would connect with extensively for the rest of my days in journalism.

Shane, who came from the quaintly named city of Albury-Wodonga, spent most of the night teaching me the intricacies of film editing. I then followed him around for a couple of days getting experience on the job. It took the phrase "crash course" to new levels.

However, it worked as when I arrived for my first shift at NBC, at least I knew how to appear competent. It was again the power of adventure and opportunity. I could have told the truth, that I knew next to nothing about professional editing, or I could have gone out and learned. Thankfully, I chose the latter.

Even with NBC shifts, work was sporadic so I decided to cut costs and booked into a YMCA. I was impressed as it was far more luxurious than its stereotyped reputation for cornering the unwashed traveller market. My room even had an adjoining bathroom and a minibar.

I soon found out why. It happened when I was handed a bill for a hundred and thirty-five pounds after three days' stay. On querying the exorbitant amount, I discovered this was no ordinary YMCA. In fact, it wasn't a YMCA at all.

It was instead a Y Hotel — a hospitality group I had never heard of and an extremely expensive case of mistaken identity.

I checked out at speed and dialled a friend of mine, Colin, asking if he could find cheap accommodation. Colin said he knew someone considering taking in a lodger and invited me to dinner at her spacious house in Battersea Rise. Her name was Nicky. If she liked me, she would possibly let out a room.

Colin picked me up at the Y Hotel, surprised to see me carrying a suitcase.

"What's that? You can't just move in."

"Well ... maybe she'll like me."

He wasn't convinced.

"Put it in the trunk. And don't take it out. She mustn't see it or she'll think you're a presumptuous jerk."

Half way through dinner Colin suddenly asked Nicky, "Do you like Pete?"

She was a bit taken aback.

"Well ... he's OK."

"He's got his suitcase in the car."

"You mean he's moving in? Now?"

"If that's OK."

To prove I would be a good lodger, I did the washing up after dinner.

The next day I called Nicky from the NBC offices. "Hi, it's Pete."

There was a brief silence at the other end. Then she asked, "Pete who?"

"You know, Pete the lodger."

"Oh — I forgot I now have a lodger," she laughed.

"I'm working late tonight so I won't be back for dinner."

She laughed again. "Pete, I'm not your mother — you don't have to tell me where you're going. You're a lodger."

From that moment on, Nicky's crowd of friends always referred to me as "Pete the lodger".

It was a dream introduction to London. Nicky was a few years older than me; a very cool, very beautiful blonde with a large circle of equally cool friends. They were the city's yuppies of the day, driving snazzy convertibles and going to country cottages for extravagant parties over weekends.

Completely by chance, I had fallen in with an extraordinary group of highly intelligent, flamboyant, fun-loving, interesting and artistic people. As "Pete the lodger", I happily tagged along.

It was a fascinating time for me. A young man from Africa living in London, one of the greatest international cities of the world, where every new experience was wildly exotic. I was meeting captivating people such as Charles Spencer, Lady Diana's brother who was the entertainment correspondent for NBC. He had lived in Cape Town for several years, so we had an instant connection. He also got me some showbiz stories, such as interviewing Rolling Stones' guitarist Bill Wyman. The ageing rocker was at that stage nudging half-a-century, and somewhat controversially, to put it mildly, was about to marry a teenager called Mandy Smith. Needless to say, it was a real rock 'n 'roll interview.

But best of all, I was covering stories without being shot at or pelted with rocks.

However, I was still restless. Extremely restless — as I discovered one morning while filming the Kings Cross Underground Fire Inquiry where thirty-one commuters perished in a Tube inferno.

It was an unimaginable tragedy, but even so, dry commissions of inquiry are not the most riveting news stories. It also was typical London weather: cold and pelting with rain, even though it was summer.

I was bored as I gazed out of the window. I desperately wanted to feel some sunshine. But I also needed money. The only way to balance that was to find an exciting job in a hot country.

The Olympic Games were about to kick-off in Seoul, and although the South Korean capital is not the Caribbean, it was definitely sunnier than London. On a whim, I phoned the British Olympic Committee and queried how to get press accreditation.

They said as long as I worked for a media company, I could apply.

I was a freelancer, which meant I would not be accredited as things currently stood. The only way around that was to create my own media company. This entailed a trip to Her Majesty's Revenue and Customs headquarters in the city centre, where I registered the somewhat grandiosely named Broadcast News Ltd. I was sole director, sole shareholder and tea boy.

With that under my belt, I managed to obtain three highly-prized press passes to cover the Olympics.

However, I was not out of the woods as the costs of getting myself, a soundman and loads of equipment to South Korea was way out of my reach. I desperately needed sponsorship.

I approached TV-am, the UK's first breakfast TV franchise, and asked the news editor if his team had anyone based in Seoul.

Jackpot! They didn't. They had applied too late and all Olympic accreditations had been snapped up.

"Well, I've got three press passes," I said. "I'm taking my own soundman and if you loan me one of your correspondents, we can work as a team."

"Perfect — we'll give you plenty of coverage. But," said the news editor, "we can't afford to fly you out."

Back to the drawing board. But at least I had guaranteed exposure.

I contacted Korean Airways, told them I was covering the Olympics for TV-am, and asked if they would like a promotional video of the airline, which I would provide in exchange for three plane tickets.

Once again, the gods were smiling. As luck would have it, the Olympics coincided with Korean Airways' inaugural flight from London to Seoul via Ankara. Yes, they certainly were interested in a promotional video to highlight this.

I then phoned Tony, a soundman/editor I had worked with in South Africa and asked him to get on the next flight to London. Tony had extensive corporate video experience and was a brilliant editor. We flew First Class to Seoul, sipping champagne and snacking on canapés as we worked.

Then we had another stroke of incredible luck. CBS had heard through the media grapevine that I was covering the Games and urgently contacted me. Like TV-am, they hadn't got applications through in time and asked if I could work something out. This was too good an opportunity to miss, so I flew Mike to Seoul and we split into two crews, servicing both networks.

No sooner had we agreed on the deal with CBS when their correspondent Adrian Brown arrived at our hotel to discuss coverage. While outlining potential stories, Adrian rather rudely — in my opinion — told me I needed a haircut. I replied there was nothing wrong with the length of my hair.

He smiled. "Trust me. You really *should* get a haircut."

Adrian even gave me the name of a barber. As soon as I arrived, I discovered why he was so insistent. South Korean barbers consider the craft of coiffure to be an art form, although the jury is out on whether it complies with the dictionary definition.

It was late summer with daylight temperatures averaging 30 degrees Celsius, so I was dressed in T-shirt, shorts and flip-flops. As I sat on the barber's chair, it hydraulically spread into a recliner couch.

My feet were placed in a basin and a Korean woman, who could have been a catwalk model on any London agency's books, gave me a foot massage in soapy water.

While that was happening, using hot and cold cloths as lubricants, the barber slid a cutthroat razor sharper than a samurai sword so closely down my face that my skin was smoother than a baby's posterior.

I was then flipped over, and a barefoot Korean woman walked up and down my back, expertly clicking vertebrae into place and massaging spine muscles while keeping her balance holding onto a ceiling rail.

All of this was completely above-board. It was included in an upmarket hairdressing salon's service, standard for wealthy Koreans, and done in the open. No clothes were removed, and there were at least four other guys having their hair trimmed at the same time.

Working for CBS news meant that we were not rights holders to actual sports coverage. In other words, we could film sprinter Ben Johnson warming up for the hundred-metre dash, but not the race itself. We covered events as news rather than sport, although there was much blurring of lines when Johnson broke the record, then failed a drugs test the next day.

In fact, a lot of the really interesting stuff didn't involve the Olympics. I got great footage of North and South Korean officials meeting on the 38th Parallel Demilitarization Zone (DMZ), the latitudinal co-ordinate that separates the two bitterly divided countries. The conference table was placed directly over the Parallel, with the line drawn exactly down the middle. Officials would discuss what military movements were happening near the DMZ, handle allegations of infringements, and generally try and ratchet down war talk.

I was lucky enough to be flown by the Americans along the Parallel, and hanging out of the 'copter with one foot on the skids, I filmed arguably the world's most fractious border. The amazing aspect was not the stark difference of booming prosperity in the south and abject poverty in the north, but the astonishing abundance of wildlife flourishing in no-man's land. It was vivid evidence of how nature thrives when humans don't interfere.

Another fascinating sidebar to the Olympics was the ferocious student protests that regularly erupted at Seoul's International University. Among the myriad of student gripes were demands for more democratic government and reunification with the North, all underpinned with virulent anti-Americanism.

North Korea is a rogue nuclear power and failed state, something that even today, more than thirty years later, has not been resolved. Consequently, many of the student demands were ideological non-starters. That's nothing new. Student protests are a rite of passage in a democracy, and South Korea was no exception.

But what was exceptional was that even in the raging vortex of a riot, everything was strictly structured — so much so that at times I thought I was watching a Monty Python parody of Oriental discipline. Both sides adhered to rules of conflict. There was even a student hotline giving the time and venue of each protest, and exactly how long it would last.

Mike and I decided to film a protest and arrived fully prepared. This entailed wearing baseball helmets as plenty of 'missiles' would be thrown, and carrying a stepladder to give us a height advantage over rival TV crews.

The riot — sorry, protest — was scheduled for two p.m., and with five minutes to spare, we set up the camera and stepladder at a road intersection in front of the University.

As punctual as a Swiss train, the students erupted from the campus and started throwing rocks and fire-bombs at the cops, who retaliated with rubber bullets. It soon spread like wildfire into the suburbs.

Mike and I followed the running street fights, eventually stopping at a corner where police and students were regrouping. I decided I would get a better shot on the other side of the road where the students were, and ran off. The camera on my shoulder was attached via an electronic umbilical cord to Mike's recording box, so he had no option but to follow me.

As I sprinted across the street, a petrol bomb narrowly missed my head, exploding with a fiery 'whoosh' on a wall in front.

That was a bit close for comfort and we turned and started running back the way we had come.

Then, for some reason, I changed my mind, spinning around and running towards to the action again. Unfortunately, I neglected to tell Mike, who was still dashing away in the opposite direction.

The umbilical cord jerked like a bungee, snapping us both backwards. I turned to follow Mike, while he turned to follow me. We careened straight into each other, collapsing in the middle of the road. Only our baseball helmets saved us from cracking heads.

The entire riot stopped in mid-violence as a result of our collision. Both police and students ran over, picking us up and dusting us down, jabbering excitedly in Korean, asking if we were all right.

We nodded, and both groups escorted us back onto the pavement, sternly telling us to remain there.

Then it was business as usual. The riot resumed with even greater intensity, rocks and rubber bullets again flying as we filmed from the sidelines.

Forty-five minutes later, exactly on cue, the riot stopped. No signal was given; it was as if some subliminal 'Time Out' had flashed. Students and police joined forces to clear up the mess, carting rocks off the road and sweeping spent rubber ammo off the 's.

Within an hour, traffic was flowing freely and the streets as peaceful as a postcard.

Coming from the chaos of South Africa, this was simply unbelievable. As I remarked to Mike, in this part of the world even mayhem was efficient. We shook our heads in amazement.

Finally, the Olympics ended in an incredible ceremony watched around the planet, again resulting in unbelievable coverage for CBS and TV-am, which was crucial for my freelance résumé.

Then, it was time to fly back to London. I was met at Heathrow by a beautiful friend whom I rather fancied called Janine Haines. Everyone called her JJ.

Her first comment was, "Wow, your hair is very short."

Indeed. I'd had four haircuts.

Chapter Ten

JJ

I T WAS CANADA DAY, 1 July 1988. I have no ties to Canada, but it is a day I remember well. It was the day I met JJ in London.

During those exuberant times, any event — no matter how obscure — was an excuse for a party, whether I knew the hosts or not. Canada Day was no exception, even for us non-Canucks.

Festivities were in full swing when I arrived. One of the girls on the dance floor instantly caught my attention. She was dark-haired and striking, moving sinuously to the music. I walked up and introduced myself.

To my surprise, she replied that we had met before. "You were bitten by a lion in South Africa," she said.

It all came flooding back. I had bumped into her while being treated at the Johannesburg General Hospital after a lioness almost severed my right hand. This required extensive therapy at the hospital's hand clinic, where JJ was also a patient. She had seriously injured a finger in a circular saw accident, and we got chatting. Right away, I thought she was gorgeous. However, she had a rather large boyfriend hovering around who wasn't interested in me talking to her, so nothing came of it.

I had long forgotten that encounter. So what were the chances of us meeting again several years later at a party in London celebrating Canada's national day? I would not have gambled good money on that happening. But it did, and I am eternally grateful.

After a not-so-subtle inquiry, I discovered that the hefty South African boyfriend had been downgraded to an "ex", and we exchanged phone numbers.

This was a promising start, but not for long. I soon lost her number, and having no idea where she lived, had no way of contacting her.

That was the end of that. Or so I thought. Then fate struck once again and we met at another party. She was rather cool towards me as I explained the reason for not contacting her. I then asked her out for a meal. She somewhat warily agreed to meet at Tattershall Castle, a pub on the River

Thames, in a few days' time. I wanted to make it a dinner date, but she insisted on lunch, and I could sense that after the debacle of losing her phone number, she wanted "neutral" ground.

That didn't deter me. In fact, this time I was determined everything would go perfectly. Except it didn't. As I was about to leave the office, a crucial last-minute meeting cropped up with the news editor to discuss our contract for the Seoul Olympics. I had to attend the meeting or else I could lose the deal. As a result, I was unable to meet JJ on time.

In those pre-cellphone days we had pagers, usually clipped to trouser belts. I was still in the meeting when mine bleeped with an irate message from JJ informing me that I was late and she was not waiting a second longer. Furthermore, I should not contact her again. Ever.

The entire office heard the curt "Dear John" message — and we hadn't even gone on our first date. This caused some amusement among my colleagues, which I obviously didn't share.

JJ was not short of suitors. Suffice it to say, it took a lot of hard work to get her to meet me again. Far, far harder than the toughest battlefront media assignments I have been on.

She has an intriguing background. Attractive, well travelled and adventurous, she is a true cosmopolitan at home anywhere in the world. Everyone calls her JJ, which she prefers as South Africans tend to pronounce her name "Jarr-neen", rather than the more melodious French "Zha-neen", as intended.

Here's her story, told in her own words.

"I was born in Switzerland, the youngest of three daughters to an English father and South African mother.

"My father, who worked in the insurance industry, travelled extensively with my mother and more or less used Switzerland as a base. As a result, we were brought up by French-speaking nannies and my sisters and I grew up speaking an unusual blend of English and French.

"Montreux, at the foot of the Swiss Alps, was my hometown, although we also lived in Uganda for about a year when I was four.

"My childhood changed when my father suffered a seriously debilitating stroke. He and my mother were on an island off Libya at the time and she flew him back to Switzerland to recuperate. My sisters were at boarding school in England, and as mum had her hands full looking after my father, I was also packed off to school there, even though I was only six years old. Basically, that was when I left home.

"My father died when I was twelve, and my mother returned to South Africa, taking me with her. I finished school in Johannesburg, then went to university in Cape

Town. I had no idea what degree I wanted to study, randomly choosing archaeology. However, it didn't take long to discover that the glorious Cape wine routes, beautiful beaches and non-stop parties were far more fun than academia, so in an attempt to avoid these distractions, I returned to Johannesburg to do an interior design course. That was when I first met Pete. It wasn't every day that you bump into a guy who'd been bitten by a lion, so although I vaguely remember him as being charming, apart from his injury he didn't make a lasting impression. At that stage of my life, all I really wanted to do was go travelling. That's what I loved most. I had travelled extensively with my parents, even going on the Trans-Siberian Express, and that's what I wanted to keep on doing."

After qualifying as an interior designer, JJ flew to Israel and lived in a kibbutz for several months before trekking around Greece and Egypt, finally returning to England and meeting me.

"I actually saw Pete a couple of weeks before meeting him at the fateful Canada Day party. He was at a Tube station, tanned and wearing a brown leather jacket, and I instantly knew he was South African but didn't recognise him as the lion guy. So it was quite a surprise meeting him at the party.

"He was a very persistent suitor and didn't give me a choice, literally sweeping me off my feet no matter how hard

I tried to get rid of him. First it was an invite to lunch, which I accepted as I figured it would just be an amicable meeting over lunch. Then he wanted me to go away with him and I said no, that wasn't going to happen. Undeterred, he then said he was going to Scotland for a weekend with friends, and it would be nice if I came along. As it was a group holiday, I agreed."

I was delighted that JJ accepted the Scottish invite and thought I was making good progress. However, the trip backfired spectacularly. We were walking in the woods in the middle of nowhere and came across a public phone box — those bright red ones Britain is famous for — and one of my friends decided to ring his mother in South Africa.

"I'm here with Pete Henderson and his girlfriend," he told her.

There was a moment's silence at the other end. "Girlfriend?" queried his mother. "But he's got a fiancée in South Africa."

JJ heard that, and I was in deep trouble. Deservedly so. Once again, my powers of persuasion were seriously put to the test. JJ was not interested in complicating her life and told me to return to South Africa and sort myself out. Her tone implied that she had no intention of sitting around waiting for me. Not only that, she might not take my call when I returned.

I also knew that I wanted to be with her more than anything else.

It was close to Christmas, and the following week I flew back to South Africa, told my fiancée Sue I had met someone else, and was returning to Europe for good. As Sue had done nothing wrong, I decided the honourable option was to give her everything I owned in South Africa. That included the house, the car, the windsurfers, beach toys, and the pets.

All I had when I boarded the plane back to Europe was a backpack, a hundred dollars in my pocket, and some clothes. But crucially, I still had my camera equipment. With that, I believed I could make a living anywhere in the world.

I knew that JJ was in Switzerland and in the throes of getting Swiss nationality. Switzerland has no birthright laws, so even though JJ was born in the country, she was not automatically a Swiss citizen.

I phoned her and told her everything was sorted. I had broken off the engagement and was now a free man — if she still wanted me. She agreed to meet me at Geneva and go skiing at Gstaad. We were both almost broke and the train fare to Gstaad further depleted our finances. We couldn't even afford to hire skis, a major problem on a skiing holiday. Instead, we went to a restaurant and collected some plastic rubbish sacks, which we used as a crude toboggan to slide down the slopes at remarkably fast speeds. It was great fun, and not something many champagne-swigging Gstaad jetsetters had witnessed before. I think we were the first to introduce extreme-budget-skiing at the elite resort.

It was now time to start considering future prospects. I knew with absolute certainty that I didn't want to continue working in London for other people, as although it's a fabulous city, it was a bit mundane for a guy used to adrenaline journalism. I wanted to see more action. Not only that, as the Seoul Olympics had proved that I could make it on my own in a strange land, the idea of starting up my own global freelance TV news outfit now seemed feasible. I also had the confidence that I could compete with the best anywhere in the world.

But where?

The question soon answered itself. The most explosive flashpoint at the time was in the Middle East. The Intifada uprising against Israeli occupation of the West Bank and Gaza, and the Lebanese civil war, were raging simultaneously. It was a flaming maelstrom, inexorably sucking the entire region into its vicious vortex. As a veteran covering South Africa's township rebellions, this was the type of white-knuckle news I was familiar with. I knew first-hand how to operate in hostile situations.

I was also sick of the grey English weather and despite its myriad of almost insoluble problems, at least the Middle East has a good climate. I think the promise of sunshine swayed me as much as the news potential.

I initially decided to base myself in Beirut. However, the Lebanese capital was one of the most dangerous cities in the world with several Europeans being held hostage and treated horrifically by jihadists. United Press International journalist John McCarthy, for example, was locked in a tiny cell for more than five years before being freed.

The more sensible option was Cyprus, where few international TV networks were based. At the time, the global news networks covered the Middle East from offices in Tel Aviv, London or Rome. This meant that big name journalists were continuously flying in and out of the multiple regional flare-ups, wasting valuable time and costing loads of money. I figured that being in Cyprus, which was only a forty-minute flight to either Beirut or Israel, would provide a crucial edge. It was similar to my thinking in South Africa when I based myself in Port Elizabeth rather than Johannesburg, a decision that paid off handsomely. In TV news, whoever gets the camera rolling first almost always wins.

My soundman, editor, and good friend Mike Mathews was also dead keen on the idea, so we already had a two-man rapid reaction crew raring to go.

But would JJ also opt in?

That was the key question. She possessed all the qualities I envisaged in my ideal woman; incredibly well travelled, fun, adventurous and exciting to be with. If anyone was perfectly suited to go on the next journey with me, she was. She was also incredibly attractive. I wanted to be with her more than anything else. Everything — Cyprus included — hinged on her answer.

I braced myself and asked her.

She thought about it for a bit, then phoned her lawyer who was sorting out her Swiss nationality. He confirmed that being in Cyprus would not affect her application in any way.

"OK, let's go," she said.

My relief was palpable. It wasn't just that she was coming with me — I discovered at that moment how exceptionally brave she was. Not only would we be in a strange country; working with me also meant she would be thrown into the deep end of the notoriously cutthroat TV industry. She disputes that courage, saying she had already travelled extensively and had no real roots in either Switzerland or England. Consequently, going to Cyprus was just another adventure in a string of them. This was truly a woman after my own heart.

We were set to go. But as we were about to board a plane from Geneva, I got a nasty shock. All my camera equipment

— absolutely vital to our venture — added up to a bill of a hundred dollars' excess luggage. It was money I didn't have.

I had no option but to ask JJ if she would loan the cash. Otherwise we were dead in the water. I don't think I have ever felt more embarrassed, as not only was I taking her to an alien country, I couldn't even pay our way.

"I only have two hundred dollars," she said, as she handed me the money.

I will never forget that. The trust she showed in that simple gesture was one of the most humbling moments in my life. I knew without question I had a quality companion.

The next hurdle was to get accommodation in Nicosia, Cyprus's largest and most important city. We had no money to pay a deposit, and trying to sweet-talk an intensely suspicious Cypriot landlord into letting out an apartment to three unkempt foreigners was next to impossible. Somehow we managed.

The apartment was to be our home and office. Our furniture consisted of two mattresses and three beanbags. We also had three knives, three forks and three coffee mugs.

I was twenty-six years old. This would be the third time I would be starting out from scratch. The first had been forming the Cape Connection film production company; the second the news bureau in Port Elizabeth. But this was something else altogether. We were setting up a business on an island we had never been to before, covering a global flashpoint we knew little about. And with no money.

It was truly a venture into the unknown.

Chapter Eleven

Missiles in the Middle East

UNABLE EVEN TO PAY rent, we had to find work fast. Or else the Cyprus adventure would wither ignominiously on the vine.

This proved to be harder than I imagined. I worked the phones non-stop, calling everyone in the media industry I knew. I had good contacts at TV-am, the BBC, CNN, NBC and ITN, and thought I could rely on that extensive network to pick up assignments. Also, I had my own camera, unlike most other freelance teams, and was based close to the Middle East hotspots.

But even so, we got no offers.

After six weeks with absolutely nothing coming our way, Mike flew back to London to earn some money to keep our landlord at bay, while JJ and I held the fort. Things looked bleak.

Just as I was on the verge of total despair, we had a breakthrough. Out of the blue, ITN's Brent Sadler called me saying he urgently needed a cameraman to accompany him to Lebanon. I agreed on the spot, but told him I had no soundman. It was a classic case of Murphy's Law. Our first job offer comes as Mike leaves for London.

Fortunately, Brent was in such a hurry he brushed that off saying we would hire someone in Beirut.

Sadler is known in TV circles as "Blazing Saddles", due to his fearless, scorched earth pursuit of any story. It suited him, and he was one of the star foreign correspondents of his time.

I met up with him at Larnaca along with 12 boxes of gear containing cameras, lights, editing equipment, and two monitors. As this was our first Middle East assignment, I was leaving nothing to chance.

We boarded the ferry to Lebanon and I soon realised this was no milk run. At three a.m. I woke to whistling rockets and whooshing water spouts. I went up on deck to see gouts of sea exploding high into the sky. We were being shelled and we hadn't even reached shore.

The fifteen-year Lebanese Civil War was a hugely complex conflict between various Christian, Muslim, Druze, communist and nationalist factions. To further complicate matters, both Syria and Israel invaded the ruined country, with the Syrians controlling the north, the Maronite Christians controlling the coastal cities and far south, and Israel the rest. Just as the hippies quipped that if you remembered the sixties, you weren't there — if you thought you knew what was happening in Lebanon, you were deluded.

At the time I arrived, General Michel Aoun, a Maronite Christian, was president and the Syrians were shelling the hell out of his army from the heights of the Chouf Mountains southeast of Beirut.

Our ferry stopped about two miles off the coast to keep out of rocket range. As I gazed towards the shore, the blood-red dawning sun outlined the shattered skyline of Beirut. Much of it was smouldering, testimony to the ceaseless bombardment of the most shelled city in the world.

Brent radioed his contacts and two speedboats came out, zigzagging between the cascading bombs. We clambered aboard with our equipment, and then charged towards Juniya, a harbour city about ten miles north of Beirut. It was like something out of a D-Day movie, with our boats dodging screaming shells spraying us with torrents of water.

ITN's Lebanese driver — an unshaven, grizzly bear of a man called Joseph — met us at the quayside, kissing me on both cheeks as I leapt ashore. It was a welcome I had not received before.

We put on bulletproof vests as Joseph piled our mountain of equipment into the back of his battered 1958 Chevrolet Impala. As we sped through the town, I remarked that the roads were in terrible condition, pitted by thousands of potholes.

"Those aren't potholes, mate," said Brent in his native Manchester accent, "They're rocket holes."

According to Joseph our driver, the best time to travel in Lebanon was when the Syrians were shelling as it kept traffic off the roads. He said it approvingly. Having now experienced both options, all I can say is give me a traffic jam any day.

Joseph dropped us off at our hotel and Brent removed his bulky bulletproof vest, telling me to do likewise.

"Are you sure?" I asked, apprehensively watching a missile shrieking out of the sky and exploding barely a mile away.

"Yes, we're safe here. The hotel is in a mountain enclave which the Syrian missiles overshoot. They can't reverse back on themselves. So we're in a little piece of paradise."

We were scheduled to interview General Aoun in a couple of hours, then drive to the Mount Lebanon district, nineteen miles east of the city. The Syrian army controlled much of the area inland, including the mountain heights, so it was a key frontline battleground.

Before leaving, we picked up a soundman from the Lebanese Broadcasting Corporation who would be stringing for us. He was an immensely likeable young man — incredibly courageous and his local knowledge was invaluable.

After the interview with the president we drove into the mountains, arriving at a strategic town called Souk El Gharb. It was a Christian stronghold controlled by the Lebanese government that overlooks much of Beirut, including the airport, and consequently extensively shelled by the Syrians.

There were two media Jeeps: myself, Brent and our Lebanese soundman in the front one, and a French photographer and interpreter in the other. Brent lived up to his "Blazing Saddles" legend and directed our driver down a road in full view of the Syrian gunners, although there were some cars parked on their side acting as barricades.

Things started to get hairy as the Syrians targeted us, but I was getting great footage of exploding rockets, soldiers firing rifles and the general havoc of a war zone.

A bunker sheltering government soldiers at the end of the road provided a modicum of protection, from which I filmed more fighting while Brent provided some lively on-camera narrative.

When I'd captured enough action footage, I suggested we get out of the area quickly as the Syrian shelling was intensifying. We had got what we came for, and Blazing Saddles agreed.

However, the French photographer refused, saying the mountain light was "picture perfect" and he wanted more photos.

I shook my head. "This is nuts, my friend. We've got the pictures. There's no point in hanging around."

"You go. We'll follow," he said.

Brent, the interpreter and I got into our Jeep, while the French photographer and our soundman stayed behind with the driver of the second vehicle.

About five minutes later we heard a tremendous explosion. Brent and I looked back, shocked to our bones. A Syrian anti-tank missile had scored a direct hit on the second jeep. It was a mangled mess of flaring metal.

We looked at each other. No one could have survived that.

Shouting at our driver to reverse up the hill, we frantically scrambled among the wreckage for our colleagues. The driver and the soundman were dead. In fact, the missile had struck the soundman dead-centre on his chest. All we found were tattered remnants of his flak jacket.

To our astonishment, the photographer was still alive. By some miracle, a bulky radio set on the seat next to him had shielded his body from the full force of the blast. But he was riddled with shrapnel and appeared mortally wounded.

There was no time to waste. Brent and I bundled the photographer and the body of the driver into the back of our Jeep with all our equipment. There was no space for anything else, so the two of us stood on the rear fender and hung onto the roof racks for dear life as our driver sped down the winding mountain road towards Beirut.

We soon realised we were sitting ducks as the road zigzagged like a snake. Even worse, the Syrians had distance markers so their artillery knew exactly where to sight.

The driver shouted that the only way to avoid certain death was to go off-road. It seemed suicidal to me but it was our sole option. We careered straight down the side of the mountain through forests of Lebanon's famous cedar trees. All I remember of that helter-skelter slalom was gripping roof-racks with white-knuckles as we bounced liked a football, ricocheting off trees, gnarly bushes and rocks with a critically wounded photographer inside. We owe our lives to our driver's off-road skills.

Joseph was waiting for us at the bottom with eyes as wide as dinner-plates. We loaded the photographer into his car and accelerated off to Beirut's closest hospital. Lebanese doctors were, for obvious reasons, among the most skilled combat surgeons in the world, and late that night they saved the life of the Frenchman.

Brent and I returned to the hotel and I got into the shower to wash off splattered blood, skin and bone fragments. As I watched the crimson water swirling down the plug, shock set in. I started shaking and crying, both from relief that I had miraculously survived an artillery bombardment, and grief for the loss of two colleagues.

That night I slept in the bath in case the bedroom windows blew out from a bomb blast or another shelling. I knew the hotel was in a safe enclave, but I was past all reasoning. Nothing made sense. Least of all the death of our young soundman on his first international assignment. Not only was it a tragic, meaningless loss, it seemed so unfair. It was pure bad luck that we had got into separate vehicles, as he had initially been travelling with us. This was no fool's bullet. His name, tragically, was on that anti-tank missile, I guess.

The next day we visited the soundman's parents to offer condolences. For both of us, it came from the heart, even though we barely knew the young man. Brent was amazing and ITN financially compensated the family, although nothing can replace a dead son.

We now needed to get out of the country and get our film to the ITN studios right away. I knew I had some good footage, but was surprised at how remarkable it actually was when I started editing it.

Apart from the fighting at Souk El Gharb, there had also been a direct hit on an oil refinery and I had flames leaping hundreds of feet into the air as a backdrop to Brent's voice-over. Including Brent's hard-hitting interview with President Aoun, the story and pictures were unbelievably powerful — perhaps the strongest I've filmed.

At Larnaca an ITN runner grabbed the tapes and rushed off to the TV station. The story led news bulletins around the world throughout the night.

I went home and collapsed on my mattress, unaware that my life was about to change dramatically. For while I was fast asleep, other networks — particularly the BBC — were scratching their heads wondering how the hell they had been so thoroughly scooped. So much so that Chris Cramer, the BBC Foreign Editor in London, told his team to track down the cameraman who had taken the battle footage at Souk El Gharb.

"It was Pete," came the reply.

One of the news editors looked up. "Hey, that's not fair. He works for us."

No, I didn't. I had offered my services on arrival in Cyprus and the Beeb had not accepted.

That was now going to be rectified. A few days later, Chris Cramer phoned saying he was flying to Nicosia and wanted to work out a deal. That set off a minor panic for us. We were promoting ourselves as a hotshot international camera crew, yet all we had in our Cyprus flat, which was also our office, were three beanbags and a couple of mattresses. This was not the most auspicious venue to do a deal with the BBC's vaunted Foreign Editor.

Fortunately, even though I had been in Cyprus for less than two months, I had made some invaluable friends. One was Chris Drake, head of the Middle East Media Organisation, and a doyen among the region's foreign correspondents.

I gave him a call. "Chris, have you got an office I can rent for a day?"

He thought for a while. "No. But there's a storeroom downstairs that is sort of like an office. We can put some furniture in, but there's no telephone line."

"That's OK. I won't be phoning anyone."

Chris Cramer arrived, and Mike and I ushered him into our 'plush' new office, in reality a disguised storeroom. Chris likes to negotiate from a position of strength and he showed this straight away by sitting behind my desk rather than in the visitor's chair. He was in control. Or so he thought.

He then plonked his feet on the desktop, leaned back in the swivel chair and said, "Henderson, how much are we going to have to pay you?"

I was expecting a bit of banter before getting down to the nitty-gritty, but this was obviously not going to happen. I decided to play Chris at his own game.

"What's your budget?" I asked, equally bluntly.

I saw he had written a figure on a cigarette packet, which he then placed face down on the desk.

In a flash, I leaned across, grabbed the packet and flipped it over. The figure was a hundred thousand dollars.

"Done," I said. "That's for a hundred days a year."

"No. That's for the whole year."

I shook my head. "A thousand dollars a day and we work exclusively for you. In return you will have the best camera crew in the Middle East. As well as editing equipment."

Chris smiled. "Done."

However, I had to pledge that I would be the cameraman working for them and reiterated that Mike and I would not do any assignments for ITN. No more of this "nonsense" with Blazing Saddles, he said.

Our next visitor was Keith Graves, BBC's legendary Middle East Correspondent. He's a real character, but I suspect the word "curmudgeon" was conceived on his behalf. He made it clear that he considered us a problem that Chris Cramer had foisted on him.

"I hear you're my camera crew," he said as I opened the door. "That's bollocks — I don't need a lens pointer. I just take NBC's pictures and edit them. And if you think I'm going to carry all your equipment around, you've another think coming."

OK, I thought. We have a real prima donna on our hands.

I could not have been more wrong. Keith Graves was not only a gifted journalist; he was a raconteur, entertainer and historian of note. He was also a total maverick, saying the most outrageous things in volatile situations and somehow always getting away with it. JJ, Mike and I spent the most amazing couple of years with him, discovering the fascinatingly rich histories of Middle Eastern nations that we would never otherwise be exposed to. On assignments, whenever possible Keith made sure we had a day off both before and afterwards to visit incredible places, such as the Wadi Qelt south of Jerusalem, where we walked the rough desert paths to visit an ancient monastery with Keith as our immensely knowledgeable guide.

He also saved me and JJ from being thrown into jail. We were in Syria, which has a bizarre regulation that not only do foreigners need a visa to enter the country, they also need one to exit. This gives the paranoid authorities control over how foreigners behave, and with the contrarian media, it's sometimes harder to get out than it is to get in.

It was December and we were filming a Christmas story for the BBC about a town called Maaloula, one of the last remaining communities that speak Aramaic, the language of Jesus. The beautiful village, thirty-five miles northeast of Damascus, leads up a craggy massif and in some sections is carved into the mountainside. It has two historically significant monasteries, and the priest in one seemed to have amnesia concerning his holy vows and took a fancy to JJ, insisting she drink all the communion wine.

That evening we went back to the Cham Palace hotel in Damascus, only to be woken at sunrise with Keith Graves banging on our door.

"Pete, JJ!" he yelled. "We have to go now."

I opened the door and Keith, looking extremely agitated, told us to pack our bags immediately. There was a taxi waiting to take us to the airport.

"What's going on?" I asked. "Are we off on another story?"

He wouldn't tell us — just urging us to pack as quickly as possible.

As we reached the taxi, JJ suddenly said, "I need to go back to the room. I've forgotten my nightie."

Keith ferociously grabbed her arm.

"Get into the cab. Now!"

We sped to the airport, pushing through passport control with minutes to spare. It was only once we were in the air that Keith relaxed.

"You guys are really lucky," he said. "The Syrian authorities checked with the hotel and wanted to know why you were booked in as Peter Henderson and the woman in your room was JJ Haines. They then phoned me to ask if you were married. I said of course you were; JJ just travels under her maiden name. They were not convinced. So we had to get out of the country fast. Or else you two would have been stoned to death in the street."

JJ and I hadn't tied the knot yet. The penalty for an unmarried couple living together in Syria was death, although even zealots may have thought twice about publicly executing a foreign newsman and his girlfriend. But even so, we were lucky Keith acted so fast.

The First Intifada, a full-scale Palestinian uprising against Israeli occupation of the West Bank and Gaza was also raging at the time.

We covered it extensively, usually staying at the American Colony Hotel in Jerusalem's Arab quarter, which allowed us to interview Palestinians out of sight of Israeli security.

However, moving around the area to film was more problematic. In those tense times, the Israeli army would cut off journalists entering conflict zones, instructing us to film an official declaration written in Hebrew that we were in a closed military area and had to leave. Anyone caught filming after that was in serious trouble. The only option was to avoid the Israeli military, which entailed sneaking around the hotspots like bandits and hiding from any army vehicle. If spotted, we quickly drove off in the opposite direction.

But the soldiers knew the neighbourhoods intimately and regularly cornered us. On one occasion I was filming some standoff and one of the soldiers pointed his rifle directly at me. I somewhat provocatively pointed my camera at him, zooming in for a mock photo. Big mistake! Through the lens I saw his finger tightening on the trigger as he pulled off a round. A bullet cracked millimetres from my ear. I jumped in my car and left at speed.

It was only while driving off that I realised how stupid I had been. A picture of a soldier pointing a gun would not have made any news bulletin. All soldiers have guns. I was just fooling around, and if that bullet hit me, it would have had "plain bloody fool" stamped on it.

The most potentially hazardous assignment, however, was not at the frontline. Instead it was in the sedate air-conditioned office of the Israeli Prime Minister, Yitzhak Shamir.

After some to-and-froing, the BBC got an exclusive interview with Shamir, and Mike and I were sent with Keith to film it. But it was no simple matter of pitching up for an on-camera conversation. The Israeli security forces instructed us to drop off every item of equipment we would be using at their offices the day before. They dismantled everything while looking for explosives, even the camera tripod, only handing it back an hour before the interview was scheduled.

When Prime Minister Shamir arrived, the first thing that struck me was how short he was — well under five foot, as I was later told. But he had a huge smile and was very welcoming.

He went to his side of the desk, sat down ... and promptly disappeared. In my viewfinder, at least. I could barely see him above the desktop, just a pair of bushy eyebrows and mop of steel-grey hair. I lowered the tripod, but even then he did not look very Prime Ministerial.

I asked politely if we could move a bulky Israeli flag from the side of the room and place it behind him to give some gravitas. He agreed and Mike offered to move it.

It was extremely heavy and Mike had to use all his strength to shift it. He managed to wriggle it closer and closer until all he needed was one final shove to get it into position. He heaved as hard as he could. At that crucial moment, the pole broke free from the base and shot straight into the ceiling like a javelin. On top was a large copper spike and as it struck the roof, it dislodged a hefty chunk of ceiling. I looked up and — aghast — saw it almost floating down in slow motion, aiming straight for Shamir's head. I could visualise the headlines in tomorrow's Jerusalem Post: "BBC camera crew assassinate Israeli Prime Minister".

Keith Graves saw it as well and said "Mr Shamir ..." about to warn him.

The Prime Minister leaned forward. "Yes?"

At that precise moment, the lethal piece of concrete smashed the back of his chair, exactly where his head had been a nano-second before. Security guards reached for their guns, unsure of what was happening.

The backrest snapped in half. Shamir, still leaning forward, glanced around, first at us, then his security team, then his shattered chair and finally at the gaping hole above him.

"I see they don't make things like they used to."

We all laughed, relieved that he didn't take the situation too seriously. We were even more relieved when the security officials holstered their weapons.

Shamir had spent his entire adventurous life fighting for a Jewish homeland. He had been a leader of the Stern Gang, labelled a "terrorist" by the British who ruled Palestine in the

1940s, and later a Mossad operative. He had numerous awards for valour. It would have been beyond irony for him to be taken out by a lump of concrete from the ceiling while being interviewed by the BBC.

But it had been a close call.

Chapter Twelve

NewsForce

NOT ONLY WERE we finally able to pay our bills, we had money to spare. We even moved into a real office, instead of some jazzed-up storeroom to impress the BBC.

This was a big event for us, so I decided it was time to form our own company, consisting of myself, Mike and JJ. I had a placard printed and screwed it onto the office door.

NewsForce.

The initial response was not encouraging. The first person who walked in was star BBC correspondent and life-president of the curmudgeon club, Keith Graves.

"What the bloody hell is NewsForce?"

"It's a company, Keith," I said. "If you want to buy some shares, you can."

"Shares? This nonsense is never going to get off the ground."

"Come on, Keith," I said. "Give us a thousand dollars and you can have a ten per cent slice. You can be a shareholder-correspondent. Bring us in some extra work and make yourself a profit at the same time."

"Bollocks, I'm not giving you one penny. Waste of money."

Despite, or perhaps because of his gruffness, we all loved Keith. I laughed. "You're going to eat those words."

I said that more in hope than conviction.

However, one of NewsForce's first assignments didn't bode well for the future. Terry Waite, a hostage negotiator who himself had been taken hostage in 1987 and held in solitary confinement, was about to be released. The handover was in Damascus, but as the BBC were banned from Syria at the time, we couldn't fly out to meet him. Luckily, the U.K. Government charted a private plane to fly Waite to the RAF Akrotiri base in Cyprus before flying him home.

Waite, who was also an envoy to the Church of England, had been seized while negotiating in good faith with Islamic Jihad, a militant cell linked to Hezbollah. They had promised him safe conduct to visit several other Western hostages, some of whom, he was told, were gravely ill. So perhaps he was too trusting when meeting the jihadists at a go-between's house in Beirut. They cynically broke their pledge and bundled him off to a building in Beirut's southern suburbs where he was tortured, beaten, and chained to a radiator for almost five years.

Waite was easily the most famous hostage in the world and his pending release was headline news. John Simpson, the veteran BBC foreign correspondent and I were standing on the roof of the Akrotiri airport when Waite and his entourage landed.

It's sometimes difficult to keep a sense of spatial awareness when squinting through a tightly framed lens and pulling focus as someone walks towards you. I zoomed in on a tall man (Waite is six foot seven inches) getting off the plane and taking his first steps of freedom across the runway to the airport terminal.

Once Waite was inside the building, I said to John Simpson, "He doesn't look too bad after being handcuffed to a radiator for all that time."

"What do you mean?"

"Well, apart from a limp, he looked pretty good."

Silence. John Simpson looked at me quizzically. "Terry Waite hasn't got a limp," he said.

Then it dawned. "Pete, you idiot — you've just filmed his brother. I hope you got a wide shot?"

I hadn't known that David Waite, who looks remarkably like his sibling, was also on the plane.

"No, I just filmed a tall guy getting off the plane. That's the only shot I got."

John stared at me, aghast. "I can't believe you missed him completely."

If ever there was a time to think on my feet, now was it. I glanced around and saw Andreas Roditis, a cameraman from Reuters dismantling his equipment. I casually wandered over.

"Andreas, I'm off to send my tape to London. Do you want me to get yours to Reuters while I'm at it?"

"Hey, that would be cool. Saves me a trip."

I hailed a taxi and rushed to the feed station. I then, as promised, sent off Andreas's tape to Reuters with perfect footage of Terry Waite getting off the plane.

I also sent it to the BBC.

At about one a.m. the next morning we were in some nightclub in Nicosia when Andreas accosted me.

"What's going on?" he asked suspiciously. "You've now bought me four drinks in a row. How come you're being so nice?"

"OK," I said. "I missed the shot of Waite getting off the plane. So I also sent your stuff to the BBC to cover my ass."

He squinted at me for a while, then burst out laughing. "You bastard," he said, wheezing as he guffawed. "You owe me one — big time."

It was no serious breach of ethics, as the BBC had a contract with Reuters that gave us access to their pictures in any event. So Andreas was not offended, particularly as he knew he could now call in a favour from me anytime he chose. Among frontline cameramen that's gold dust.

South Africa was my initial baptism of fire, but the white-hot crucible of the Middle East taught me even more about being ready for any eventuality. In South Africa, few of the rioting township 'comrades' were armed. In the Middle East, everyone was.

Driving around Beirut was particularly challenging, and I'm not just talking about dodging the Syrian artillery. Various factions controlled different sectors and on any given day we needed at least three press passes to drive across the city. I always kept them in separate pockets, but the trick was to remember which was which. If I pulled out a Lebanese Forces pass at a Lebanese Army checkpoint, it could be the last thing I did. Wrong answers often were a death sentence. Fortunately, our Lebanese drivers usually could tell who was who, although we had some close shaves.

The all-pervasive climate of fear and suspicion was palpable in its intensity. On one occasion a photographer was taking a light reading and as he pointed his meter at the sky, an Israeli jet hurtled past. We were with a group of Palestine Liberation Organisation fighters, who then demanded to see what the photographer was doing. They grabbed his light meter and unfortunately the reading was F16 — coincidentally the model of the Israeli fighter jet. He had a torrid time trying to explain that the tiny machine was merely advising him what F-stop, or camera aperture, to use. We backed him up as best we could, but he was lucky not to have been executed on the spot.

NewsForce started growing rapidly. We became known as the go-to company for breaking news stories, which in the cutthroat media industry was priceless endorsement.

Not only were we fortunate in being at the right place at the right time, we also had the right business model. It wasn't rocket science — in fact, it was simplicity personified. Mike and I worked on the basic premise that the minute one of us walked out of the office, someone else footed the bill. All expenses, from travel, hotels, ferries and taxis, were charged to the client, usually the BBC. Assignment overheads were zero, apart from our time.

Also, a camera had to earn at least one per cent of its market value each day it was operational. This meant our production gear had to be on assignment for at least a hundred days a year, and earnings above that were ploughed into a capital expenditure fund for new equipment, which was replaced every two years.

However, we soon hit a speed bump with our rapid growth. Mike and I were contractually bound to work only for the BBC, as per the initial Chris Cramer agreement. But now with NewsForce's growing status, more and more networks were banging on our door.

We had to expand to exploit this windfall. We needed more crews out there and more cameras. Consequently, Mike and I decided that while we would honour our personal deal with the BBC, NewsForce would recruit other teams to feed the rocketing demand from rival TV stations.

The first person I called was Shane Macdonald, the Australian who had taught me to edit in London when I got my first freelance break with NBC.

Shane was part of a coterie of highly skilled Aussie cameramen, sound engineers and editors. It was a network that became invaluable to us, and the Australian connection soon proved to be a key factor in NewsForce's impressive surge.

I also knew from hard experience that it was imperative to hire the best we could, which meant paying well. We never made money out of our people. Whatever daily rates the TV networks paid us for freelance staff, we funnelled directly to our crews, ensuring not only top-class results, but also loyalty.

Instead, our profits came from equipment hire. As I discovered in South Africa, a cameraman earned five hundred dollars a day, but a camera could earn up to seven hundred. However, you first needed at least fifty thousand dollars upfront to buy a camera, which understandably resulted in a lot of highly skilled freelance operators without equipment. So they worked for us.

Shane spread the word among his compatriots and soon we had up to eleven camera crews on call, all top professionals hungry for stories.

Aussies are famous — or perhaps infamous — for their work hard play hard attitude, but in the broadcast media this seems doubly true. As a result, Cyprus became renowned in media circles for wild parties. It was the perfect sun-drenched island for correspondents and crews to de-toxify and escape from the realities of the conflict barely forty minutes away. We spent much of our free time driving souped-up Harley Davidsons up mountains, bungee jumping, sailing, water-skiing — then going the back to Lebanon or Israel to dodge rockets and bullets.

Our key selling point was that if anybody could get into an almost impossible situation, NewsForce could. This provided us with a great opportunity to expand beyond the Middle East. Hot spots were erupting all around the globe, and we were following the news wherever it broke. For example, in

1989 the rusting Iron Curtain finally collapsed, Russia invaded Chechnya, reducing the capital Grozny to rubble, Bosnia went up in flames and Somalia descended into anarchy not seen since the Dark Ages. Also, an Ebola epidemic flared across West Africa, and we had teams filming the crisis and creating awareness before most of the world knew it was happening.

Our services were now in such high demand, and we knew we had 'made it' when Keith Graves bumped into us outside our offices. He said one of his biggest mistakes was not taking us up on our initial offer to buy ten per cent of the company for a mere thousand dollars.

He was now eating his words after all.

Chapter Thirteen

Gulf game changer

THE FIRST GULF War, triggered by Iraqi President Saddam Hussein's invasion of Kuwait, was a pivotal game changer for NewsForce.

It may have stretched our resources to the limit, but it also showed how adaptable we were — far more than I anticipated. Even more crucially, it sparked a trailblazing breakthrough in broadcast news that would change the industry forever.

Kuwait became an independent nation in 1961, a move bitterly opposed by Iraqis who believed the tiny sheikdom had been artificially concocted by British imperialism. Kuwait, Saddam insisted, was historically and geographically a province of Iraq.

Perhaps of more importance was the not inconsequential matter of an outstanding thirty-billion-dollar debt. Kuwait had loaned the money to Saddam during Iraq's war with Iran that ended in a stalemate a couple of years previously, and were now demanding payment in full. Suffice it to say that Saddam was less than keen on complying.

The phone jangled next to my bed, jerking me out of a deep sleep. I looked at my watch: five a.m. The date was 2 August 1990.

"Saddam's invaded. Get to Kuwait now." It was John Mahoney, the BBC's foreign editor.

I rubbed the gritty tiredness out of my eyes, thinking furiously. "OK, but Kuwait will probably be shut down by now. How do I get in?" I asked.

"Don't know. Just go. Hire a plane if you have to."

That was NewsForce's speciality. Getting into places others considered impossible.

The story started unfolding in snippets. No one knew exactly what was happening, but the Iraqis had apparently crossed the Kuwait border at two that morning, tanks storming across the desert as the Kuwaiti government fled into neighbouring Saudi Arabia. All I knew was I had to get there. And fast.

I called Arab Wings, an executive jet charter company operating out of Amman in Jordan that NewsForce had used before. A spokesman cut me short. With the current emergency, he said every jet they owned had been snapped up.

I then phoned the Larnaca airport information desk and asked if there were any flights to Kuwait.

"Haven't you heard?" The voice on the other end of the phone was incredulous. "Kuwait's closed."

"Then where's the closest open airport?"

"Well ... either Cairo or Jeddah."

"Do you have a plane I can charter?"

Again, the incredulous tone crept back in. "We're a national airline, not a charter company."

"OK, what's the smallest plane you've got?"

"We have a BAC One-Eleven."

"Can I rent — not charter — that?"

"I can ask the Operations Director."

"What's it's going to cost?"

"Where are you going?"

"Like I said, Kuwait."

"Yes, but you may not be able to get there."

"OK, charge us as if we're flying to Kuwait. If we can't get in, we'll land somewhere close."

I heard the telephonist talking to the Operations Manager. "One hundred and eighty thousand dollars. That's the rental fee."

I whistled through my teeth and phoned John Mahoney.

"Flippin' hell, that's a lot of money," he said. "Hold on."

I heard John barking orders. Crucial minutes were ticking by.

"OK," John came back on the line. "I've got NBC and Reuters to share costs, so book it. Now."

"Umm ... John, that's a bit above my credit card limit. By about four zeroes."

He laughed. "I'll fax the airline confirmation."

We met the media team at Larnaca airport two hours later. The BBC correspondent was Michael Macmillan and with him was Greg English, a photographer for news agencies sharing the hire costs. In total, there were eleven of us aboard a ninety-nine seat plane that came fully-equipped with a full complement of cabin crew. This took personalised service to new heights, if you'll excuse the pun.

There was no radio response from the Kuwaiti air traffic tower so we decided to land first at Cairo to transmit footage for the midday news. Once there, we rushed off to the Egyptian TV station, placed Mike Macmillan in an Arab street scene with a mosque in the background where he broke the first news from an Arab country that Kuwait had been invaded.

We then sped back to the airport through Cairo's kamikaze traffic, our taxi driver shouting and hooting as he swerved wildly from lane to lane.

We were airborne when the news broke that Kuwait City was now in flames with fighting in the streets and Iraqi tanks rumbling through the central business district. We also heard that the airport runway had been bombed and air traffic control wasn't operating. Flying in was now out of the question.

Our pilot radioed Bahrain requesting the go-ahead to land in the small Arab state. The airport authorities asked for identification and the nature of our business. When we said we were from the BBC, we heard a voice curse "*sahafa*" (press) and flatly deny permission. They didn't want journalists around during these troubled times.

We turned right and headed for Dubai, touching down soon after dark. The tiny Emirate at the time was far removed from the mega-boom city it is today. In fact, there were only three hotels, so we chose the closest, the Airport Hotel.

There was no time to spare. Deadline for the nine p.m. news loomed, and in journalism, deadlines are sacrosanct. We rigged up a spotlight outside the hotel, positioned Michael Macmillan again under a tall palm tree sagging with dates — perhaps the Middle East's most iconic emblem — where he gave a breaking news summary of what was happening. He ended off saying, "This is Michael Macmillan reporting from Dubai."

We rushed into the TV station to feed the footage into the satellite. But first we had to get permission. This can be, and often is, a bureaucratic nightmare as most Middle Eastern countries have strict internal censors and all material has to be vetted.

The government censor, Abdullah Aziz shook his head when he checked our report. We could not send it out, he said. I expected him to dispute some facts, or highlight perceived security issues, but that was not the problem.

"You cannot say you are reporting from Dubai," he told us.

I pleaded with Abdullah. "This is the lead story. We haven't time to change it. We have to broadcast now."

He wagged his finger at me. "No mention of Dubai. Nothing."

I grabbed Mike. "We have to do it again."

"We haven't time."

"Just come!"

We sprinted down the stairs to the car park. I re-rigged the lights and Mike did a flawless one-take report in 90 seconds flat. It was a superb piece of high-pressure broadcast journalism.

Crucially, this time he ended by saying, "This is Michael Macmillan reporting from the Middle East."

The censor was happy. But it was likely we would miss the nine p.m. news. The next bulletin would only be aired the following morning, and we would lose all exclusivity. I was determined that was not going to happen.

With seconds to spare, we connected via satellite to Broadcast House in London.

"OK Pete," the BBC engineer's voice came through calmly over the speaker. "Your report is going directly out onto worldwide transmission. Raw and unedited. So when I say push the red button, make damn sure you push the right one."

"Got it," I said, with more conviction than I felt.

"Push," came the command.

I then heard the cultured voice of the newsreader, my old boss in South Africa, Michael Buerk, as clearly as if he was in the same room. "It's been an extraordinary day in the Middle East and we have an exclusive report from our correspondent Michael Macmillan ..."

We had done it. It was the first piece-to-camera televised reporting on the Gulf War from the Middle East.

We returned to our hotel, excited, exhausted and proud. Hero-grams — as mentioned earlier, journo-speak for congratulatory messages — started flooding in from the BBC, applauding us on a magnificent job.

It had indeed been an incredible day; from persuading a national airline carrier to rent us a plane, to breaking the news of the Kuwait invasion from a key Arab country, to the first live report on what was soon to be called the Gulf War. What made it even sweeter was that while we were on air, our main rival ITN was still being cleared for take-off at Stanstead Airport north of London. We were a whole day ahead.

I was twenty-eight years old at the time. I put much of our success down to sheer tenacity and perseverance. The enormous financial risk of hiring a ninety-nine-seat plane and the physical risk of trying to fly into a country at war are risks most people wouldn't dream of. But to me, they were simply actions we needed to take to capture great, exclusive footage.

It wasn't long before NewsForce had teams in Saudi Arabia, Syria and even in Baghdad itself with journalist Peter Arnett and CNN. Peter had a New Zealand passport, allowing him access to Iraq, and gave the first live global broadcast from the city as it was being bombed in real time.

I opted to base myself in Israel as the BBC used us for all news coverage of that country, whether there was a war on or not. They may have sent in star correspondents such as Carol Walker, Michael Macmillan and Keith Graves, but NewsForce was the service provider.

Globally, there was never any doubt that Saddam would be brutally punished for the vicious hijacking of a sovereign country. Apart from breaking international law, the fact that a dictator now controlled twenty per cent of the world's oil supply was simply untenable. Massive retaliation was on the cards. The only question was when.

It was soon answered. On 24 February 1991, a coalition army consisting of soldiers from thirty-five different nations poured across the Saudi border. The invasion was led by America who also provided the overwhelming bulk of soldiers, equipment, expertise, finance — and pretty much everything else.

I was at the American Colony Hotel in Jerusalem having dinner with a group of journalists when we got the news. All hell broke loose with sirens blaring and pagers pinging us to contact our offices.

Without finishing our food, Mike and I sprinted for our rented Volvo and headed for Tel Aviv. In fact, we left in such haste that we didn't pay our bill, which the hotel did not forget. The next time I visited I had to pay in advance.

Although we had an office in Jerusalem, both of us believed Saddam would bomb the commercial capital rather than the administrative one. Jerusalem is considered a holy site to Islam as well as Judaism and Christianity, not least because of Temple Mount known to Muslims as Haram esh-

Sharif. It was unlikely Saddam would risk destroying sacred land with a Scud missile.

Bombing Israel was a key strategy for Saddam. He believed he could goad the Israelis to retaliate, forcing Arab states such as Egypt and Saudi Arabia to desert the American-led coalition — or even side with Iraq. He was banking on Arab brotherhood and hatred of Israel trumping distrust of Iraq.

We arrived at Tel Aviv at four a.m. and were greeted by a huge cloud of what looked like a mist rolling towards us. Mike and I looked at each other anxiously: Has Saddam already bombed the country? Could this cloud be deadly gas? Or nuclear fall-out?

We grabbed masks, hurriedly pulling them over our faces, as well as rubber gloves to cover hands and arms.

At the time, it was widely believed Saddam possessed weapons of mass destruction, a logical assumption as he had already used chemical warheads against Kurdish dissidents in Mosul as well as in the war against Iran. He even claimed to have nuclear weapons. Our dread that this mist could be nerve or mustard gas was terrifyingly real.

I remember thinking that if the Israelis were being gassed in their homeland, it would trigger a global apocalypse. It was forty-five years since the Second World War, and many survivors of the holocaust were still alive. Most Israelis had relatives or friends who had been gassed in Hitler's death camps. If history was repeating itself, it could be an Auschwitz-scenario with unimaginable consequences.

With massive relief we realised, the mist was just peasouper fog rolling off the Mediterranean Sea.

We arrived at the television network offices in Herzliya, an affluent city in the northern part of the Tel Aviv district, where I was interviewed by CNN. It was basically a "what can you see out of your window" interview. Everyone was terrified that chemical warheads would come screaming out of the sky, but the truth was nobody knew what was actually going on.

The next morning, I rented the entire top floor of the Herzliya Hilton as an office. I chose the Hilton because the Americans and Israelis had an antiballistic Patriot Missile battery on the side of hotel's car park. If nothing else, we were guaranteed spectacular footage of rockets being fired.

The rest of the day was manic, setting up cameras at the best vantage points on the roof, securing microwave satellite feeds, and making sure everyone knew exactly what to do to keep as safe as possible. All TV crews wore flak jackets and chemical suits. We were convinced the worst scenario would unfold.

Then at about six p.m., Tel Aviv's sirens started wailing. The cry went out: "Incoming!"

The Scuds were clearly visible in the star-studded sky. We rushed to our cameras, filming through an emotionally charged haze of absolute awe and horror. It was almost hypnotic witnessing these huge balls of fire, the size of double-decker buses, streaking through the stratosphere at supersonic speeds.

Some landed behind us in the sea, some in the desert sand. Others were taken out by Patriot surface-to-air defence missiles. But some got through, exploding in the streets of the coastal cities, inflicting civilian casualties. Israel discovered what it had long feared; its antiballistic defence system was not infallible.

We were busy filming this lethal firestorm when suddenly furious Israeli soldiers boxed us in, shouting commands. They manhandled and unceremoniously frogmarched us off the top of the building to a basement. There, an incredibly angry Israeli general confronted us, saying we were all going to be shot for treason.

We looked at him, completely confused. "What's the problem?" someone asked.

"You people are an electronic forward observation post," he ranted. "Who do you think is watching your pictures in his bunker in Baghdad? Who do you think is tuned into CNN and the BBC? I'll tell you who — Saddam Hussein! Your live pictures are being shown in Baghdad and he is seeing exactly where his Scuds are landing. All he has to do is instruct his artillery to adjust their sights accordingly."

He turned and stared at us one by one, incandescent with rage.

"Showing all this live coverage means you are spies. You are colluding with the enemy."

Hang on, we replied. Israel is a democracy and that means we as journalists had every right to film the war blazing around us.

"Yes, but you have no right to put Israelis' lives at risk," he shouted.

We all agreed on that.

"So," I said. "How do we handle this? The war is happening. We cannot ignore it."

I then pointed out that we had a correspondent in Baghdad, which meant what was happening in Tel Aviv was the same scenario there in reverse. The Americans could see where their missiles were landing in the Iraqi capital.

Everyone calmed down a little, and a lengthy debate ensued. At least the Israelis agreed that the war could not be ignored by the media, so we had some common ground. We finally reached a compromise whereby we would not film any Scuds landing. We could show the missiles in the sky and the aftermath of a blast, but we could only report that it had landed somewhere in Israel. Nothing else. This meant that

Saddam, hunkering down in his bunker with his hand on the hotline to his artillery — as the Israeli general claimed — would not know if his gunners were on target

We all honoured that agreement. None of us wanted to compromise the lives of civilians.

This was before the days of round-the-clock news saturation, so TV crews would usually pack up around eleven at night. But there was no talk of going to bed and getting some sleep. The adrenaline rush of the day blazed too bright.

Instead, journalists would converge at the Bagdad Café, which held nightly "End of the World" parties, the doomsday prediction ghoulishly advertised on a board outside.

The irony that the pub was called Baghdad Café — and that people were getting blasted by alcohol if not shrapnel — was not lost on the revellers. Everyone partied like there was no tomorrow, especially the Israelis. Music pumped, drinks flowed and plenty of beautiful raven-haired girls dressed in military fatigues with Galil rifles slung over their shoulders danced on the tables. If the end of the world was coming via a toxic Scud, no one was sitting around moping.

Often sirens would start screeching, resulting in carousers pausing for a few seconds to pull on gas masks as they continued jiving, periodically easing aside the canister to take a fresh swig of booze.

These end of the world parties usually ended at about three a.m. with the world still intact and we would stagger off to bed, ready to face another possible Scud attack in a few hours' time.

Despite fun and games at the Baghdad Café, the reality on the ground was awful. Everyone was convinced chemical attacks were imminent and all homes had plastic sheeting taped over windows to be as airtight as possible. People wore gas masks while jogging and I even saw a Jack Russell terrier with a mask being taken for a walk.

The BBC correspondent in Tel Aviv, Carol Walker, wanted to film a documentary on ordinary Israelis living under this dreadful physical and mental siege. As a result, we were invited to film a family celebrating the Sabbath.

We hired a taxi and were driving down a street in the suburbs when a rocket alert beeped ominously on the car radio. Israel has a sophisticated missile alarm system, immediately detecting when a Scud is fired and where it would most likely land. The fact that we were getting a direct alarm indicated the rocket was heading straight for us.

The procedure was that all cars pull over to the side of the road and wait for an all-clear signal. The driver told us he had to stop, but Carol ordered him to keep going. I could see he was torn between obeying the laws of his country, or the extremely urgent demand of a paying customer. He chose the latter and continued driving.

It saved our lives. Barely thirty seconds later a Scud exploded with a massive blast exactly where our taxi had just been. Widows from surrounding apartments shattered, showering glass and debris like a hailstorm, and a car parked on the side of the road behind us burst into flames. The vehicle in front did as well.

Miraculously we were unscathed. I soon saw why — there was a building site directly adjacent to us and a mound of recently excavated earth deflected the lethal, rippling shrapnel and shockwaves. It was tantamount to being in the calm eye of a hurricane with thousands of steel fragments flying around. Even so, we were hurled across the road like a spinning top.

I was filming it all so Carol got an extraordinarily powerful video of us almost being taken out by a Scud. I knew it was going to be pretty hair-raising watching it on the news that night, so quickly phoned JJ in Cyprus to tell her we were all right.

At the same time, our team in Saudi Arabia was following the coalition forces into Kuwait. They had bought a 4x4 off-road truck from a local at an exorbitant price, and re-sprayed it from sky-blue to desert-khaki to be as inconspicuous as possible.

As they were bouncing about on desert dunes, they became increasingly irritated by something rolling around on the floor of the car. Thinking it was a beer can, one of the guys put his hand under the seat to grab it. His fist closed around a live grenade. Fortunately, the pin was still in but even so, he threw it out of the window as quickly as if he had grabbed a live snake.

Soon afterwards they realised they were lost. Not only that, they had also just driven through a minefield and astonishingly had not been blown up.

They carried on driving aimlessly until they saw some vehicles ahead. It was the American advance force, the elite tip of the invasion spear, super-fast and massively armed.

The armoured vehicles swivelled their machine guns on the approaching civilian pick-up, screaming orders for the occupants to evacuate. Our two guys did exactly that, throwing their hands in the air shouting, "Don't shoot, we're Australians."

The Americans were stunned. "Australians? What the fuck are you doing here?" shouted their commander.

"Filming the war."

"You're meant to be behind in the main convoy with other journalists," he said. "In fact, five miles behind."

"Aren't there journalists with you?"

"Fuck no! No fucking newsies allowed. We're the attack team that's going to retake the airport and secure the country," he said.

The soldiers knew exactly what to do with captured combatants. But not so much with captured journalists. So our guys were told to tag along behind, behave themselves and stay out of the way.

Thanks to that unbelievable good luck in not only driving unscathed through a minefield but linking up with the advance strike force, our team were the first journalists into Kuwait City. They filmed the Americans liberating the country, getting one of the most iconic shots of the war when soldiers raised the Stars and Stripes in front of the American Embassy. They even filmed a hovering helicopter lowering a bright-red Coca Cola vending machine as the flag was hoisted, which perhaps was as close to a visual metaphor of normality returning as one could get.

They then contacted me in Tel Aviv. "Pete, we've got these incredibly valuable pictures sitting in our cameras. But how do we get them out?"

We couldn't. There was nothing to do except wait. We were being held hostage by inferior technology and it was only the next day when an ABC truck arrived with a giant satellite dish that we were able to transmit our exclusive footage. I swore we would never be hostages to other network technology ever again. I didn't realise it then, but that vow was a turning point in my life.

I was absolutely exhausted, burnt out from continuously living on the edge where at any second we could be taken out by a six-and-a-half-ton missile. It had already almost happened. I had to take a break and go home. I did not want another melt down like in South Africa.

I landed at Nicosia's airport, catching a taxi home. JJ was waiting for me outside our apartment.

"Don't unpack," she said. "We're leaving."

She turned to the taxi driver. "Back to the airport, please."

It was not the homecoming I expected. But little did I know that I was in for one of the most wonderful weeks of my life.

We caught a plane to Cairo, stayed at an exquisite old palace in an area called Zamalek, visited the pyramids, the Cairo Museum, then flew to the Valley of the Kings at Luxor and boarded a hotel boat to Aswan. Our penthouse suite had full-length French windows that provided a panoramic view of the majestic Nile. Thanks to the war, there were very few tourists.

JJ instinctively knew exactly what I needed. It was incredibly therapeutic, returning from absolute mayhem and madness to the most magnificently tranquil setting imaginable.

Fully rejuvenated, we returned to Cyprus and without actually planning to do so, I started gradually withdrawing from frontline camera work. I began concentrating on the logistics of managing NewsForce's rapidly expanding teams, visiting our people in the various centres and making sure everything was running smoothly.

Within six months Saddam was on his knees, a humiliating surrender that festered like a pus-filled wound. The final culmination was the Second Gulf War eleven years later, with an even more crushing defeat. The murderous dictator was finally captured hiding in a spider hole near his hometown of Tikrit, and executed.

Our coverage of the war had been hugely successful, transforming NewsForce into one of the most recognised names in international news gathering. We also learned valuable lessons, which would enable me to take the company to the next level.

But first I did something far more important.

I got married.

Chapter Fourteen

Dishing up the goods

THROUGHOUT THE rollercoaster days of establishing NewsForce, JJ was at my side, not only as my girlfriend, but my best friend.

In May 1991, we decided to make it official. She would still be my best friend, but my wife as well.

The ceremony was superb, one of the best days of our lives. We were married by the Mayor of Nicosia, in a short and intimate ceremony. JJ looked stunning in her wedding dress as we walked through the cobbled streets to our favourite Italian restaurant, the Romantica, for celebrations with friends and family.

After the big day, events became a little less conventional. As my mum and stepfather were in Cyprus, I invited them to join us on our honeymoon in Israel and Turkey.

This, unsurprisingly, was not exactly what JJ had in mind. Even worse, in Jerusalem I got a call from the BBC informing me that John McCarthy, the longest-held hostage in the Middle East, was being released in Damascus. Could I cover it?

Almost without thinking, I said "of course". It was my default reaction to most news stories.

JJ was dumbstruck. How could I even consider rushing off on an assignment during our honeymoon? What was wrong with me?

I assured her I would be back within forty-eight hours. The withering look on her face spoke volumes. I knew that if I didn't play this carefully, my parents would be my sole honeymoon companions on my return.

John McCarthy had been seized by Islamic Jihad, the same radical group that had kidnapped Terry Waite and held him in a cell for more than five years. The handover would happen at the British Embassy, and as McCarthy was a journalist, many of the media crowding the consulate in anticipation were close colleagues. Most, including his family, had long believed they would never see him again. The atmosphere was extraordinarily emotional and with the highly charged crowd jostling for position I could barely hold my camera steady. I willed myself to hold still out of respect for this amazing man. It was the most important day of his life and I wanted to do it justice.

Then a warning light flashed in my viewfinder. The battery was running low. I stupidly had not checked it. There was no time to insert a new one so I kept filming, agonisingly watching the power haemorrhaging away. It would be a bitter irony for me to botch this assignment when I should rather have been on honeymoon.

Then just as the battery died, McCarthy was whisked out of the room for medical checks and other engagements.

I knew I had strong footage that I had to rush to transmit to London, not to mention getting back to my new wife whose saint-like patience was wearing thin. Our honeymoon could finally continue without further hitches.

But the gods of fortune decreed otherwise. As our taxi sped towards Damascus's TV station, one of my young Australian cameramen, Hedley, wheezed in a strange voice, "Pete, I've got a pain in my chest."

"You need to get fitter," I quipped.

"No, something is wrong. We must go back to the hotel."

Sweat blistered on his ghostly-white forehead. I then realised this was no fitness problem. Hedley was in the throes a major heart attack.

I shouted to the taxi driver, "Hospital — now!" He floored the accelerator, and ten minutes later Hedley was wheeled into an emergency theatre where adrenaline was injected straight into his heart. Arab cardiac surgeons are world renowned and thankfully they managed to get his heart pumping again.

They had saved his life, but he was still in a critical condition. I needed to get him to specialists in London as soon as possible, not to mention getting myself back to my wife.

However, as JJ and I had previously discovered when we inadvertently booked into a single room without the benefit of a marriage certificate, it's often easier getting into Syria than out. Hedley did not have an exit visa, and without that, could not leave.

The next day I went to the Ministry of Information to get the visa, stressing Hedley's medical situation was the reason he could not apply in person. The officials were not interested. The fact that Hedley had almost died was no reason to relax the rules. The Australian Consulate would have to vouch for him.

I phoned the embassy and got a delightful first-hand dose of cheeky Aussie diplomacy.

"It's Pete here from the BBC," I told the woman on the end of the line. "My Australian cameraman has had a heart attack and needs an exit visa to get to London."

"Heart attack, mate?"

"Yes. He's only twenty-two."

"Fuck me," she said.

It was not the polished reaction I expected from an embassy attaché, but she said she would send someone to the hospital to do the paperwork.

I spent the next few days with embassy staff as we sorted out the visa. While we waited, they were kind enough invite us to an Aussie 'barbie' with meat flown in from Australia.

The BBC are great at looking after their own people, even if they are freelance stringers. Hedley flew back on a medically equipped jet to Guy's Hospital in London, where he had a pacemaker fitted. He fully recovered, and today is one of the best cameramen around, winning all sorts of international awards.

I finally got back to JJ having missed her in Israel and giving her the unenviable job of getting my folks out of the country and onto a ferry travelling to Athens. A day later, we flew out to Fethiye, where we chartered a yacht to sail the glorious Turkish coastline. Visually glorious, that is. All my poor wife remembers is being cooped up in a tiny cabin next to her in-laws, whom she barely knew at the time. To this day she reminds me that I owe her a proper honeymoon.

I decided that now I was married I would gradually ease out of warzone work. I am the first to confess I'm not the greatest cameraman. My talent was having an uncanny instinct of being in the right place at the right time, rather than technically perfect photos. In other words, I'm an opportunist — something I'm very happy to admit. We all know life is not fair, and this perhaps is even more true in the fleeting world of fast-breaking news where flare and luck often trumps creative ability.

However, with the rapid growth of NewsForce, I was now surrounded by highly skilled battlefield cameramen, many of whom were equally good opportunists as well.

For example, when I was in Tel Aviv during the Scud attacks, I phoned cameraman Greg Timms in Cyprus requesting him to bring more flak jackets.

That sounds like a simple request. But at the time, Israel was in lockdown and all airports closed. The only marginally possible route into the country was through Egypt, which entailed flying into Cairo, crossing the Suez into the Sinai Desert and then basically going on bended knee begging Israeli border guards at the Red Sea port of Eilat to open the gates.

No problem for Greg. Not only did he blag his way through Egypt, Israel's sworn enemy, with what was essentially military cargo, he also somehow convinced the notoriously edgy Israelis that a suitcase full of body armour was routine luggage. That may sound amazing, but if you didn't have the ingenuity and *cojones* to routinely pull such stunts off, you had no chance in our line of business.

We did have some misfits, however, such as the editor who phoned me from a hotel in Damascus saying there was a "massive problem". The editing machine was not working.

I told him to check the fuse.

"That's the problem," came the reply. "I can't plug it into the wall. It doesn't fit."

In other words, he had a square three-prong British plug that he was trying to ram into a round two-prong Middle East socket. All he needed to do was cut the plug off his bedside lamp, rewire it and connect it to the machine. If he couldn't figure that out, it didn't bode well for future scenarios where it would be vital — sometimes a matter of life or death — to think on your feet.

Needless to say, he didn't last long working for NewsForce.

Hotspot journalism is as much about resourcefulness and survival as it is about creativity. Crossing borders that may or may not be open, getting past roadblocks manned by drugged-up militias, sweet-talking belligerent combatants into giving interviews, and convincing warring factions you're on their side, are essential tools of the trade.

It's also about attitude. Being able to get along with people in incredibly stressful situations when you are scared, dehydrated, starving and missing loved ones is paramount.

Then there's the constant uncertainty, wondering if you were going to get out of an ugly situation in one piece — or what the hell were you doing there in the first place.

But the flip side is the addictive adrenaline and camaraderie that is shared only by a unique and privileged few. For me, it was incredibly stimulating and exciting. Having a ringside seat at the epicentre of tectonic global upheavals was not just a privilege but an unimaginable seat-of-the-pants ride.

I knew I was going to miss it.

I summoned the entire NewsForce team back to Cyprus, not just to tell them I would be taking a more managerial role, but also to hold a full-scale brainstorming session. The central theme was to distil what we had learnt from the Gulf War into a concrete vision.

For me, a key moment was when we had the iconic photos of American soldiers raising the flag at the embassy in Kuwait, but were unable to get them out. To us at NewsForce, this was the Achilles heel of television journalism. The Gulf War had glaringly shown us that unless we were able to transmit our own footage, we would always be hostage to rival machinery.

The solution was obvious. We had to get our own technology, our own satellite dish. But not the massive, ungainly flying saucers perched on TV station roofs. We needed a small, highly mobile transmitter that we could take anywhere, exclusively tailored for our specific needs.

This not only made good technical sense, it was a sound business strategy. If NewsForce became totally self-sufficient, able to cover assignments live, editing and transmitting in real time no matter how difficult the situation, it would give us a huge advantage over competitors.

This became my new obsession. Once again, it was thanks to JJ's belief in what I was doing and her extraordinary support and patience that allowed me to pursue it. Here we were, freshly married, and instead of talking about new curtains, kitchen cupboards and lounge suites, we talked about taking satellite dishes into warzones.

I approached a company in London called Advent, which specialised in such equipment, explaining to the owner Steve McGuinness exactly what I wanted. He asked some questions, scribbled a few notes and said it would cost a million dollars.

A million? That was a huge chunk of NewsForce's capital, earned through high physical risk and buckets of sweat. Could we afford to blow it on one item?

It was an agonising decision. What should we do? JJ and I were financially secure for the first time, so shouldn't we rather start planning for a more stable future with insurance policies and investments? A new house?

Or should we gamble it all on something with possibly huge potential, or just as conceivably, a very expensive dud?

I took a deep breath.

"Go ahead. Build me the machine," I told Steve McGuinness.

Still riddled with doubt, I went to our bank in Cyprus and instructed my long-suffering manager George Theodorous to cable the money to London.

He looked at me, flabbergasted. "A million? In one instalment?"

I nodded. "One hit."

I slept on it that night, and slept badly. In the morning I decided it was too big a gamble. It was too much money for unknown rewards. I was risking too much too early. Technology was rocketing at an exponential rate. Maybe if I waited something cheaper and even better would soon be on the market.

I picked up the phone. "George, have you cabled the money to London yet?"

"No. It's going out at ten o'clock."

Whew! I had dodged a bullet. Or so I thought.

"Don't do it," I instructed.

Then I phoned Steve. "Sorry mate, I'm cancelling the order."

"But Pete, I've already started building the dish."

"I can't go ahead," I said. "It's a shedload of money to spend on one asset. I don't even know if it will work."

"Oh, don't worry about that. It'll work perfectly."

"Are you sure?" I asked.

"Without doubt." He was adamant.

I phoned George back. "OK, I've changed my mind. Cable the money."

I could sense his unease. This was the third conflicting instruction I had given in as many days.

"Are you sure?" He repeated the figure as if tormenting me. "A million?"

I was anything but sure. But decided there was no turning back.

Some weeks later the dish arrived from London — twenty industrial boxes stuffed with what looked like a giant Meccano set weighing twelve hundred kilograms, or 1.2-tons. This was our 'mobile' unit.

I had no idea how it worked, let alone how to assemble it. It looked like witchcraft and I needed someone who grasped technical sorcery to piece it together.

Fortunately, a friend recommended a former British Army signaler, Ken Suckling, who was said to be a genius with such new-fangled wizardry.

He was. Over the next few days he connected the close-on seven-foot antennae, reflector, actuator, feed horn, amplifier, circuit boards as well as stuff I had never heard of, then bolted the whole contraption together.

We held a collective breath while he did transmission tests. To my utmost relief, it worked. But Ken — whom we suspected of having close ties with elite British special force units — wanted to test it out in anger, so to speak. He took it to the outbacks of Afghanistan where various factions, including the Taliban, were fighting it out after the Soviet withdrawal in 1989. We couldn't get wilder badlands than that.

The dish passed every trial. We could broadcast from wherever we chose. Never again would our crews be reliant on other networks.

It was a game changer in more ways than one. We were now for all intents and purposes an independent broadcaster, providing live links directly from any hotspot we chose. Instead of billing a single client two thousand dollars a day, we charged multiple clients two hundred dollars for a minute of feed. It was repeat business in its purest form, resulting in profits rivalling our wildest dreams. And our clients were happy as they were paying solely for footage used.

It also changed the face of frontline reporting forever, and few would disagree that this was a key factor in the boom of round-the-clock TV news.

Our timing was unbelievably fortuitous. The 1990s will go down as one of the most globally turbulent decades, starting with the communist bloc imploding like the rickety house of cards it was and the meteoric surge of the oligarch class in the former USSR.

These events led to an unusual spin-off. A South Korean TV company wanted to film the breakup of the Soviet Union as a real-time documentary and approached me to advise on logistics. I told them that not only could I do that, I also had a mobile satellite dish that was prefect for the job. They immediately hired it at top rate, but I warned they would need a plane to fly it around Russia, the largest country in the world.

No problem, they said. Just charter one.

However, that actually was a problem as there were no private companies in the collapsing USSR, let alone private charter companies. The only person who owned a jet was the president.

Once again, the power of adventure and opportunity, the lodestar of my life, loomed large before me. Without the plane, the lucrative South Korean deal would collapse. Do I give up, stating the obvious that there were no private jets in the country? Or do I ask President Boris Yeltsin if I can borrow his?

I chose the latter. Yeltsin, bless him, said yes.

That sounds pretty cheeky, but it's worthwhile remembering that post-communist Russia was cautiously dipping its toe into capitalist waters. Yeltsin's office obviously liked the idea of making money out of his Presidential toy.

We hired the sixteen-seater executive jet for the month, and the irony of using the Russian leader's wings to film the demise of communism in his own country was delicious in the extreme. It also gained us massive street cred, arriving at various airports in the boss's jet.

Having an entire documentary screened live in South Korea was great marketing for our new acquisition. We were now acknowledged as leaders in the field. While it was true most of the TV network giants had their own mobile satellite dishes, these were manned by engineers who got the same wage whether they were in a warzone or back in their hometown. There was no powerful incentive to get the story out — in fact the opposite when bullets zinged past — whereas we had both financial and professional motivation in spades.

Another factor was that networks were increasingly reluctant to send their far larger state-of-the-art dishes into volatile areas at exorbitant expense. And why do so when they could buy a five-minute feed direct from us at a fraction of the price?

Also, I could make executive decisions about where and when we should go, whereas the networks ruled by corporate committee. Consequently, we were far leaner and quicker off the mark, supplying live footage while others were still talking about it.

But even with our sophisticated new gadgetry, it was not always plain sailing, as one of our staff discovered during a rather hairy situation in Libya.

It happened when the country's leader, Muammar Gaddafi, hired us to film him holding Friday Prayers, the most important weekly ritual in Islam, at a secret location in the desert where he was hunting with falcons.

Gaddafi loved to broadcast images of himself praying. As a survivor of multiple assassination attempts, it not only showed Libyans that he was still alive, but how devout he was.

Even though the undisclosed location was far out in the Sahara, we knew we would be able to beam into Arab-Sat, Libya's satellite system. As it was a fairly straightforward assignment, our engineer James Middleton went out on his own to handle it. Libyan TV had a crew that would do the filming and commentary; we just needed to transmit it.

The fact that we thought it would be a simple job probably kyboshed it from the word go. The day after James arrived, I got a frantic call from him somewhere in the Sahara saying he was being driven around in ever-increasing circles. It had been eight hours since they left Tripoli, and they still hadn't reached Gaddafi's hunting camp. When would he be able to assemble the dish?

I said don't worry, it was merely the secret police stalling as they were reluctant to reveal the obsessively-paranoid Gaddafi's exact location. They would probably only go to the camp early Friday, which would still give James several hours to set everything up before noon prayers.

That was wishful thinking. Soon afterwards James's vehicle ground to a halt with a puncture. A security cop told the driver to change the tyre. The driver shamefacedly admitted he didn't have a spare. The enraged cop then drew his pistol and shot the driver in the foot. The man hobbled off screaming into the desert.

James again frantically phoned me. "Pete — they've just shot my driver."

"Dead?" I asked, stunned.

"No, in the foot."

"Why"

"Well ... we had a puncture."

"Are you at Gaddafi's camp yet?"

"No. And I have no clue how we're going to get there with a flat tyre. Unsurprisingly, our driver has run off."

There was not much I could say apart from warning James to be careful. I doubt that gave him any comfort.

Somehow they patched the puncture and the press entourage started moving again, eventually arriving at Gaddafi's hunting camp in the late morning. James had scant time to get the dish operational.

He assembled it as rapidly as possible, then told his interpreter to phone the TV station in Tripoli to check for a signal.

After some animated conversation, the interpreter shook his head. No signal.

Time was running out at breakneck speed. The worst nightmare scenario was unravelling like a ball of string tossed off a cliff. James turned knobs and tested wires like a man possessed.

Twenty minutes before Gaddafi started praying, James again phoned. "Pete, they still can't see me in Tripoli."

"Any failure lights flashing on the machine?"

"None. I'm pretty sure I'm beamed in on the right satellite. But Tripoli can't see my test bars or signal generator."

I phoned Algiers TV, which also had an Arab-Sat connection, and asked if they could see our signal. Yes, they replied. It was rock solid.

I called James back. It was five minutes to noon. The midday prayer session was about to start.

"You're definitely on the satellite," I said. "It must be Libyan TV's fault. Get your interpreter to give the station your exact channel and transponder frequency, and make sure they have polarisation on the left pole, not the right one."

At that moment Gaddafi emerged from his Bedouin tent, clad in flowing white robes. Aides rushed to spread his prayer mat in the sand. Just two minutes to go.

James was fast reaching panic stations. The bullet in his driver's foot was still fresh in his mind.

His phone rang. An excited voice in Arabic gabbled the good news. They had locked onto the signal.

It was that close. As James later remarked, if the guards thought nothing of crippling a driver because of a flat tyre, imagine what they would have done to him if the broadcast of their 'dear leader' praying had gone belly-up?

I shudder to think.

Chapter Fifteen

Despots and democrats

THE BOOMING VOICE of Steve Cassidy, CNN's head of foreign news was so loud he could have been in bed next to me.

Thankfully, he wasn't. But it also woke JJ. She was not happy.

I was used to being woken up at all hours by Steve as he was based in Atlanta, U.S.A., which is seven hours behind Cyprus. As a result, we almost always got his calls in the small hours, which understandably irritated JJ trying to get some sleep.

Even worse, Steve's standing joke whenever I picked up the phone was, "When I say jump, what's the answer?" The correct reply in Steve's opinion was "how high, how high

Steve," which was sometimes difficult to find amusing at three a.m. six thousand miles away.

This time the "how high" joke — which is now a cliché — was followed by the revelation that something "massive" called Operation Restore Hope was about to kick off in Somalia. The American military would be "storming" into Mogadishu, the dysfunctional capital of the country, armed with an Everest-high amount of emergency aid for the beleaguered population. The plan was also to get rid of the vicious warlords ruling the city. I needed to be there within twelve hours.

I shook my head. Most network editors may be great at their job, but not that great on geography. Steve was no exception. Getting into a collapsed country ruled by warring thugs thousands of miles away was problematic no matter which way you looked at it. Doing so in a day was almost impossible.

"You know we're in Cyprus, Steve. It's an island. Somalia is on another continent."

"I'm not asking you to swim. Get a plane. But get there soon. Rival camera crews are scrambling as we speak."

I sighed. Catching a plane to Somalia was infinitely easier said than done. Few were flying into the war-torn country, officially recognized as the world's biggest basket-case. In fact, the only national airline that could get us close was

Kenya Airways. But as there were no direct flights from Larnaca to Nairobi, we would first have to jet to Heathrow to link up.

Being a freelancer means solving problems, not creating them. So I assured Steve we would be in Mogadishu within twenty-four hours with more bravado than I felt. If we had to backtrack all the way to London, it would set us back by at least eight more hours and every cameraman and his dog would be in Somalia before us.

Luckily for me, I was surrounded by immensely creative staff. One was my accountant, Roula Crisp, an absolute genius at solving problems, both administrative and logistical. I phoned her and gave her what I considered an impossible task, then left her to weave her magic.

She went through all possible routes, trying private plane suppliers in nearby countries such as Israel, Lebanon and Greece. Nothing was available. She thought as a last resort to call Panicos, an agent that we used at Larnaca Airport to help us in tricky situations. Instead of turning Roula down flat, he said, "I'll put you through to a friend in Traffic Control to see whether we can do something with scheduled flights."

After twenty minutes or so on the line, Roula was connected to the controller who confirmed that there was a Kenya Airways flight in the air that had left Heathrow, heading to Nairobi. For the right price, the pilot would deviate his course to land in Larnaca, to pick up our crew. After negotiation with the pilot, Roula got this deal for a mere seventeen thousand dollars. It was a miracle!

I hurriedly called a team together, packed our equipment, and drew fifty thousand dollars from the bank. Roula may have negotiated a bargain basement price, but I knew I would need a lot extra when the pilot saw our excess baggage.

As Kenya Airways didn't operate out of Cyprus, there were no notification boards at the airport. I went to the information desk. "Is there a Nairobi flight scheduled to land at four p.m.?"

I think it was the first time a Cypriot airline clerk had dealt with such a query, but to my relief she confirmed that there had been a last minute diversion by a Kenyan Airways plane to pick up four passengers.

On board were scores of journalists and camera crews from networks around the world, getting the same tip-off as CNN about Operation Restore Hope. All were chomping at the bit to be the first on the ground in Somalia. Then suddenly, in midair, they were informed they were being diverted to Cyprus, meaning a nine-hour flight had now turned into thirteen.

To say they were spitting mad is understating the case — doubly so, when they discovered the diversion was to pick up a rival CNN crew. We weren't exactly given a rousing welcome when we boarded, even though I knew many of the photographers and correspondents.

To further rub salt into the wound, they watched in open-mouth fury as we were ushered into business class. I then handed a flight attendant the suitcase stuffed with dollars, who took it to the captain.

Once we had landed in Nairobi, there was a mad dash as correspondents scrambled about trying to rent planes. There were no scheduled flights to Mogadishu so the only option was to charter.

I used my African contacts to hire a plane from a company called Bluebird operating from Wilson Airport on the other side of Nairobi. The company had recently hired Bulgarian pilots, who may be good, but couldn't speak a word of English. This meant we also had to bring along an interpreter to communicate with air control.

We chartered a BN2-Islander, which could take twelve hundred kilograms of cargo and three passengers. That was the exact weight of our satellite dish. But with myself, a sound engineer and the hefty interpreter, we were significantly over the total weight limit.

This proved to be a problem when we discovered we were using more petrol than anticipated. The pilot indicated he would have to refuel at an airstrip on the Kenyan-Somali border.

A mobile avgas pump was ready as we landed, and the tanks on the Islander's wings filled to capacity. I told the pilot to hurry, but he shook his head. There was now another problem. The rudimentary runway was too short and the temperature too hot for us to take off. We had to ditch some gear.

That was not going to happen. We needed every bit of equipment stowed in the hold. This resulted in a standoff with me refusing to off-load our stuff, and the Bulgarian refusing to take off.

The only solution was to eject the interpreter. He protested vigorously, but I told him it was my charter, and the pilots would pick him up on the way back.

Somehow the Islander cleared the runway, but our next problem was communicating with Somali Air Control who obviously did not understand Bulgarian.

Fortunately, I had studied for a pilot's licence in South Africa and knew how to operate a radio. I read out our call sign and declared our flight plan.

Then our radio crackled. An officious American voice barked at us, "Yankee Mike Alpha Five Zulu. You must return immediately to Kenya. This is a closed military zone. Do you copy?"

Military zone? This was meant to be a humanitarian mission. I replied, "Please identify yourself."

"This is King. We're an American AWAC and you need to leave immediately, or risk being shot down."

An AWAC is basically a huge-winged flying command centre, controlling airspace directly surrounding a battle area. If it threatens to shoot you down, you had better listen.

I had one last card to play. "Please give your name, rank and number because your commanding officer, President Bill Clinton, is really going to be pissed off with you for not allowing CNN to fly into Somalia and film what is going to happen in a few days' time. If you are prepared to accept that responsibility, I'll turn around immediately. Or else, let us in."

There was a momentary pause. "You're CNN?"

"Affirmative."

"Stand by."

Less than a minute later, King was on the air again.

"Permission to proceed."

I think the fact that CNN was an American network gave us the edge. Few — if any — other charter flights were allowed in that day. As a result, not only did we seriously delay the Nairobi-bound plane carrying most of the press, we added insult to injury by being the first media guys into Somalia.

Soon we were sending back real-time footage of the attempt to bring some semblance of order to the chronically failed state. This was the first time the rest of the world glimpsed the extent of the Somali horror, where close on ninety per cent of the capital city's population was starving.

We filmed American soldiers landing on the beaches, leopard-crawling up the sand dunes, guarding Red Cross distribution centres that were regularly looted by militias driving "technicals" — the local name for Toyota pick-up trucks with a 50mm cannon mounted on the back.

We went into the hospitals and photographed stick-thin mothers without milk for their newborn babies, children with corrugated rib cages and grossly distended kwashiorkor bellies, and listless Somalis sprawled on the sidewalks, too feeble to move. We videoed young men with bloodshot eyes stoned sky-high on khat, the local narcotic, brandishing AK-47s and chanting blood allegiance to the various warlords who were the root cause of the anarchy.

It was a mesmerizingly tragic portrayal of a country completely on its knees, a heart of darkness way beyond what most in the developed world could comprehend. Many journalists, no strangers to horror and despair, were deeply affected by what they witnessed. I saw more drinking and drug taking among the press corps in Mogadishu than anywhere else.

Sadly, Operation Restore Hope did not live up to its name. Nine months later the infamous Black Hawk Down battle erupted, when American soldiers attempted to arrest one of the most barbaric warlords, Mohamed Farrar Aidid. This resulted in a fifteen-hour street battle that claimed the lives of eighteen Americans, including two Delta Force soldiers whose mutilated bodies were dragged through the streets by a cheering mob. It's not known how many Somalis were killed, but probably more than a thousand. Two Black Hawk helicopters were shot down during the operation; hence the name of the battle.

Soon afterwards, the Americans withdrew from Somalia, unknowingly convincing another warlord that American politicians had no stomach for a fight. That warlord was Saudi, rather than Somali. His name was Osama bin Laden.

The rest is history.

Conversely, hot on the heels of the bloodshed and anarchy in Somalia was the success story of the decade, not only for Africa, but the planet. In 1994 a genuinely democratic election took place in South Africa, where for the first time in the country's troubled history, all races participated. If ever the world needed a good news story, this was it.

We had extensively covered the release of Nelson Mandela in 1990, so the election in which he would be sworn in as president was a natural follow-up. Apart from Mandela's release being an unrivalled historic occasion, we also had a good laugh at the South African Broadcasting Corporation's hilarious attempts to downplay the momentous event after spending the better part of three decades labelling Mandela a "terrorist".

Their political reporter Clarence Keyter was dropped off outside the Victor Verster Prison, where Mandela was being set free, with instructions to provide a five-minute commentary before switching to the main news. Routine stuff, he was told.

However, Mandela's release was delayed, and Keyter's five minutes' ad-lib turned into an agonising two-hour thumbsuck that has few comical equals in the annals of airwave debacles. Due to its antagonism towards Mandela, the SABC refused to allow Keyter to interview the adoring hundred-thousand-strong crowd jostling outside, or to insert context or archives on Mandela's life into his floundering commentary. That would be too "positive".

Instead, through no fault of his own, Keyter was reduced to risible observations such as the Victor Verster Prison being the "most beautiful jail" in the world, which may have surprised the inmates. Another gem was, "The sun is baking down on us. The sun is not only needed for growing grapes, but for growing South Africa."

As a result, the SABC was reduced to a global laughing stock on one of the most pivotal days in history.

However, for us not bound by straitjacket ideology, the release of Mandela was also a dry run for what we would face when covering the first fully democratic elections four years later. This time we had our own satellite dish, and had no need, nor desire, to be beholden to the SABC to transmit footage.

But we soon struck a major snag, which had the potential to torpedo our entire project below the waterline. South African satellites worked on a system called C band, used in countries without dense populations and not needing multiple high frequency signals.

In other words, our much-vaunted mobile transmitter was basically useless in South Africa. If we didn't sort this out immediately, I was in big trouble as I had several contracts to honour.

We figured the best way to make our small dish that transmitted high-frequency Ku band compatible with C band was to digitalise the signal. But digital pictures had never been used on a satellite before, so this was entering unknown territory. We had no idea if it would work, but we had no other option.

With engineers Jeff Mann and Ken Suckling, we took our dish to New York where there is an 'Earth Station' that tests satellite signals. Without getting too technical, we wanted to experiment with encoders utilised by cable TV companies that compressed analogue into digital, decoding the signals into broadcast quality video. We bolted together components of various coding systems, switched on the digital signal and beamed it onto a satellite.

The results were beyond our most optimistic expectations. The signal was not only rock solid, but crystal clear.

This was a massive breakthrough in broadcasting technology. We were responsible for pioneering the first Digital Satellite News Gathering (DSNG) system. We did it not only by exploring new technology, but by taking existing technology and reformatting it in a way that had never been done before.

High fives were exchanged, and I decided that as a special treat, Jeff, Ken and I would fly back to London on the supersonic Concorde.

This was going to be a trip of a lifetime and there was great excitement when we arrived at JFK Airport. However, I was a little surprised when we boarded the ninety-nine seat plane as it was much smaller than I imagined. There were only twenty-nine passengers and two seats on either side of the corridor that ran through three cabins.

We were in the front cabin. The Captain welcomed us aboard and said it would take two hours and forty minutes to cross the Atlantic from Newfoundland to the edge of Scotland. It was simply unbelievable to grasp that we would be flying at double the speed of sound.

The Captain then said that at precisely twenty-seven seconds after take-off, the conical nose of the plane would adjust and there would be a change of engine noise. This was because he would be switching off the afterburners as he didn't want to blow out the windows of "our neighbours in New York".

The roar of the engines as we rushed down the runway was remarkable. But about halfway down the runway there was a sudden load bang. We all looked at each other. The pilot had said nothing about that. We took off.

No one was unduly worried and he came on air a little later apologising for the noise. He said it was similar to a car backfiring, except that as it happened in a supersonic jet, it was a little more intense.

"We've checked all systems and everything is working fine," he assured us.

The view was spectacular as we were flying at fifty-nine thousand feet and could clearly see the curvature of the earth. The sun had just set and the horizon was a magnificent blue and black glow. I looked at the information screen on the bulkhead as I ordered the three of us a second gin and tonic and noticed we were flying at Mach 2.

Suddenly there was a deafening noise — another big bang — but this time far louder. The plane shuddered and shook like a wet dog, then nosedived straight towards the Atlantic.

The lights went off. The engines turned off and went silent. The flight attendant serving our gin and tonics was knocked flat on his back. The drinks trolley careered right over him, slamming into the door of the cockpit. He valiantly tried to crawl up the corridor using seat legs as handles, all the while shouting that there was nothing to worry about.

In pitch-blackness, we sat rigid in our seats, absolutely stunned and terrified to our bones. Amazingly, there was no screaming or panic. Apart from the floored flight attendant's assurances that all was well, there was silence. Except for one passenger in Seat 1A, who loudly declared that this was "very inconvenient".

"I hope they give us double air miles," he said.

Talk about a stiff upper lip. There were a few nervous giggles, but otherwise absolute quiet for the next three minutes. It was the longest hundred-and-eighty seconds of my life, and I imagine in every other passenger's as well. Even worse, there were no updates from the cockpit. No one had any idea of what was happening except that we were freefalling towards the sea.

In those heart-stopping minutes, we plummeted thirty thousand feet — ten thousand feet a minute. It was like being in an elevator when the cable snaps, but high in the stratosphere rather than an apartment building.

Suddenly the plane levelled out, ramming us back into our seats, flattened by the enormous G-force thrust. My body felt five times its normal weight.

Then the engines spluttered into life, recharging the batteries and switching on the lights. The absolute relief was indescribable, boosted even more so by the sound of the Captain's calm voice.

"Ladies and gentlemen, I apologise for not talking to you sooner. But as you can imagine we have been rather busy up front trying to regain control of the plane, which I am pleased to say is now fine. The aircraft is stable but we have to assess the damage, which was due to another engine surge, and decide where to land."

I was aware that a Concorde cannot fly across the Atlantic at less than the speed of sound as it doesn't have the range. We would run out of petrol and nosedive into the Atlantic, except this time with absolutely no hope.

After another few minutes the pilot came back on air and said we would be returning to New York.

"We have no option but to dump our fuel over the sea, and we will engage in a full emergency landing."

We had only been flying outwards for about 20 minutes, but it took an hour and a half to limp back to JFK. The intense elation of passengers when we saw the iconic New

York skyline and the illuminated Statue of Liberty was palpable.

Even more exciting was the emergency landing. A fleet of ambulances, fire engines and foam-throwers charged along the runway next to the plane as we touched down and eventually stopped at the terminal building.

The gangway folded out and to our amazement, there were twenty-nine flight attendants to greet us. One for each passenger.

"We're terribly sorry Mr Henderson," said the attendant assigned to me. "We have a couple of options. You can fly out in half an hour, first class on United Airlines and continue your journey, or we will put you up in a hotel of your choice with all expenses paid. You can then take the nine a.m. Concorde tomorrow back to London."

Ken, Jeff and I decided we'd had enough flying for one day and chose to stay at a hotel near Madison Square Gardens.

It was getting late, but luckily the bar was still open and we went in to celebrate being alive. This was particularly true for Geoff as he initially thought the explosion was his fault as it happened the exact moment he plugged his earphones into the seat socket.

I generously announced to the entire bar that drinks were on me. My offer was taken up with gusto. No problem, except for some reason I decided to repeat the offer for the next round, not a wise choice in a five star New York hotel.

Luckily for me, the bartender rang the bell and said the bar was now closed, which was a relief for my credit card.

The next morning a limo took us to JFK, and as we were getting ready to board, an attendant asked if everything had been to our satisfaction.

"The service was excellent. Except I now have a hangover and a very expensive bar bill," I joked.

She asked if I had the receipt. I presented it to her.

"My goodness, you did have a good night."

She wandered off into the BA office and came back a few minutes later with twelve crisp hundred-dollar bills.

"Here's your reimbursement for the night. Thank you for flying BA and sorry for the trouble."

The flight back was uneventful.

And yes, to the relief of the magnificently unflappable gentleman in Seat 1A, we did get double air miles.

Chapter Sixteen

Heart of darkness

WE FLEW OUR newly modified dish to South Africa, ready to make broadcast history, or so we hoped, with the first digital coverage of a general election.

Not only that, it was also the first fully democratic hustings in the country of my birth, which for me was a nice twist.

There was no denying this was a big risk, as we had no guarantee our system would work. So much so that even my long-time anchor client, the BBC, refused to give us exclusive rights to provide their feed. They said our technology had never been proven in the blazing cauldron of breaking news, so booked slots with the European Broadcasting Union

(EBU). However, they pledged that if our feed worked, they would switch back to us.

I knew that was the best deal I was going to get, so had no option but to go ahead. This meant that over and above the mega-dollars spent on reformatting our equipment, the exorbitant costs of flying out three engineers and close on two tons of equipment in the hope that everything would pan out gave me more than a few sleepless nights.

Our engineers installed the dish on the roof of the BBC offices in Johannesburg, which had been transformed into an informal nerve centre for the foreign media. They turned it on for the first test run while I paced restlessly in NewsForce's London office.

Several hours later my phone rang. It was my engineer, Geoff Mann.

"Pete, we've completely messed up our calculations."

My stomach sank. That was the last thing I needed. If we had miscalculated, the entire project would implode like a derelict building. It could even be the end of NewsForce with our reputation in tatters.

"It's the amplifiers," he said.

"What do you mean?" I barked down the line. "We bought the best amplifiers we could."

That was true. We had a capacity of eight hundred watts, hugely boosting the strength of our signal.

"I know. But we only need eighty watts," Geoff said.

"So? That's … umm, good, isn't it?"

Geoff started laughing. "I'm winding you up, mate. This beauty is over-performing like you won't believe. The picture is crystal clear. The signal is rock-solid. The guys in London are gobsmacked."

I exhaled like a burst balloon and started laughing with him. Perhaps a little hysterically, considering my relief.

"But I can tell you where we do have a problem," Geoff continued. "There's a queue outside our door with every network and his dog wanting to transmit through us. They've seen the quality, and now want a slice of it — so much so that we don't have enough satellite capacity."

The EBU, our rival transmitter, was sending an analogue signal, which was almost twice the cost of digital and not as clear. It was based in the SABC office, a ten-minute drive away. That meant with our system working like a dream, we now had another significant advantage as well — the old axiom of location, location, location. Not only were we cheaper and transmitting better quality, we were conveniently in the same building as the rest of the foreign media. ITN, Reuters — in fact, all the major networks — were barely a few strides down the corridor. Instead of having to drive to the SABC office, go through torturous security checks and find a seat at a bank of EBU computer screens, camera crews could stroll into our office, get a mug of coffee and bowl of popcorn, slip their tape into our machine and send it straight to Europe.

This was a lucrative bonus that literally fell into our laps. We hadn't bargained on non-clients wanting to buy transmission time from us. Now we had them lining up demanding exactly that.

"I had better book some extra slots," I said.

"Mate, don't just book *some*," said Geoff, his Strine accent twanging across the line. "You need the entire bloody transponder. Book it around the clock for the whole week."

I phoned Intelsat, the Washington-based company selling satellite space, and asked to buy some circuits.

"No problem. How many?"

"One hundred and thirty-two."

"What?" He had been expecting two or three.

"Yes, and I want them all next to each other, on the same frequency, and on the same channel."

I could sense some head scratching at the other end of the line. "Never heard of that before. But OK, we can do it. How long do you want it for?"

"A week."

He guffawed. "A week? You're kidding. We only sell by the year."

"How much is that going to cost?"

"Thirty-two thousand dollars payable each month. So multiply that by twelve."

Three hundred and eighty-four thousand dollars! That was considerably more than I had budgeted.

But hang on, I thought. I punched a few keys on a calculator and suddenly the figures didn't look too bad. We would be selling single ten-minute feeds at a thousand dollars, so to break even for the first month I only had to hawk thirty-two slots on the biggest news story of the year. We could easily do that. Anything above would be pure profit that hopefully could tide us over for the rest of the rental year.

Having done due diligence, I also discovered there was another loophole I could exploit. The satellite covering South Africa was an old one, which the industry called an "inclined orbit". In other words, it was not geostationary and moved around in a figure of eight, meaning our engineers would have to track it. For that inconvenience, Intelsat gave a fifty per cent discount, bringing the final monthly rental figure down to sixteen thousand dollars. That was somewhat more manageable.

"OK, I'll buy it."

I now had my own satellite for a year. The question was, would I need it for that long? There was no doubt that the first month would more than pay for itself. The queues outside our office door were getting longer as all the big names, ITN, BBC, Channel 4, CNN were sending footage through our dish. We somehow had to sustain that momentum after the election.

With only three engineers, we were stretched to the limit. I flew out from London to help — not in the technical sense, but more to percolate gallons of coffee and serve mountains of popcorn.

Yet despite my lowly status as corn popper and coffee brewer, I am eternally grateful I made that trip. Never before has the "right time, right place" cliché proved so true for me.

It happened several days after I arrived when a man came into our office clutching a packet. It was nothing unusual, as there were always hordes of people hanging around, but something about him caught my attention. I have no idea why as he looked pretty ordinary, averagely dressed and very polite. There was nothing to suggest he was about to hand us media dynamite.

I stood as he came directly towards me, taking a video out of the packet.

"Have a look at this," he said.

We walked over to a recorder and I put in the cassette. I will never forget the first image. It was of a river choked with bodies from bank to bank. There was a shallow weir across the water, and corpses flowing downstream were stacked like cordwood as they bobbed over the barrier. It was so shocking that I thought it must have been Photoshopped. But there was no doubt that the video was raw, unedited, authentic footage.

"Where the hell is that?" I asked.

"A place called Goma."

"In the Congo — the DRC?"

He nodded. "But the bodies are from Rwanda. The Hutu are slaughtering the Tutsis. The country is awash with blood. The world needs to see this."

"Who took the video?"

"I did."

He was a Rwandan and had flown one thousand seven hundred miles to South Africa to get genocide footage to the international press. Someone directed him to the BBC building. Noticing the queues outside our office, he concluded we were the most important people on site and came to us. He didn't ask for money, or any other compensation. He wanted the killing to stop. Simple as that.

In doing so, he handed me the first graphic evidence of the Rwandan genocide, a savage scar on humanity that has few equals. It was the biggest, saddest, bloodiest and most barbaric ethnic cleansing massacre since the rise of Hitler.

"I will get this out," I vowed, my voice rasping with shock. "The world will see it."

He thanked me and left. To my infinite regret, I didn't get his name. However, I take some solace in keeping my pledge to him, as it was television cameras as much, if not more than anything else, that finally stopped the slaughter.

The contrast was enough to make one weep. While covering the best feel-good news story of the decade, I was handed proof of the most evil. On the southern tip of the continent, a bloodbath many believed was inevitable had been averted. Yet in the Great Lakes of Africa, an even worse bloodbath was actually happening.

I showed the video to other networks; this was no 'scoop' we wanted for ourselves. But the reality was that we were the only people who could get on-the-spot footage out of a backwater like Goma. No one else had invented the mobile equipment we were using. No one else could beam it live to global audiences at such short notice.

The Tutsi and Hutu of Rwanda, and also neighbouring Burundi, have been tribal enemies for eons. The Tutsi are originally believed to be a Cushitic people, but have been in the Great Lakes for at least four centuries. They are, generally speaking, taller and slimmer than the Hutu, but years of intermarriage have eroded many physical variances. They both speak the same language and their cultures are similar. To most outsiders, the differences are difficult to detect. Yet the blood feud persists.

On 6 April 1994, a plane carrying Rwandan President Juvénal Habyarimana was shot down as it was about to land at the capital city Kigali. Habyarimana was a Hutu moderate wanting peace with Tutsi rebels fighting his government.

The next day, Hutu extremists seized power, blaming the Tutsis for the murder of the president. Local militias armed with a plethora of rudimentary weapons ranging from machetes to sharp sticks set out to kill every Tutsi they could. As tribal identities were stamped on every Rwandan's ID card, it was easy to determine who was who. In the rural areas, where Tutsi and Hutu had lived cheek by jowl since time immemorial, it was even easier.

Within a week, seventy per cent of the Tutsi population were slaughtered. Those still standing fled for their lives to adjoining countries, mainly to Goma in the Democratic Republic of Congo. That was where I sent my engineer Jeff Thorpe-Willet, an ex-British Army signaller, and cameraman Anthony Brooks.

The DRC is the size of Western Europe, but there are virtually no roads outside the run-down cities. The only way to travel efficiently was by air. But there were no scheduled flights to Goma, so the best we could do was get Jeff and Brooksie a ticket to the capital Kinshasa and hope for the best.

They booked into the Intercontinental Hotel and went for a beer to discuss the next move. In the bar, they bought a tough-looking white man a drink. He said he had been a former French Foreign Legion pilot. Yeah … right, thought Jeff and Brooksie. The continent attracts its fair share of Walter Mittys, and in Francophone Africa, to claim to be an ex-*legionnaire* is a common fantasy.

It turned out that not only was he the real deal, he also owned an Alouette helicopter. To Jeff and Brooksie, this was like winning the lottery and somehow they talked him into flying them to Goma, nearly a thousand miles away.

Goma, with a population of two million, is a sprawling shanty-city at the foot of Mount Nyiragongo, an active volcano housing the world's largest fluid lava lake. It's also on the shores of Lake Kivu, which has vast quantities of dissolved methane in its waters. If a large cloud of the toxic gas is 'burped' up, it could kill the entire population.

In short, Goma doesn't have a lot going for it.

The border post with Rwanda is little more than a pole on a road with a sign, and that's where Jeff and Brooksie started filming. I watched as the first video streamed through. Thousands upon thousands of people were straggling down the road, many nursing gaping wounds from machete slashes. Some were crawling, others dragged by those who could walk. Silent children, traumatised beyond comprehension, physically unable to scream or shed further tears, gazed vacantly as the camera panned across an unfathomable vista of human misery. Far more than words, the video captured the haunted souls of those who had escaped an inconceivable apocalypse of satanic savagery.

Unlike Hitler's gas chambers, this genocide was up close and personal. People were hacked, stabbed, clubbed, slashed, strangled or simply pulped to death. Many collapsed and died as they crossed into the relative safety of the DRC, their last desperate ounce of will to survive evaporating.

It is believed that more than a million people were massacred. The overwhelming number were Tutsi, although moderate Hutus and Twa, a pygmy tribe, were also slaughtered.

We put the harrowing photos on the satellite feed and I phoned clients such as the BBC and CNN asking if they wanted the link. They jumped at it.

Then Jeff Dubin, head of the European Broadcasting Union's news division phoned me.

"I see you've got a feed-point working out of Goma. Can I book?"

"What time slots do you want?"

"The lot."

"You're booking 24-hour slots? You realise we charge by the minute."

"No problem. We've got so many people lined up that we need the feed full-time."

Not only were we providing the sole live footage, we had our own satellite. The gamble I took in booking an entire transponder for the year had hit the jackpot, although I certainly had not known that at the time.

But even so, the story was too big for us to handle alone. With EBU's multiple clients the dreadful news of the genocide would get out far quicker. The overwhelming priority was to stop the carnage.

For the next twenty-four hours, the world watched in shocked horror as our team in Goma filmed around the clock. I only realised the extent of our coverage when Jeff phoned a couple of days later and said, "Pete, do you realise I owe you 1.2-million dollars?"

It was astonishing. So much money started pouring in that I invoiced the EBU daily instead of weekly to make it more manageable.

This was great for the company, but obviously horrific for the victims. I had a huge problem trying to reconcile that. How could we be making so much money out of so much misery? It was impossible to grasp.

I was visibly wrestling with this dilemma — making money broadcasting misery is a quandary war journalists face at some stage of their careers — when one of my engineers called me aside and pointed out that it was thanks to us that there was now a global humanitarian movement to help the victims. Without that initial broadcast at the Goma border, where Jeff and Anthony Brooks live-transmitted the first traumatic footage of terrified, machete-hacked people fleeing for their lives, the slaughter would have continued. The victims now had food, shelter, medicines, blankets, and clean water. Above all, they had safety. I took some small consolation from that.

Almost exactly a year after the Rwandan ethnic cleansing ended, we broke the news of another genocide. This time in the Balkans.

We had been covering the violent breakup of Yugoslavia and its seismic aftermath since the early 1990s, so my crews were familiar with the conflict. The biggest flashpoint was in Bosnia and Herzegovina, where the region's three largest ethnic groups, the Serbs, Bosniaks (Muslim Bosnians) and Croats were at each other's throats. The Bosnian Serbs were the best armed of the militias as they were supplied by neighbouring Serbia, while the Bosniaks and Croats had formed a loose, often uneasy, alliance against them.

It was a particularly nasty war for journalists to cover, mainly because of the number of snipers targeting people in the streets. People were killed going to a store for a bottle of milk. In fact, the main boulevard of central Sarajevo —

Bosnia's capital — was known as Snipers' Alley due to the alarming number of assassins picking off civilians at random. Journalists were no exception. In fact, they were possibly prized targets among the predominantly Serbian shooters.

We needed to protect our client crews, which meant keeping them off the streets and transporting them around the beleaguered city in armoured vehicles.

However, few networks owned such vehicles, so most journalists and cameramen relied on the largesse of the various peacekeeping forces under the auspices of the U.N., which was not always forthcoming. This meant journalists often braved shrapnel and snipers' bullets whenever they left the hotels to do their jobs.

NewsForce was known as an innovative company. It was key to our "can do" reputation. We had just invented digital news gathering, so I thought we needed an equally creative concept to keep journalists safe while reporting on the Bosnian conflict.

The obvious solution was to get our own armoured vehicle, something big enough to carry camera crews and our gear that included more than a ton of satellite equipment. I searched around and discovered a Scottish company in Dumfries that manufactured Armoured Personnel Carriers (APC) for the British military.

I phoned to place an order. Their first question was which army did I represent.

I replied that I was a private individual, which threw them off track a bit. However, they said they had a demonstration model constructed to full NATO ballistic-protection specifications that could carry twelve people. Did I want to buy that?

I did. APCs, which look like tanks, are also known as battle busses or battle taxis as they ferry troops to the frontline. It was exactly what we needed. However, ours had no weapons and I stressed it had to be painted white rather than camouflage or khaki. We were journalists. The last thing we wanted was to look like military.

The next step was to get the vehicle U.K. number plates. I was in Cyprus at the time so phoned Bill, a friend of mine in London, asking if I could register a vehicle with his home address. I forgot — conveniently, of course — to mention that said vehicle was actually an APC. Bill got quite a shock to get a knock on his door one evening by a policeman asking if he owned a tank. It wasn't illegal. Just highly unusual, and the police were curious. I could picture Bill muttering "bloody Henderson" under his breath as the cop left.

The tank's first outing also caused quite a stir when we drove it to Heathrow Airport laden with satellite equipment. We parked it in the drop-off zone, and soon had security police swooping like a pack of bewildered dogs. They barely allowed taxis to pause for more than a few minutes — and here was a tank right at the airport entrance. Even worse, a bunch of motley-looking journalists about to leave for Somalia emerged from the back carrying loads of boxes. I think we triggered every security alarm possible.

We caused an even bigger stir when I decided to show off our new toy to potential clients. The interior was customised to accommodate the flyaway satellite dish, which unfolded like a pizza box through a porthole in the roof. We festooned the vehicle with NewsForce stickers and drove it to a hotel near the ABC network offices in London. I bought several crates of wine and beer, then invited the foreign media to come and inspect the "first armoured mobile satellite news gathering vehicle".

The name didn't exactly trip off the tongue but there was massive interest, particularly as a fair number of the journalists present had been shot at before. I signed a contract with CNN on the spot, but the deal stipulated that the vehicle had to be delivered to Croatia, where a news team would be waiting.

We put the APC on a ferry to Belgium and one of my engineers drove it to Split, a distance of almost one thousand and eight hundred miles, crossing five international borders. The look on customs officials' faces when a bulky tank towering over Citroens and Skodas arrived at the various border posts was priceless — but that's what NewsForce people were skilled at doing.

At Split, we linked up with the CNN team led by my old friend Brent "Blazing Saddles" Sadler. Our troop carrier then surreptitiously slipped in behind a United Nations convoy delivering humanitarian aid to Srebrenica, a small mountain town in eastern Bosnia. The decision to paint the APC white worked beautifully; no one suspected it was carrying journalists and cameramen, let alone a mobile satellite dish.

We arrived in Srebrenica in the nick of time. Bosnian Serbs laying siege to the town had recently massacred eight thousand Bosniak men and boys in a detention centre while U.N. troops from the Netherlands stood by helplessly. In fact, every atrocity imaginable was being committed under the radar without the world knowing.

In the middle of the vicious street fighting where Bosniak males were buried in mass graves and their women gang-raped, a white armoured troop carrier arrived. Then, to the astonishment of the militias, a turret popped open and a satellite dish appeared. As it did, a cameraman started filming while Blazing Saddles delivered a hard-hitting commentary on the reality of an on-going genocide. As he spoke, damning evidence of atrocities were beamed to the rest of the world. It was the first time the extent of the ethnic cleansing against Bosniaks was revealed.

As the news spread globally, enraged Bosnian Serbs targeted the white tank and the media crew inside was fired upon repeatedly, as well as multiple grenades hurled. So much so that the APC had more dings and pockmarks on its paintwork than a teenager with a severe case of acne. But the heavily reinforced vehicle was impervious to bullets and shrapnel. Not one journalist relying on us for safety was injured.

That was how the awful story of Srebrenica went viral, and there is no doubt its huge impact was because it was being beamed live from actual killing zones. That was solely because we had the technology to do so.

We now had to get the troop carrier back to the U.K. for a service after its intense baptism of fire. This wasn't something we could take to the local grease-monkey for an oil change — it was a highly sophisticated, computerised vehicle. We had to bring it back to Scotland.

Our engineer who had driven the APC to Split was given the job. He knew the vehicle well, so was the obvious choice. However, when several days passed without any contact, I started to get worried.

Eventually he phoned. There had been a problem, he said. He had fallen asleep while driving along the mountainous

Croatian coastline and careered off the road, ploughing through a forest of pine trees, eventually stopping at the edge of a sheer precipice that plunged into the sea.

I sent out a flatbed from Dumfries to winch the mangled wreck up the mountainside. The reinforced chassis, built to withstand landmines and artillery blasts, was twisted like a corkscrew. How the driver escape with his life is a mystery.

Sadly, the APC was irreparable. As no sane broker would insure it, we had to write it off as a loss, as well as the excessive recovery costs.

However, on the plus side, the success of our battle taxi was phenomenal. It only covered one story — but what a story. Indeed, the U.N. Secretary-general Kofi Annan described the Srebrenica massacre as the worst crime committed on European soil since the Second World War. The International Court of Justice at The Hague concurred, and the Bosnian Serb leader, General Ratko Mladić was later convicted of war crimes and jailed for life.

For me, our white tank symbolised not only NewsForce's lateral thinking, but also the power of adventure and 'can do' approach, which as I have said is the lodestar of my life. We could have shrugged, saying it was too dangerous to go to Srebrenica. We could have waited until the situation calmed.

Instead, we chose to take full responsibility for our crew's protection, with gutsy journalists venturing into insanely hostile areas in our own armoured vehicle.

I bet Ratko Mladić wishes we had chosen otherwise.

Chapter Seventeen

Ayatollahs and aristocrats

MY EXTREME GOOD luck in life was choosing to be a TV cameraman during one of the most newsworthy periods of the century.

This was no great achievement on my part. I was just happy to be part of it all, often pinching myself wondering how someone born in South Africa, not exactly the epicentre of global affairs, found himself reporting on flashpoints around the world.

Even better, now that I owned a news gathering operation, I could choose which events I personally wanted to cover. You don't get luckier than that.

One story that springs to mind was reporting on the death of Ayatollah Ruhollah Khomeini in June 1989. But what was far more interesting than the funeral of the hardline cleric was travelling around Iran, where Westerners are often openly targeted.

We booked into Teheran's Laleh Hotel (a former InterContinental), where a giant poster on the wall behind reception welcomed us. Perhaps "welcome" is the wrong word, as this was not exactly a genial greeting, as you would expect from the city's premier hotel. Instead, the message was "Down with America, down with Britain!" accompanied by crude caricatures of Ronald Reagan and Maggie Thatcher. As I was with Mike Mathews and Keith Graves representing the very British BBC, this did not invoke a warm and fuzzy feeling.

A group of journalists were then invited by the Minister of Oil to fly down to Abadan, the country's leading fossil fuel producing region. Although we were on a civilian flight, our pilot was from the Iranian Air Force who wanted to demonstrate his 'Top Gun' credentials. He taxied out of the hangar at speed, pulled the equivalent of an aeroplane handbrake turn, and screamed down the runway at full throttle.

We reached Abadan in record time, then visited the oil refineries, most of which had been bombed during the recent Iran-Iraq war.

From the wrecked petroleum plants, we drove to a military base to interview the oil minister, who blamed everything on the "Great Satan" America as well as Israel and, to my surprise, South Africa.

At this stage, Keith Graves remarked in a stage whisper that echoed around the room, "Henderson, how much will you pay me not to tell them you're South African?"

I ignored him, hoping fervently the Iranians would as well.

Back in Teheran, we visited the notorious Evin Prison where an English businessman, Roger Cooper, had been jailed for life on flimsy "spying" charges. He shared a tiny cell with thirty other people, including the previous Shah of Iran's brother. It was so small that not all inmates could lie down simultaneously, so they slept in shifts.

While interviewing Cooper (who was released two years later), a Dutch journalist wanting a different news angle left us and wandered off down another corridor.

He soon got the shock, rather than story, of his life when a guard grabbed him, hurling him into one of the congested cells shouting "Spy! Spy!"

The entire press corps ran towards the commotion with cameras poised. The first thing I noticed was the journalist's bloody hand jammed in the cell door as he frantically tried to prevent it from being slammed shut.

We managed to wrest open the door and release the Dutchman. He was extremely fortunate. If we hadn't got the cell open, he would probably still be there.

For some reason, the press junket was organised in the middle of Ramadan, a time of strict Muslims fasting, so we were unable to order freshly prepared meals during the day. We could only get tinned food, hotel management informed us. We shrugged philosophically. When in Rome ... but then discovered that tinned food included Caspian Sea caviar.

Soon there was a shuttle service delivering the delicacy to our hotel rooms. So much so that one of my abiding memories of Iran was flying home laden with caviar and exquisite Persian carpets, which were an absolute bargain.

Another enduring memory was being invited to meet an Iranian brain surgeon married to an Englishwoman. He had lived in the U.K. during the reign of Shah Pahlavi, the last King of Iran, but decided his talents would be better utilised in his homeland with Khomeini's triumphant return. The couple lived in the majestic mountains skirting northern Teheran, but had to downgrade their mansion due to official hostility towards wealth. Their swimming pool, for example, had been filled in.

After a sumptuous meal, we were offered a glass of wine. However, as we left, our English hostess stood at the door with a plate of chewing gums sticks. I declined to take one, but she insisted.

"If the religious police smell alcohol on your breath, you could be stoned to death on the side of the road."

I took the gum.

In fact, the religious police did harass one of our party, the AP photographer Greg English, who had long blonde hair. Greg left the hotel one morning after a shower and hailed a taxi with his hair still damp. As he got in, another vehicle sped up and forced the taxi to stop.

It was the religious police wanting to know why a "blonde woman" with wet hair was alone in a taxi.

Fortunately, Greg was able to convince them he was not a woman, but it was a classic example of the endemic paranoia in the country.

In stark contrast to the austere Iranian elections, I also covered the far more convivial presidential hustings deep in the beating heart of the "Great Satan" itself — America. It was in 1992, when the incumbent president George H. Bush was being challenged by a little-known former governor of Arkansas, Bill Clinton. Most people thought Bush would be a shoe-in for a second term.

I first met Clinton at a TV station in the Midwest when he walked into the studio for an interview. I introduced myself, said I represented Sky News, and we chatted for a while. It was a fascinating encounter, and whatever one thinks of Clinton, he is one of most charismatic world leaders I have met. Unlike many of the ruling elite, he is engaging and looks directly at you when speaking. I was captivated by his energy and presence and thought maybe people were wrong about Bush being the likely winner.

Bush was also a likeable man, but far more old-fashioned. With a horde of other journalists, I joined him and his wife Barbara on a whistle-stop rail tour. This is a peculiar American way of campaigning where the candidate hires an entire train, holding rallies at multiple stops on the same day.

One carriage had been converted into a media room with rows of tables sagging with refreshments. Gorgeous blonde women carrying trays brimming with Hershey Bars and M&M's dished candy out to newsmen, which I thought was great, albeit as close to actual bribery as one could get.

The train stopped at most stations, where Bush would address crowds of varying sizes gathered on the platform. A fleet of cars then ferried the press to the nearest TV station where we would edit our footage and beam it off to our various head offices. Once done, we would board the train again at the next stop.

It was a fascinating experience watching the two most powerful people on the planet campaigning. I couldn't help comparing it to other leadership contests. For example, when I met Jonas Savimbi, he was blowing up Angolan trains rather than using them for whistle-stop election campaigns. In Iran, the only "blonde woman" was Greg English's mistaken identity, not some beauty laden with candy bars.

Both the Iranian and American elections were mainstream stories, but we were continually on the lookout for more obscure features that other networks overlooked. One I remember most was a documentary on the bitter conflict in Kashmir, which only NewsForce could cover thanks to extensive contacts forged from years at global flashpoints.

Kashmir is a heavily occupied militarised region carved up between Indian and Pakistan in the far north of the subcontinent. Four wars have been fought over it since 1947, and as both countries are nuclear powers, it is perhaps the world's most volatile state. It's divided by a Line of Control, with soldiers squaring up on either side.

It was not a good place for any foreigner, let alone Westerner, to visit. In fact, it's downright dangerous and few tourists venture into the area. I knew I could get into Indian-occupied Kashmir, but the Pakistani side, known as Azad Kashmir, was another matter altogether. Many districts were controlled by fundamentalists who were the forerunners of today's Taliban.

I phoned my good friend Riva Levinson in Washington, whom I knew had contacts in a "Free Kashmir" movement. Some years previously she had organised my Angolan trip to meet Jonas Savimbi, and if anyone could get me into a no-go zone, she could.

Riva called back suggesting I fly to Pakistan the following week where she and political consultant Matthew Friedman would meet me.

I landed in Islamabad with Israeli cameraman Chris Whitefield. I told Chris I had little idea of what type of story would eventually emerge, but we would have one hell of an adventure along the way. That alone was enough to convince him to sign up for the ride.

At Islamabad's airport, officials whisked us past passport control and a state vehicle drove us to a hotel where we met Matthew and Riva. Thanks to them, our trip had been sanctioned at the highest level. No other TV network at the time could get that sort of access.

Early next morning we boarded a helicopter and flew to Muzaffarabad, the capital of Azad Kashmir. The passenger door was off and with feet dangling in the air, Chris and I filmed the extraordinary valleys of the Hindu Kush below.

At Muzaffarabad, we interviewed the governor who authorised a visit to a refugee camp where we spoke to people fleeing from Indian-occupied Kashmir. Most had escaped across the freezing Himalayas, so apart from horror stories of torture and abuse, they were suffering from hypothermia and frostbite.

I then said what I'd really like to film was the Line of Control (LoC) — the literal "line in the sand" between two nuclear powers. It would be graphic footage of the most dangerous standoff in the world.

No problem, said Matthew. We would do so the next day.

We woke early in the bitter cold. An hour or so later, we reached a flimsy wooden bridge across a deep ravine. Fearing we would plunge into the valley below, I suggested to Matthew that being the lightest, he should walk in front of the car to test the planks.

He agreed, and it was extremely fortunate that he did. Some slats could barely take his weight, let alone that of the vehicle. We solved that problem by reinforcing the weak boards with loose planks that we had already driven over.

Just before the LoC, we got out of the vehicle and walked up a hill for a better view. In the distance I saw an Indian soldier waving a flag.

"What's he waving that for?" I asked one of the Pakistanis with us.

His mouth dropped opened in shock. "Get down! Get down!" he shouted. "They're going to shoot!"

We all hit the dirt.

Our Pakistani guide then explained that protocol stipulated soldiers on both sides of the line waved flags as warnings before opening fire.

Fortunately, the Indians didn't shoot as we scampered back to our vehicle.

The next step was to film the story from the Indian side. But if the Indian authorities discovered we had been in Azad Kashmir, we would be in serious trouble. Or at the very least, not be allowed into the country. So we left our film and equipment in Islamabad, taking only two high-quality handheld video cameras on the plane to Delhi.

There we were met by a man who ostensibly owned a carpet shop, although was obviously up to his neck in one of the Kashmir liberation movements. He gave us plane tickets to Srinagar, the largest city in Kashmir, where we were met by another man holding a board with our names.

He ushered us out of the airport to a Tuk-Tuk moped taxi and told us to hide under a pile of blankets on the back seat.

The taxi dropped us off at Dal Lake on the perimeter of the city where we boarded a beautiful houseboat, hand-carved out of rare rosewood. Chris and I were shown our plush *en suite* bedrooms covered with exquisite Kashmiri carpets, then invited to dinner. On the aft deck overlooking the lake, a magnificent stretch of water also known as the Lake of Flowers, we feasted on a delicious meal of Kashmiri chicken.

The next morning our host took us to a guerrilla training camp somewhere in the mountains. As we approached, we were surrounded by a group of fierce-looking fighters with faces covered by keffiyehs and cradling AK-47s.

It was surreal. In normal circumstances, these people would have happily slit our throats. Yet thanks to Matthew and Riva, here we were filming their stories.

However, the footage was highly subversive from India's point of view and we would have been thrown into jail if caught. The only option was to smuggle it out.

Our host instructed Chris and I to seal the film in plastic bags, which were stashed under trays of freshly caught fish and sneaked out on a truck to Delhi.

As an added precaution, we also took reams of tourist videos featuring Kashmir's spectacular scenery. It was a good thing we did as we were arrested at Srinagar's airport where customs officials searched our luggage with microscopic thoroughness. They screened our videos, but I think eventually got fed up watching endless vistas of mountains with Chris and I grinning inanely in the foreground.

In Delhi, we picked up the smuggled tapes from the carpet dealer's shop, then flew to Islamabad to fetch the rest of our equipment.

Back in Cyprus, I hired Keith Graves to narrate a cracking one-hour documentary. It was a story most people knew little about and I was convinced I had a winner. With huge optimism, I flew to London to market it.

I hailed a taxi at Heathrow Airport. As we hit the road the cabbie said, "Bleedin' shame that Maggie has resigned, isn't it?"

I jerked upright in my seat.

"What?"

"She's gone. Knifed in the back by her own party," he said. "Bleedin' shame."

As I had been travelling, I hadn't heard that Margaret Thatcher had just resigned as Prime Minister.

I slumped in my seat. My dismay was total. From a purely selfish point of view, the "bleedin' shame" was that my timing could not have been worse. I knew with cold certainty that for the next fortnight, every non-Thatcher story in the U.K. would shrivel into total insignificance —

including my exclusive documentary. The BBC and Channel 4 wouldn't even spare me a minute to discuss it.

In desperation I called CBC, the Canadian broadcaster, and was put through to bureau chief Hillary Brown. I had a few seconds to do a sales pitch on one of the most complex stories of the time.

"I've got amazing stuff on Kashmir with exclusive footage on the Line of Control and interviews with terror groups. It involves two nuclear powers. Would you be interested?"

Hillary, a veteran journalist, knew the Kashmir crucible could detonate at any minute. She knew how significant it was, but even she baulked.

"Sorry. Everything is focused on Thatcher at the moment."

"I know, but that's going to pass. You must have a look at this."

Canada, like Kashmir, was part of the Commonwealth, so Hillary half-heartedly agreed. I dropped the tape off at her office and waited. There was not much else to do as every minute of broadcast news was choked with the latest on the Thatcher saga.

Three days later, Hillary phoned.

"Four Corners love it," she said. "We're buying."

"World rights?"

"No. Just Canadian."

That meant I would get half the price I was hoping for. However, Four Corners was a prestigious travel series, and maybe other networks would also bite.

They did. I sold it to about half a dozen stations, including CNN, but even so, I didn't make huge money. However, the excitement and adventure of getting the exclusive story under the nose of edgy nuclear powers was one of those crazy moments that inject so much adrenaline into journalism. The thrill and buzz of once again being in the crosshairs of history with a camera was intensely visceral.

Queen Victoria famously remarked that the Indian subcontinent was the "jewel in the crown" of the British Empire. So it was serendipitous that three years after the Kashmir story I met Victoria's great-great-granddaughter, Queen Elizabeth, at the 1993 Heads of Commonwealth meeting in Cyprus.

The Commonwealth is the sole remnant of the once-mighty Empire and I was covering another story abroad when the Royal Yacht Britannia sailed into Limassol Port. However, I arrived back in Cyprus just in time to accept an invitation to meet Her Majesty at a press function on the aft deck.

Fearing I was late, I sped from Larnaca's airport, blagging my way through Limassol Port security and drove straight to where the Royal Yacht was berthed. As I was running up the red carpet gangway a voice boomed from the deck.

"Excuse me Sir, who are you?"

Panting with exertion, I stammered, "I'm Pete, here to have drinks with the Queen."

That was not quite what it said on the invite, but the cut-glass British accent didn't waver for a second.

"You are most welcome Sir. But you should use the aft stairs. These are Her Majesty's."

Red-faced, I did a speedy U-turn and ran to the other gangway.

On the aft deck, I was puzzled to find I was the only person there. Only later did I discover that the Queen's Press Officer, Dickie Potter, had been briefing the media on royal etiquette at a nearby hotel. By the time they arrived, I was on my third cucumber sandwich and second gin and tonic. This garnered some wry comments from the rest of the press who had to sit through a dry lecture on how to behave.

As Her Majesty arrived, we stood in a line while Dickie Potter introduced us. When she came to me she said, "Isn't this a wonderful view from the ship?"

I agreed.

"The last Commonwealth Conference was in Zimbabwe," she said. "I went on safari and an elephant put its trunk on the Land Rover bonnet. It was rather scary."

This was gold-dust information for me, particularly as she had no idea I was from Africa.

"Your Majesty, you are right to be concerned about wild animals," I said. "I was once bitten by a lion."

"You were what?"

I showed her my scarred hand. She held it, through a glove of course, for a closer look. She had never seen a lion wound before.

Dickie Potter went quietly ballistic. The key thrust of his etiquette brief was that you never, repeat, never touch the Queen. Yet here she was holding my arm.

"Your Majesty ..." he started

"Wait a minute Dickie. This is fascinating."

I told her the story, then ended by saying, "Your Majesty, one last thing ... I want to thank you for sending a telegram to my grandmother who turned one hundred last year."

"How is she?"

"She's wonderful. Still very active."

"Sounds a bit like my old mamma."

"Well, actually my brother once met your old mamma." As I said that, I could see Dickie out of the corner of my eye throwing his hands in the air. I'm not sure if that's because I, a mere commoner, was referring to the Queen's Mum as "old mamma", or because I was hogging valuable time.

"When was that?"

"He's the Regimental Sergeant Major of the Transvaal Scottish, which is linked to the Black Watch."

The Queen nodded. Her mother was the proud patron of the Black Watch, the Royal Regiment of Scotland.

"I remember that. It was just after mamma had swallowed a fishbone and had to be rushed to hospital."

"How is she, Your Majesty?

"She is doing very well and I'm pleased your old mamma is as well. What a fascinating story and wonderful to meet you."

It was a great event for me, but thanks to the irate Press Secretary, I was never invited to a royal occasion again.

Chapter Eighteen

End of an Era

SOON AFTER MEETING the Queen, JJ and I left Cyprus and moved to England. It was time to change base. Cyprus had been wonderful; we lived a hectic social life, and the initial idea to be close to the action when the Middle East was flaring had been a sound commercial one. However, with demand for our highly mobile news gathering outfits soaring, we now needed a presence in more countries.

We had already opened offices in Singapore, Johannesburg and Sydney, with plans to expand in Caracas as our South American bureau, and Delhi to give us a foothold on the vast Indian subcontinent.

Most importantly, we needed an office in London, as that was where much of our business was generated.

Also, on a personal note, our daughter Jessica would soon be turning two and JJ was pregnant with our son Tom. It was time to move back home.

We bought a large house in Farnham in the South East of England, which bizarrely reminded me of purchasing my initial mansion in South Africa years ago on a whim. That was my first attempt at being a grown-up rather than a nomadic cameraman. But the key difference now was I had a wife who shared my outlook on life, waking up in the morning thinking everything was amazing — enjoying the thrill of pushing boundaries and doing stuff others say is impossible.

News gathering is tantamount to feeding a voracious monster. As the old cliché goes, today's headline wraps tomorrow's fish and chips. Obviously that was in the days of print, but it's even more metaphorically valid now with the advent of insatiable, round-the-clock TV news.

Unfortunately, it's often either famine or feast, and a good crisis is needed to nourish the gluttonous beast. I now had thirty employees around the world, and despite turning over millions of dollars a year, it was a precarious business model as cash flow depended on dramatic events. But such events are invariably outside our control — so how do freelance news outfits prosper when there isn't some plague, earthquake, or psycho starting a war?

The answer stared us in the face. We had mobile satellite technology that no one else did. We could broadcast and edit from anywhere. So why not also use that for non-news coverage?

I would like to take credit for the genius idea, but it actually fell into our lap when I was in South Africa. We were beaming out footage of Nelson Mandela's presidential inauguration when a flamboyant, cigar-smoking man walked into our office.

He had one question. Pointing to our digital set-up, he asked if it could be used to transmit a sports match.

"I don't know," I replied. "We haven't used it for anything longer than 10 minutes." This was before the Rwandan genocide.

The man's name was Roger Philcox, a larger than life character, who was also head of ITV Sport. He was in South Africa on a fact-finding mission, investigating various options to broadcast the World Cup Rugby extravaganza the following year.

He said the bog-standard method would be to send live footage from the sports stadiums to the SABC studio in Johannesburg via micro-links, which would be relayed to the massive C band satellite dish at Hartbeespoort Dam fifty-five miles away, and finally beamed to ITV in London.

It all seemed rather cumbersome as each game would, in effect, be transmitted three times. And as they would be filming from multiple sports grounds around the country, there would be significant loss of broadcast quality.

I told him I had a better idea. "We can set up our mobile dish in any stadium car park and transmit the game direct to London."

Roger was amazed. That was a fraction of the effort compared with the conventional route. But he was still cautious, wanting me to sign a six-month contract and only for selected matches.

"I can't do that," I replied. "We are primarily a news organisation. I don't know where I will be in six months. There might be a war on.

"But," I continued, "if you give me a contract for every match, I'll buy another digital dish and dedicate it solely to World Cup coverage."

"What will you charge?" he asked.

"A thousand dollars a minute."

"Flipping hell! You realise a game is ninety minutes long?"

I nodded. "But if you do it the normal way, you'll probably pay the same without the quality."

Roger reluctantly agreed. We got the contract for all matches. It was a massive success and the 1995 Rugby World Cup was the first sports event to be broadcasted digitally from a production truck in a stadium parking lot. It was also a fairy-tale ending for the host country when South Africa, playing for the first time as a 'rainbow nation', beat New Zealand with a drop-kick goal in the dying minutes of the match.

This snowballed into other sport broadcast contracts, including cricket where five-day tests literally printed money. For those matches, we charged for the signal delivered rather than a daily rate, which meant more broadcasters bought in as well. We even got a contract from ESPN in America to cover cricket in the Caribbean. This was a surprise bonus as Americans consider cricket an arcane idiosyncrasy rather than a sport.

Soon sport was almost rivalling news in generating income. This spread to other events, such as the 1996 Miss World pageant in India where more than a hundred and fifty countries took our feed.

However, the biggest live event was the return of Hong Kong to China after more than a century and a half of British rule.

This was in 1997 and the BBC hired us for logistical expertise as well as mobile satellite technology. It turned out to be one of NewsForce's most intensive projects and we flew out almost three tons of equipment and a dozen people to the island.

My mission, as always, was to beat every other network — not only journalistically, but also creatively. To do that we had to scout the best vantage spots, no simple task on a tiny, traffic-congested, skyscraper-studded strip of land.

We scoured every nook and cranny, finally discovering that the most panoramic angle was on top of the Academy of Performing Arts in the bustling Wan Chai commercial district. I banged on the Academy director's door and stressed that not only would we would be recording history, we wanted to do so from the roof of his prestigious institution. He loved the idea, granting us the best position overlooking a spectacular sweep of the waterfront with Kowloon in the background.

The other prime spot was more difficult to secure. In fact, almost impossible. It was the roof of the ultra-exclusive Royal Hong Kong Yacht Club (RHKYC), situated on Kellet Island with an unparalleled vista of the famous Victoria Harbour. It's one of the oldest and most prestigious sailing clubs in the world. The entrance fee for a married couple is US$17,600. So offering to pay for a position on the elegant clubhouse's roof was not going to cut much ice with their well-heeled members. The club had more wealth and status than we could begin to imagine.

As neither hard cash nor the reputation of the BBC was going to work, I decided the only options were either sweet-talking the club committee, or going down on bended knee and begging.

That may have done the trick if I had got through the door, but soon discovered it was easier to break into Fort Knox with a claw-hammer than for a non-member to get an appointment with the commodore.

I had one final trick up my sleeve. My step-father Peter Carr was commodore of the Emmarentia Sailing Club in Johannesburg's northern suburbs, which compared to the RHKYC is a mere puddle. However, yacht clubs are big on reciprocity rights, so I got Peter to fax me a letter inviting the RHKYC to be "honourable reciprocal members" of the "esteemed" Emmarentia Sailing Club.

This time, establishing myself as a sailor from Africa, I was tentatively allowed to set foot in the commodore's office. After a few minutes of polite conversation, I handed over the letter granting RHKYC members reciprocity in the unlikely event they wanted to sail a dinghy on a tiny urban pond in the concrete heart of Johannesburg.

"Saving face" is big in Chinese culture, and if some obscure club in Africa granted RHKYC members such benefits, then it was only right and honourable that they reciprocate.

It was approved right away, as well as — crucially — a prime position on the roof overlooking Victoria Harbour to film the ceremony.

This earned me double-kudos. Not only did I by some fluke wangle the best lookout spot on the island, I was also extremely popular with the BBC crew, who now spent their evenings sipping exotic sundowners in arguably Asia's most exclusive bar.

It poured with rain on the day of the handover, which dampened the "sun setting on the British Empire" pitch most newsmen planned to use. But that did not detract one iota from the magnificence of the occasion. The last governor, Chris Patten, formally returned the territory to China in an evocative ceremony resonating with pomp and pageantry, while Prince Charles sailed out of Victoria Harbour on the Royal Yacht Britannia. It was a privilege to be there, and with our two exquisite vantage positions, we got the jump on other networks.

The return of Hong Kong was the end of an era. Not just for the British Empire, but for me too. I barely admitted it to myself, but I was considering a "new era" as well. Deep down a question nagged: was it time to do something different with NewsForce?

As any entrepreneur will attest, it's lonely at the top. The rewards can be great, but so are the perils. The wins are shared by many; the losses by yourself.

Entrepreneurs live with stresses that few in the corporate world experience. I liked that, but it can take a toll, mentally and physically. Maybe I needed to think the unthinkable and get a partner to share the risks.

This was no Damascene moment, where my future was laid out in a blinding flash of light. On the contrary, it was triggered by a trip to Las Vegas, perhaps the last place to have a cerebral epiphany. However, in retrospect it was a fitting venue as I was possibly rolling the dice with one of the biggest gambles in my life.

Vegas is not only a casino magnet. It also is a hub of industrial trade fairs and exhibitions, such as my favourite, the National Association of Broadcasters (NAB).

The annual NAB Expo attracts the biggest names in broadcasting with the latest technology and innovations on display. As NewsForce was now as much of a pioneering tech company as a news organisation, we had a stand.

However, due to some chaotic mistiming, I hadn't booked accommodation. I called up a hotel at the last minute and was told there wasn't a vacant square foot in the city due to the NAB event.

"That's a pity," I said. "Because I'm a big gambler."

"Oh ... in that case I've just found a room for you."

"What's the cost?"

"It's free for gamblers."

I quickly phoned five colleagues giving them the hotel's number with instructions to tell the receptionists they were high rollers.

That year, 1998, the NAB fair was one of the biggest, and parking outside the convention centre was impossible. Fortunately, there was a Harley Davidson shop nearby, and the NewsForce team hired powerful hogs that we could park at will. To me this was not vanity; it was symbolic. After being first in Rwanda, Kuwait, Bagdad, Mogadishu ... you name it, I believed my team had earned their chutzpah stripes.

While showing off our technology, I got chatting to a guy who had recently sold a broadcast solutions company for multiple millions. I was intrigued and mentioned I was considering getting an investor in NewsForce. He agreed that due to the unpredictable nature of my business, it would make sense to find a partner. As he had just gone through a similar process, he offered to help.

"What you should do is write to possible buyers, then negotiate with those interested. Hire me as a consultant and I'll put together an offer memorandum and let's see what comes out of that."

He then asked which type of companies would be most interested. I pondered for a while. It was not only about who would be interested in NewsForce. Equally important was who would I be interested in working with. I wanted people who had something to offer, not just cash.

As the most expensive single cost in digital news is satellite time, an ideal partner would be a satellite owner. That meant access to vital technology as well as investment.

My new consultant agreed, and we drafted memorandum offers to Canadian Telecom, French Telecom, British Telecommunications, Deutsche Telekom, and IntelSat.

The Canadians, Germans and French replied in quick succession. I exchanged information with the Canadians, but decided they were logistically the weakest link as they were far away. A European partnership would be easier to manage.

I then spoke to representatives from Deutsche Telekom and it went well. I decided I could definitely do business with them.

That left France Telekom (FT). I finally met Michel Combes, the CEO, who flew out to London for talks. To make a good impression, I took him to the upmarket Carlton Club in Piccadilly for lunch. It's an exclusive gentleman's establishment, and although I knew doing business there was discouraged by the posh club management, I didn't suspect by how much.

As Michel arrived, the doorman took his coat and also relieved him of his briefcase, saying he could not take it into the restaurant. No business, he stressed. Michel was somewhat taken aback, but like most Frenchman, probably thought all Brits were mad.

Then, over a superb meal, he took out a notebook to jot down some points.

A waiter approached and told him notebooks were not allowed.

At that moment Michel's cellphone buzzed. The waiter politely informed him that he should have left his phone with the doorman. If he had to take calls, he must please do so outside.

Michel ignored him, and I could see his eyes widening as he listened to a rapid-fire torrent in French. One of their clients had beamed pornographic content on the FT satellite and they had to remove it immediately to avoid global embarrassment.

While Michel was trying to sort this out, the waiter continued requesting he switch off his phone. Michel uttered a few choice words in French, then went outside, standing on the pavement in the pouring rain trying to get pornography off his satellite.

He returned, then defied the waiter by taking notes of our discussion on a paper napkin that disintegrated under a ballpoint pen.

What a disaster, I thought, as he left to catch a flight back to Paris. Here I was trying to sell a portion of my business over lunch in a club that banned business discussions, while he sorted out outer-space smut.

To my surprise, not only did I get an offer from France Telecom a couple of days later, it was twice as good as anyone else's. They wanted to buy forty-nine per cent, which left control in my hands without having to worry about cash flow problems.

I needed help drawing up an information memorandum for the sale of shares and chose Kevin Fleischer, who is not only my best friend but one of the brightest men I know. He was a star Morgan Stanley investment broker and did what many dream of — retiring in his thirties. He thrives on these types of unusual entrepreneurial deals.

We flew into Paris and were ushered into France Telecom's impressively dignified boardroom. As we sat, one of the directors asked what we were going to call the project.

"Project Padda," Kevin replied, quick as a flash. I could barely hide my grin. "Padda" is Afrikaans for frog. We were lucky none of our French friends understood the word.

"*Tres bien*. Project Padda it is," said the director, writing the name on his folder.

The French had done their homework, hiring two top accounting firms to examine my business in microscopic detail. They were complimentary.

"The structure of the NewsForce setup is extraordinary," said one board member. "After consolidating the various international offices, your overall tax is only seven per cent. You must have paid a huge amount of money to set this up."

I shook my head. This was no stunning accounting feat. We had simply winged it ourselves as we acquired new offices in different countries with different tax requirements. I basked in the warm glow of being considered a financial wizard, but it was a brief moment. This was a backhanded compliment.

"Unfortunately for us, it's too tax efficient," said the FT spokesman. "And by a long way. Anything under eleven per cent is taxable in France under much higher rates. So we'll have to restructure the entire company and set it up as a single offshore Dutch Antilles corporation with fourteen per cent tax."

I was not entirely happy as that meant I was doubling my tax, as well as handing over almost half of my company. However, on the credit side, I was getting unimaginable access to satellite capacity.

For the next nine months my office was an airline seat, flying between Amsterdam, Paris, London, Cyprus, Singapore and Australia to complete the deal. It took much time and sweat, as well as lost revenue as I was concentrating on intricate contractual details rather than the core business of news reporting. Cash flow was tight — so much so that I had to close the agreement with FT before the end of the year or would not be able to pay January salaries.

Then as the December deadline loomed, France Telecom phoned. Sorry, the spokesman said. The deal was off. Dead in the water.

This could completely ruin me. Regaining my composure, I asked, "Why?"

"We've had another look at the structure and decided we're not interested in buying a minority stake."

I was silent. Then the FT spokesman said, "For the deal to proceed, we need fifty-one per cent."

The penny dropped with a clang. The deal was not dead in the water after all. The buggers — they had planned this all along. They had played me from the start. I didn't like it, but I knew from hard experience that business is not a game for ninnies. I had been outmanoeuvred. They knew that after all the time, money and energy spent fine-tuning the deal, I was in a desperately tight corner.

I thought quickly. "OK, that'll cost you another two million dollars."

The alacrity to which they agreed confirmed my suspicions.

But there was another far more profound issue. If I no longer controlled the company, how deep would my commitment be? It's a question every entrepreneur asks. And as most come up with the same answer, I added a kicker.

"You also will have to buy the rest of my shares within a year."

That took them by surprise.

"No. That's too short. We need three years."

I then knew with certainty that despite the obvious advantages, I didn't want to be working for France Telecom for the rest of my life.

I agreed to three years. But in return, I got them to agree that we would only have one conference call each month and meet twice a year as long as NewsForce met budget. That would be their level of involvement. FT signed that off, which allayed fears that the board was going to suffocate me with micromanagement. To its credit, it never did.

Barely had the ink on the contract dried when we scooped a massive story on an Ebola outbreak in West Africa. Once again, we were the first there and doubled our projected income figures.

But when I sent my report off, instead of getting a hearty pat on the back, Michel Combes was confused.

"Peter, why have you sent us these amazing figures?"

"Because that's what we did."

"*Non* — impossible."

"Look again."

"OK, but that means I have to go to my board and explain why I am more than ten per cent out on variance of results expectation."

"Michel, this is not a telecoms business. It's a media business and you get ups and downs. Celebrate that this is an up."

"Can't you put some of the revenue into next month?"

"It's already in the bank."

The first year of the FT partnership continued in that highly profitable vein. As always, conflict is the biggest news generator and, among much else, the Kosovo War in 1999 provided that. We were way above budget. I knew this was a wave to ride hard as we were in the ficklest of fickle businesses.

I was right. The next year was a lean news cycle, and our results showed exactly that.

However, at that time I had a chance encounter with an amazing man that literally pitchpoled my value system. He was in his late seventies, and either by fate or luck, sat next to me on a plane. He asked what I did for a living.

I told him, and it turned out he owned one of the largest global media companies. We had much in common. He led an extremely eventful life, a multi-millionaire and alpha achiever, and our conversation for the next few hours was totally absorbing.

I eventually asked if there was anything he would have done differently. He nodded emphatically.

"I would have sold the company when I was forty. Then I would still have a family."

He could see the surprise on my face. I, too, was approaching my fortieth birthday.

"I had a great wife, three kids and everything was going well. We didn't need more money, but I was a workaholic and when I came home, I was too tired or absorbed in my business to do much else.

"Before I knew it, my wife had other interests, and the kids didn't want to go to a ball park because I had never taken them there before.

"The inevitable divorce followed, with alienation from my children that I provided for materially, but neglected emotionally.

"Today I am still working and making millions. But at night I am all alone in a one-bedroom flat overlooking the Potomac River."

It was a classic case of a life filled with regret. Outward success, inward remorse.

It was also a severe wake-up jolt for me. JJ and I had three children — just as my new friend had. I was away on business trips for most of the year — just as he had been. Like him, I was missing out on so much of my family's life. My children were growing up without me.

That fateful encounter exposed an uncannily accurate mirror of my own life.

I was lucky. Unlike my friend, I had time on my side. It was not too late. But it soon could be.

When I got home I said to JJ, "Let's sell the whole company to the French."

She looked at me, surprised. It was the last thing she expected me to say. I then told of my meeting with the media mogul. I didn't want that to happen to me.

The fact that our second year with FT had not been as successful turned out to be my trump card. I was able to persuade the board to buy me out a year earlier than contractually agreed.

It was a bittersweet moment as I closed the office door for the last time. NewsForce was the defining experience of my professional career. It had been incredibly successful, and even more fun. Thanks to my team, whose enthusiasm, vivacity, *joie de vivre* and courage that at times bordered on insanity, we got stories no one else did. We were the souped-up Harley-Davidsons of news gathering; something I don't think my competitors would begrudge me saying.

It was now time to move on.

Chapter Nineteen

Wild countries

MY NEW life dawned as my fortieth birthday loomed.

Suddenly I had time on my hands. I watched the kids play sport. I attended their cricket games, tennis matches and school plays. I drove them to school.

I was learning how to relax, a new experience for me. So much so that I considered moving the family to Australia, buying land and becoming a gentleman farmer.

JJ was not keen. Australia is not only in another hemisphere, it's on the other side of the world. Getting there involves sitting on a plane for twenty-two hours. She argued it would also mean cutting ties with England, where we had a great life.

The issue remained unresolved until we visited my brother and his family in Kenya for Christmas, 2001.

Stewart worked for a South African insurance company in Nairobi and eager to show off this stunningly beautiful country, took us to a beach cottage in Kilifi, an Indian Ocean resort northeast of Mombasa. JJ and I were standing barefoot on a jetty at a boatyard wearing bright kikoi sarongs and sipping Tusker beer from ice-beaded bottles when my sister-in-law Linda remarked, "Why don't you come and live in Kenya?"

She didn't have to say much else. The spectacular scenery of sun-bleached sands and turquoise water, so clear you could see the bottom thirty feet down, did the hard sell on its own.

JJ immediately agreed. I was intrigued, asking why she was so adamantly against Australia and so pro Kenya.

"Just look at this," she said, waving an arm at the dhows bobbing at their moorings on the translucent lagoon. "It's far easier to adapt our lives to include Africa than Australia. We won't have to sell our house in England. We can regularly go back home for holidays. The countries are in the same time zone. It makes far more sense to move here than somewhere so far away."

Our kids, Jessica (10), Tom (8) and Rex (6) were born in England and went to school there. With Kenya less than nine hours flying time compared to Australia's aerial marathon, we could easily keep our English roots. At the same time, we could introduce them to the passion and adventure of Africa that I had grown up with. JJ and Linda were right. Africa made sense.

Far-flung Australia was now out of the question, and, while we could have considered South Africa as an alternative, I harboured too many negative feelings about my homeland as the country was still raw and angry, only recently emerging from nearly five decades of apartheid.

So, on my fortieth birthday at home in Surrey, I told my friends we were going to Kenya. Then we were off, arriving in style as a friend's Boeing 747 ferrying fresh vegetables and flowers flew our two Land Cruisers to Nairobi, which we drove off at the Jomo Kenyatta Airport.

Two days later my brother organised a trip to Lake Turkana involving a safari through the starkly beautiful Northern Frontier District. Turkana is the world's largest permanent desert lake and it was an expedition in the middle of nowhere, with our children sitting on the roof of a Land Cruiser watching wild animals just yards away. At night we camped high on the banks of crocodile-infested waters, and apart from that obvious danger, I also warned the kids to watch out for scorpions. They thought I was joking, but one of my friends said there was a scorpion lurking under every third stone. My kids put that to the test — and sure enough, under the third rock was an evil-looking black arachnid, its body as long as my index finger with a wickedly curved tail poised like a venomous whip.

They believed me after that.

We brought all provisions with us along with several armed guards as Somali cattle raiders were prowling in the area. This was real frontier country where stock rustlers shoot to kill.

Every day was a vibrant new experience for the kids. Six-year-old Rex learned to drive on that trip, but was so short he disappeared under the dashboard whenever he depressed the clutch to change gears. His head then popped up to see where he was going as he flattened the accelerator.

For me, the greatest pleasure was sharing this excitement with my family, as so many of my escapades had been on my own. We were now doing something together, having a thrilling adventure jointly for the first time.

Within a few months, we had bought a house with ten acres of land bordering a giraffe sanctuary outside Nairobi. Each morning we woke to magnificent views of the Ngong Hills, where Safari guide Denys Finch Hatton, lover of 'Out of Africa' author Karen Blixen, is buried after perishing in a plane crash. Indeed, our house often resembled an Out of Africa scene as the kids fed giraffe and warthogs wandering freely in the garden. I half-expected Meryl Streep and Robert Redford to emerge from the star-speckled night.

More importantly, our children were doing things they never had before — floating down wild rivers, climbing craggy mountains, swinging from trees, working in orphanages and other life-enhancing experiences. It was far healthier, physically and mentally, than being glued to an iPad or obsessed by social media.

I loved Kenya right away. It didn't matter what school you went to or how much money you had, it all boiled down to a passion for life in Africa. The expat community, who came from around the world, were a vibrant, fun-loving and interesting bunch.

However, it is important to remember that Africa is not always comfortable. I knew that as I had not only grown up on the continent, I had filmed the savage birth pangs of democracy in South Africa. Although Kenya didn't have the same tortured emotional baggage, there were still serious social and political problems that we could not pretend didn't exist. Just outside our secluded sanctuary was a turbulent world of slums, overcrowding, political upheaval, tribal animosity, and random violence. Once, driving past an intersection outside our house, we came across the bodies of three robbers bloating in the sun. They had been shot by police and left on the side of the road. JJ quickly pointed to a giraffe in the bush so the children looked the other way.

It was certainly living on the edge compared to our sedate lifestyle in England. However, as I had spent much of the last twenty years filming conflict, my 'normality' was chaos. I thrived on it.

Having said that, in the seven years we lived in Kenya, I was only attacked once. It happened on Boxing Day when I took Tom and Rex to the coast on a kitesurfing trip near the small town of Watamu. I had recently bought Tom a surfing kite, which we attached to a go-kart with sand wheels to zoom down the deserted beaches, reaching amazing speeds in the blasting offshore gusts. However, access to the beach is off the beaten track so we asked an African pedestrian for directions. He said he would show me and got into the car.

I was on the beach with Tom, rigging the kite, while Rex was swimming when six tough looking men carrying machetes and sjamboks approached. I realised instantly what had happened. Our 'guide' had seen valuables in the car and had told some local thugs.

"Sit down," one of the men barked at me.

I shook my head. "No."

A split second later I was on the sand. The man had walloped me as hard as he could with a sjambok.

"OK, relax," I said, teeth gritted with pain. "I've got some money. I'm going to give you that on condition you take it and go."

The car was parked on the beach and I had about a thousand U.S. dollars in the glove compartment. They took it, and everything else of value including Tom's prized possessions; his surf kite, a cellphone he had got for Christmas the day before, and his sunglasses.

They also took the car keys. We were potentially stranded, miles from anywhere. I shouted to the robbers disappearing into the scrub-covered dunes, "Hey, please leave the keys."

The men knew we couldn't chase them, and one found a stick, shoved it into the sand and hung the keys on it. The tide was coming in fast and if he hadn't done that, we would have lost the vehicle to the waves.

Fortunately, Rex had not seen the attack. But for Tom, it was traumatic. Not only did he watch his dad being nastily assaulted, but much of the stuff seized had been his. He was in shock and understandably upset.

"Why are you crying?" I asked.

"All my stuff has been stolen."

I put an arm around him. "You've got your life, your health and your dad ... so it's not that bad. It's just stuff."

He nodded. At that moment, Rex came running out of the sea.

"What's up?"

I told him what had happened, thanking my lucky stars that he hadn't been with us. Tom was two years older and by virtue of that, a little more resilient.

"This was a terrible experience," I said to both of them. "But if you learn anything from it, it's never to panic. There's always a choice. In this case I could have fought back and lost, as it would be one against six. Instead, I negotiated. I told them I had money which I would give them if they left. I gave them what they wanted and although I negotiated from a position of weakness, the main thing is that we were not hurt. We even got the car keys back."

The boys also learnt that there's no point in being a victim. We all went kitesurfing again. Today Tom is a Sandhurst-trained British army officer, while Rex is leading an adventurous life travelling the world.

Not long after our arrival in Kenya, JJ reminded me of what my mother had said to my stepfather, "I married you for better or worse, but not for lunch." It was her not-so-subtle way of telling me to get out of the house and find a job.

That's what I did, going back to what I had cut my professional teeth on — a warzone. Not only that, it was a conflict I knew well. The Gulf.

A year after Al Qaida terrorists flew passenger planes into New York's Twin Towers, George W. Bush decided to finish off what his father George H. had started twelve years ago; get rid of Saddam Hussein once and for all. Although there was no evidence linking Saddam to Al Qaida, Bush believed that Iraq — which he named as the "axis of evil" with North Korea and Iran — had Weapons of Mass Destruction and therefore Saddam must go.

This culminated in the Second Iraq War, starting on 19 March 2003, when close on 180,000 coalition soldiers stormed the country. Within twenty-one days, the American 3rd Infantry Division took Baghdad. Saddam Hussein was on the run in one of the biggest manhunts in history.

A couple of weeks later, Riva Levinson, who a decade earlier had paved the way for my extraordinary trip to Kashmir, phoned our beach house in Kilifi, where we were holidaying. She said the American State Department was about to establish an interim government in Iraq and their favoured candidate was Dr Ahmed Chalabi, leader of the Iraqi National Congress (INC).

Chalabi had been in exile during Saddam's rule, and as a presidential contender, his administration needed a crash course on sophisticated communication equipment such as satellite phones and the internet. Would I be interested in setting it up for them?

"Who would I be working for?" I asked.

"You'd be an independent contractor for an organisation called Special Operations Low Intensity Conflict — or more simply, SOLIC. You will have full autonomy, unrelated to any government department. Your mission will be solely to provide comms for the INC."

As she spoke, my adrenaline fizzed like champagne. This was right up my street with my NewsForce background. First, I flew to Turkey where some of Chalabi's people were based, and also met a group of Kurds who were going into Iraq to find and kill Saddam, wherever he may be. Just a cursory chat with them left no doubt how deeply they hated the deposed dictator. If they caught Saddam before the Americans, his final moments would not be much fun. They asked if I wanted to come with them.

It was true I needed to get to Baghdad to link up with Chalabi, who by now had secured premises for his government-in-waiting, but I opted for the more conventional route through Jordan.

I checked into the Intercontinental Hotel in Amman, only to find Jordan was chock-a-block with journalists also trying to get into Iraq. This was not easy, as all Iraqi airspace was a civilian no-fly zone. The only way in was by road, which was, without exaggeration a dice with death. Basically, it involved hiring an SUV or truck at daylight robbery rates and driving for fourteen hours across the Western Desert.

That was the best-case scenario. The more likely one was being shot by desperado remnants of Saddam's routed army, or ambushed by lawless desert tribesmen robbing hapless motorists at will.

In short, the road to Baghdad was the most dangerous motorway in the world. The true highway to hell. I probably would have been safer going in with the Kurds.

On the plus side, the Jordan border was open, which was not the case with Kuwait on Iraq's southern perimeter. There were also no visa formalities. All I had to do was hire an old GMC pickup that cost a thousand dollars and keep my foot on the gas until I reached Baghdad.

I spread the word at the hotel and managed to get two passengers to share costs. They said they were journalists but I soon discovered they were from Israel, which scared the hell out of me. The last thing I needed was to be caught in no-man's-land with people Iraqis hated even more than Americans. But even so ... I somehow liked the almost poetic symmetry. I had covered the First Iraq War from Tel Aviv, and here I was barging into the Second with two Israelis as companions.

I was aware of the American "shock and awe" (also known as "rapid dominance") bombing of Iraq, but totally unprepared for the results. It was something out of a 'Mad Max' movie. Blown up trucks and gutted lorries littered the side of the blitzed road, while scores of bodies swelling in the desert sun lay discarded like sacks. Some bridges had been destroyed, so we drove through *wadis* and medieval villages, hoping the sullen stares of the inhabitants would not erupt into open violence.

Finally, the outline of Baghdad appeared shimmering like an illusion on the horizon. The relief was visceral. We had made it.

I dropped my passengers off at the Palestine Hotel, where almost all the media was staying, then drove to an address provided by Riva: a plush Middle Eastern villa called The Iraqi Hunting Club.

Despite its name, it was not a shooting lodge in some desert wilderness. Instead, it was in the heart of Baghdad's affluent Mansour district, an exclusive retreat previously frequented by the Iraqi elite, including Saddam's sons Uday and Qusay.

Outside the cast-iron gates, I was stopped by Chalabi's guards. The gates clanged open and I entered a quadrangle with an Olympic-size swimming pool and verdant palm tree gardens. This was the headquarters of the Iraqi National Congress, destined to be one of the key players in the rebuilding of the country.

However, I wasn't the first non-Iraqi to get access to the INC inner circle at the club. As I entered the reception, I noticed a striking woman with a laptop wearing an eye patch. I recognised her instantly: Marie Colvin, the famed Sunday Times war correspondent. I didn't know her personally, but certainly by reputation. She was one of the most courageous journalists of our time and had lost her left eye in an ambush while covering the Tamil Tigers' insurgency in Sri Lanka.

She greeted me like a long-lost friend, but I suspect it was because she knew I was there to connect the club with satellite internet. She could soon send stories out instantly, which was absolute gold dust for any journalist in the post-invasion chaos.

The other foreigner was Colonel Ted Steele, an American security expert seconded to Chalabi by the U.S. State Department. Apart from making sure everyone was safe, his job was to scout resources for Chalabi's administration in the ruined city. This ranged from computers, printers, desks, chairs and cabinets, to pens, paper and anything else a normal office takes for granted. Anywhere except Baghdad, that is. I liked him instantly, and we teamed up, scavenging what we could from destroyed offices and ransacked shops. Much of the salvaged equipment was what I needed to do my job as well.

We also needed a fleet of vehicles to ferry the INC to meetings and political rallies. There were obviously none legally available, so all we could do was scour deserted dealerships and drive off vehicles that had not been stolen. Sure, it was technically theft, but this was the reality in post-apocalypse Baghdad. It was a world of mayhem, a world without order. The only law was the law of the jungle — in this case, a concrete one. It was the only way to survive.

Soon The Iraqi Hunting Club had an infrastructure, of sorts, up and running. As far as I was concerned, my job was done, albeit not in the most conventional manner. The potential interim administration had a communication system and the basic skills they needed.

However, I was strangely reluctant to leave. Here I was deep inside the belly of the new Baghdad. The Iraq War was the biggest story of the year by galaxies. And I was at the epicentre. How exciting was that?

I couldn't help myself — my journalistic juices flowed in full torrent. To grossly misquote a well-worn phrase, you can take the boy out of NewsForce, but not NewsForce out of the boy.

To make it even more alluring, journalists regularly arrived at the club, pleading to be let in to interview Chalabi. I watched this, thinking how lucky I was. I was already inside the gates. I had a running start, an unparalleled advantage. I would be crazy to squander it.

The main problem was I didn't have my camera equipment. It was stashed at home outside Nairobi. I kicked myself for not bringing it.

However, one of the French journalists banging on the gate, who I personally let in, changed that. He was Damien Degueldre, a top cameraman and winner of the prestigious Rory Peck Award. As I swung open the barrier, I looked enviously at his top-of-the range video camera.

Like me, he was not only a camera operator but an editor, producer and entrepreneur. We hit it off right away. He asked where I was staying and I pointed to a tent at the bottom of the garden. I had bought it in Jordan as I had no idea what accommodation, if any, I would have in Iraq.

He laughed. "Why aren't you in the main house?"

"I'm not an INC guy. I'm not affiliated to anyone and I don't want to be in that building in case Chalabi's enemies bomb it."

He shook his head, grinning. Journalists were used to five-star expense accounts, and here Chalabi's communications guru was squatting in a tent in the garden.

"Hey," I protested. "It's a big tent."

Once again, I looked jealously at his TV camera. I urgently needed him to team up with me.

"It even has a spare room, if you want it," I said.

He thought about that for a moment. "Do you have any beers?"

"Funny you should ask. I think we should get some."

We went into the city and found a refrigerator in an appliance shop strewn with shattered glass and bought a few cases of Efes Turkish beer.

I now had a lodger who crucially had a camera. To celebrate, I invited others at the club to pop in for a drink at the tent, which started a new tradition. From then on, each night interesting people from all walks of life arrived for what was basically a lengthy "happy hour", discussing the intricacies and absurdities of Baghdad life over copious bottles of Turkish brew. My humble tent was christened The Baghdad Café — coincidently the same name as the pub we frequented in Tel Aviv during the First Gulf War.

Even Chalabi's daughter Tamara was a patron. She's an extremely interesting person, Harvard educated, and more than held her own as an Arab woman in a fiercely male-dominated society. I once went to a rally with her where most of the audience were old-style tribal leaders in full Bedouin regalia. No one was interested in listening to a woman, which they made abundantly clear when Tamara stood to speak. With icy dignity, she silenced the room. She explained that the demise of Saddam's appalling dictatorship heralded a new era and everyone had to work together. She was so impressive that some started shouting "Tamara for President."

"No, no, no," she yelled above the din. "That's my dad!"

This passionate forum beneath a megawatt desert sky was hugely stimulating. The Baghdad Café, aka Pete's Tent, was not just a meeting place. It was a classic information highway where no topic — be it salacious gossip, wild conspiracy theories or Machiavellian politics — was off-limits. In other words, a journalist's dream.

This became even more evident when I noticed that several people asking to see Chalabi were well-known faces on the famous "pack of cards", issued to every American soldier. This was a deck of playing cards, but instead of kings and jacks, there were photos of the most-wanted members of Saddam Hussein's inner circle. The idea was that if soldiers saw someone suspicious, they consulted the deck for verification. Saddam was the ace of spades, while the aces of clubs and hearts were Qusay and Uday.

Some high profile "card" members had come to give themselves up and believed the INC could get them a better deal than going directly to the Americans. As the communications guy, I questioned them, while Damien filmed the interviews. These were then sent to the States to be assessed by intelligence agencies who decided whether to grant asylum or not.

However, as we were freelancers, the videos belonged to us. So I went to the Palestine Hotel where the media was based to sell exclusive footage of the most wanted people in Iraq spilling the beans. Every time I showed a clip, there was a stunned reaction: "How the hell did you get that?"

We even had an interview with Ali Hassan al-Majid, better known as Chemical Ali, who was responsible for gassing thousands of Kurds. He had come to The Iraqi Hunting Club for a visit and we got an interview, possibly one of his last before being captured and executed for war crimes.

Equally riveting for Damien and I, but scarier, was the hunt for Weapons of Mass Destruction (WMD), either biological or nuclear. Saddam repeatedly bragged he had them, so perhaps the rest of the world could be forgiven for believing him.

The American Special Forces, mainly SEALs, were tasked with finding WMD and for the Bush administration this was the maximum priority after finding Saddam himself.

Luckily for us, a group of SEALs based themselves at the club and were regulars at the Baghdad Café. Consequently, they thought we had top-level security clearance. This was something we subtly encouraged without actually lying, so they took us along whenever there was a raid.

The result was several roller-coaster weeks of intense action. Our day often started at three a.m., woken by a bunch of the hardest looking guys I'd ever seen. Some had Rambo bandanas knotted around their foreheads, others bandoliers crisscrossed across their chests, and it must have been quite a sight as we sped through the suburbs of Baghdad in Humvees, storming into factories, bunkers and warehouses. The SEALs reacted purely to tip-offs, and with every mission, we thought we would strike gold. Each time it was a dud. The warehouses were empty, the bunkers wrecked, the factories ransacked. Tip-off after tip-off proved fruitless.

However, it was downright terrifying rushing into a building not knowing whether it was radioactive or not. Or if stragglers from Saddam's army or Al Qaida in Iraq, under the murderous Abu al-Zarqawi, were waiting in ambush. After a couple of raids, I bought a civilian Humvee for us to follow behind the SEALs as we were convinced we would eventually run into a lethal firefight.

As the entire world knows, no WMDs were found. If they had been, I could have retired on the spot. Damien and I would have had the exclusive to the most elusive story of the decade.

WMDs or not, these were edgy times. The Iraqis, almost to a person, hated the Americans and the all-pervasive mood was palpably hostile. Suspicion was so rife that even the CIA was spying on the hunting club in an attempt to discredit Chalabi. There were huge differences and distrust between the Secretary of Defence Donald Rumsfeld and the CIA over who should rule Iraq. As a result, it was not just Iraqi against Iraqi, but also American against American. On one occasion a man wearing aviator sunglasses, skin-tight jeans and a muscle T-shirt pitched up at the gates claiming to be a TV cameraman. He was so obviously CIA that he was a caricature. I told Chalabi and we quickly got rid of him.

Apart from journalists, politicians, pack-of-cards fugitives, SEALs, Green Berets, and CIA cartoon spooks, we also had genuine tribal chiefs arriving on camels from distant parts of the desert to debate, discuss and figure out the future of their ravaged country. Some carried suitcases of priceless relics, possibly dating back to Babylon, for safekeeping in an attempt to stem the total destruction of the country's national heritage.

I shook my head in despair. Every day was a reminder that this land had been brutalised beyond belief. Removing Saddam would not bring stability. The historical hatreds and vendettas ran far deeper than any fossil fuel in the ancient sands. We regularly saw heads impaled on stakes at the side of roads as blood feuds were settled, many of which the West could not imagine, let alone understand.

I couldn't see a single person unifying the tortured country and Ahmad Chalabi, who died in 2015, wasn't the man. He never did lead Iraq, although he was briefly the deputy Prime Minister in 2005, despite the best efforts of the U.S. State Department.

This frenetic lifestyle, searching for WMDs with men who made Rambo look effete, living hard with constant danger, and drinking profuse quantities of Turkish beer continued for six weeks. The adrenaline pumped, the booze flowed, but the bottom line was it wore us all down.

It was time to go home.

That turned out to be the strangest adventure of all.

Chapter Twenty

The Branson of Bagdad

DAMIEN AND I were sitting outside my tent, talking about going home. While both homesick and keen to leave Iraq, we had the same harrowing thought in our minds.

"I'm dreading the drive back to Jordan," I said. "The road's a death trap."

Damien nodded. "Highway to hell."

"Why don't we fly out?" I asked.

"You crazy? Iraq's a no-fly zone. We'd be shot down on the runway."

At that moment, the local "Mr Fix-it", Colonel Ted Steele arrived.

"Hey, cheer up," he said. "You guys are going home."

I looked at him for a long moment. If anyone could bend rules, Ted could. "Can you get us permission to fly out?"

I expected a loud laugh of derision. But Ted was used to dealing with the seemingly impossible. He also knew first-hand about running the lethal gauntlet out of Baghdad.

"Let's speak to the guys at the airport."

We drove in a military convoy to Baghdad's airport and marched into the Command and Control Operations Centre. This was the heartbeat of military aviation in Iraq and every computer screen was blinking with what was probably highly classified information. I should never have been allowed in, but as I was with Ted, no one batted an eyelid.

Ted strode up to the Officer in Command and introduced me.

"This is Pete. He wants to fly in and out of Baghdad."

Ted is not big on formalities, and I was about to say I only wanted to fly *out* — certainly not in. I expected the OC to say that was impossible, when he smiled and turned to me.

"You need to speak to RAMCC." He pronounced the acronym "Ramsee", which stood for Regional Air Mobility Control Centre.

Huh? I could not hide my surprise. "How do I get hold of them?"

He lifted the phone on his desk and dialled a number. "That's how," he said, handing me the receiver.

A few seconds later, I had the chief of RAMCC, based in Doha, on the line.

"Hello. This is Pete from … um … Air Baghdad." I liked the sound of that. "I'd like to arrange civilian flights. Both in and out of Iraq." Ted had given me an idea, albeit a crazy one.

"When?"

"As soon as possible."

"How many flights a week?"

I said the first credible number that popped into my head. "Three."

"We may be able to do that," he said.

I couldn't believe my ears. But there were two strict conditions.

"Your pilot will have to know how to operate in a military theatre of operations and your flight slots will be subject to change at short notice in the event of military activity. If you accept that, we can give your three slots a week."

"That's great. I accept."

"What are the flights for?"

"Bringing in journalists and other civilians because the road from Jordan is so dangerous."

"OK. That's done."

I was still in a daze when I returned to the hunting club. I had slots, but no planes. But I had a plan. NewsForce had regularly used Arab Wings, a Jordanian-based commercial aviation company, so I phoned up contacts there.

"What's the biggest plane I can charter?"

"Dash 8."

"How much will it cost, and how many passengers can it take?"

"It's a forty-eight seater at nine thousand U.S. dollars a flight."

"Book it," I said. "Three return flights a week."

"Do you have insurance?"

That floored me. Insurance? In a war zone? That alone could be prohibitively expensive.

"We can't book the plane unless you have insurance," my friend at Arab Wings said.

I phoned Lloyds in London and got a surprisingly acceptable quote considering the hazards. But there was another hitch; Lloyds could only insure the plane if I had United National approval as Iraq was strictly a civilian no-fly zone.

This was getting more and more complicated. I now needed the nod from some faceless U.N. bureaucrat. How the hell would I get that? It could kill the project stone dead.

As luck would have it, that night I was invited to dinner with Dr Chalabi and a few select guests. During a lull in conversation, I tentatively asked if anyone at the table had contacts with the U.N.

To my surprise, a woman raised her hand. "My husband works there."

I told her about my dilemma, then looked at my watch. "It's about three p.m. in New York now. Can we call him now?"

I took a satellite phone into the garden and she dialled her husband. She handed me the phone and I told him about Air Baghdad and all that stood in the way was U.N. approval.

"What do you want the plane for?"

"Flying in journalists."

"That won't cut it with my bosses. You need a better reason than that."

I thought quickly. "Well … we're also flying in boxes of medicines and other … you know, emergency stuff."

"That's much better. I'll phone you back."

A day later we had UN approval. We were ready to rock 'n roll. I just needed passengers.

I drove to the Palestine Hotel where a group of journalists from various TV networks were propping up the bar.

"You guys know anyone who wants to fly in or out of Baghdad?"

The response was overwhelming. I was virtually mobbed. "How much is a ticket?" was the repeatedly shouted question.

I thought quickly. Nine hundred dollars was a nice round figure, and still cheaper than hiring an SUV from Jordan.

Then one of the TV producers asked what I was charging for excess baggage. Again, that was something I hadn't considered, but another potentially lucrative side-earner. "Ten dollars a kilo," I replied.

I filled up a week's worth of flights on the spot. All bookings for the inaugural journey were paid in cash, so I arrived back at the tent carrying a bag bloated with more than fifty thousand U.S. dollars.

I now needed a base, so went back to the Palestine Hotel to hire a room as an office, as that's where most of my clients would be staying. As it happened, there was an old Air Iraq office underneath the reception area that had been completely trashed in the post-invasion rioting. Damien and I cleaned it up, brought in desks and chairs, and hired two Iraqi women to staff it. We even kitted them out in uniforms.

Next we needed a vehicle. This was solved by the simple expedient of running into the street and flagging down the first bus with an air-conditioner. The driver stopped, and we negotiated a fee for a tri-weekly airport passenger service.

We now had a plane, the paperwork, and more passengers than we could handle. I was on course to be a millionaire mogul with my own airline. The Richard Branson of Baghdad.

Or so I thought. On the eve of the inaugural flight I was at my tent, or more correctly the Baghdad Café as happy hour was in full swing, when Reuters phoned asking for an interview. Great publicity, I thought, and outlined the birth of Air Baghdad and its benefits.

The next morning my phone rang again. It was the Arab Wings pilot, about to fly the first load of passengers into Iraq.

"Are you in the air?" I asked.

"No. Unfortunately, we can't take off."

"Why?"

"We have been grounded because our flight plan says the destination is Saddam Hussein International. It's no longer called that."

"Well ... call it Baghdad International. Anything — I don't care."

"I can't. That name is not recognised by international aviation. We can't take off because we are flying to a destination that officially doesn't exist."

Somewhat in shock, I phoned my contact at RAMCC, who confirmed there had to be a recognised destination on the flight plan. Even though everyone and their dog in aviation circles knew where Baghdad airport was, those were the rules.

There was nothing I could do. But how did it all go so terribly wrong so quickly?

The penny dropped. That morning The Jordan Times had published my interview with Reuters on its front page, and other airlines went ballistic. Who — or what — was this upstart airline called Air Baghdad? And why had it been granted permission to enter a no-fly zone when they had not?

As a result, the American-led Coalition Provisional Authority (CPA) that governed Iraq panicked. They cancelled my flight under the flimsy pretext that it had not gone out to tender.

I said that was ridiculous as it was a commercial operation, funded solely by myself and I didn't need to go through a government tender process. They then lamely stated the destination was incorrect.

I fumed. You could not miss Baghdad Airport no matter what it was called. Not only that, I was saving people's lives by giving them an alternative to the most dangerous road in the world. A road that their military couldn't protect.

The CPA wouldn't budge. The flight was cancelled.

I may have lost that battle, but I sure as hell won the publicity war. The propaganda fallout was massive. I don't think Paul Bremer, head of the CPA, and his team knew that the flight was crammed with angry journalists. Every one wrote a scathing report slamming the CPA. The gist of the stories headlining the world's most influential broadcasters and newspapers the next day was the same — the provisional administration claimed it wanted to rebuild Iraq, yet the first commercial operation could not even get past the starting post. Was it because I was not American or Iraqi?

Even so, the bottom line was that bureaucracy triumphed and I had to return all ticket payments, as well as paying off the short-lived office staff and bus driver.

I lost a lot of money, but despite that, it had been huge fun. I mean, who gets to set up a bones-of-the-butt airline in a no-fly war zone? That alone was worth the price. To this day, I'm convinced I would have pulled it off if I hadn't given that Reuters interview. Everything would have slipped silently under the radar. My planes would have flown.

I now had to drive out of the country, negating the sole purpose for setting up my own airline. Thankfully, the border with Kuwait had just opened, a far safer but longer route taking little more than six hours at top speed. I sold my Hummer in Kuwait City and flew back to Kenya.

Back in the bush and sun, I again needed something to do both for gainful employment and mental stimulation. Otherwise JJ would be on my case again. My experiences in Baghdad, setting up communications in a ruined city, made me consider doing the same in Kenya. While Kenya had not been through a war like Iraq, the internet system was equally atrocious.

I launched a company called Indigo Telecom, initially to provide myself and friends with a decent internet service and keep me occupied. It expanded rapidly, and the next thing I knew I had a green light from the Kenyan government to provide a satellite phone service in remote rural areas.

This was a massive task, but a big breakthrough came when I was speaking to an old friend, Malcolm Brew. Malcolm lived on Bute, a rugged, gale-swept island off Scotland's west coast, and suddenly a question popped into my head. It was an obvious one and I wondered why I hadn't considered it before. If Malcolm lived on a gusting sandstone speck in the heaving North Atlantic that was as remote as much of Africa, how come we were connecting so effectively via computer?

"Malcom, what's your phone number?" I asked.

"Don't have one, mate. No landline."

"But you're on the web. How do you do that without Wi-Fi?"

"TV White Space."

I'd never heard of that before. Malcolm explained that when TV switched from analogue to digital, there had to be space between channels to avoid regional signal interference. Those channels, known as White Space, could be shared for other uses. Most important for my purposes was that White Space used lower frequencies than Wi-Fi and mobile networks, so the signal travelled far further.

"All you need is a TV aerial to pick it up," said Malcolm. "I'm getting my signal from the University of Strathclyde and it's really strong, even though I'm on the far side of a hill. The signal pulses over mountains and forests so it's great for remote areas."

In other words, tailor-made for wild Africa.

"How much does it cost?" I asked.

"Nothing. It's free because they're old TV channels. They're empty."

I was intrigued and flew over to Scotland to see him operate first-hand. It was a fascinating trip, not just tech-wise, but just to get to Bute involved planes, trains, boats, and finally a taxi to the far side of the island where Malcolm lived.

I was bowled over. White Space was incredibly high speed and powerful, and as its signal tracked terrain rather than line-of-sight, a single TV mast could cover at least a hundred and twenty square miles. It was exactly what we needed for far-flung rural schools and villages in Kenya.

I flew back to Nairobi and got an appointment with Bitange Ndemo, Minister of Telecommunications. He, like most of the world, had never heard of White Space. I showed him how it worked.

"This is what you need," I said.

His eyes lit up. He saw the amazing benefits right away. "Definitely. Go ahead and do it."

I then spoke to Microsoft, who agreed to partner me and we jointly ploughed a million dollars into the first TV White Space network in Kenya. We called it Mawingu, which appropriately means "cloud" in Swahili.

The first town to get the network was Nanyuki, about one hundred and twenty miles from Nairobi in the foothills of Mount Kenya. We erected a TV mast and the entire community, including four over-crowded schools, a large government administrative complex and a Red Cross Centre now had access to an electronic cloud of connectivity costing a few cents a month. Almost overnight, we provided life-changing technology. Barefoot schoolchildren learned how to use computers. Villagers emailed relatives around the country, if not the world. Government offices downloaded critical data that before would take weeks to reach by post. The success was spectacular.

Sadly, too spectacular as it was extremely disruptive to other mobile companies and network operators. White Space was simply too efficient and cost-effective. While mobile companies such as Safaricom outlaid a thousand dollars to deliver a megawatt of signal, we did it for sixty. Their antennae had to be as high as trees, often towering two hundred feet into the air, plugged into an overloaded grid. Ours were barely forty feet, powered by solar panels.

All of this was done under a trial permit, but to go further we needed a commercial licence. The Kenyan authorities, so enthusiastic to start with, suddenly got cold feet.

I soon discovered why. They didn't want to upset 3G licence holders who were among the country's largest commercial taxpayers.

Like Air Baghdad, where I recently head-butted with stubborn bureaucracy, I realised this was a fight I couldn't win. I had little option but to withdraw from the agreement.

Microsoft's founder Paul Allen, a philanthropist with far deeper pockets than me, persevered, and Mawingu is still providing a valuable service in Kenya. But sadly, it hasn't been allowed to roll out across the entire country as we hoped. The true victims, of course, are the desperately poor rural people, particularly school kids, deprived of cheap internet access.

However, the Mawingu experience steered me onto a new course. It instilled a desire to combine classic entrepreneurship with good causes.

That became my new passion.

Chapter Twenty-One

Stumble in the jungle

LIFE IS FULL of surprises. But few are more unusual than being invited to travel to a bush hideout in the vast forests of Central Africa and meet John Garang, the charismatic guerrilla leader of the Sudanese People's Liberation Movement (SPLM).

I jumped at the opportunity. This was possibly exclusive footage I might be able to sell to the global networks. This time I took my camera, unlike my blunder in Iraq.

Sudan, at the time the largest country in Africa, was nearing the end of almost twenty-two years of bitter civil war between the Arab North and the African South. Garang was both the military and political leader of the South. He was not only a trained soldier, but also highly educated with a PhD in

Economics from Iowa State University, and referred to by his followers as "Dr John".

A bearded, imposing man (the Dinka tribe are among the world's tallest people), invited me to a village called New Site on the border with Kenya.

Two things struck me right away. Firstly, the almost messianic loyalty he inspired among his followers, and secondly how remote his headquarters were. However, Dr John assured me that was deliberate. The village was the perfect location as the thick Nilotic rainforest prevented aerial attacks from the North Sudanese Air Force.

He had a point. Well, sort of. The tangled bush surrounding the village may be a good defensive barrier, but there was no denying he was logistically isolated.

Having set up a network for the Iraqi National Congress in Baghdad eighteen months ago, I saw first-hand how essential sophisticated communications were for any political organisation, let alone a liberation movement fighting for its life.

"So how do you speak to your people?" I asked.

"On the radio."

"Don't you have a satellite phone network? Email? Internet?"

He shook his head.

I continued, "How can you, the leader of a freedom movement, only be able to reach your followers with transistor radios? You really need a more modern network."

Dr John agreed. "But how can we set one up here? This is a warzone."

I outlined what I had done for Dr Chalabi, and also my attempts to electronically connect rural Kenya with the Mawingu project. He was fascinated.

"Can you do something like that here?"

I nodded. "It won't be easy, but it can be done. What you need is a twenty-foot container with two satellite dishes, high speed German internet and U.S.A. dial tone, air conditioners, computers and an email address."

He seemed pretty overwhelmed, which was to be expected. "But how do I get all that?"

"I'll bring it."

"Yes — but how much will it cost?"

I thought for a moment and took a deep breath. The Sudanese civil war, the longest in Africa, could soon be over as a peace treaty granting South Sudan full autonomy and eventually independence from the North was nearing its final stages.

I looked around. Suddenly, instead of huts and forest, I pictured aerials and people with phones and internet access. The cellphone has lifted more people out of poverty than any other gadget in Africa. It has empowered ordinary people to make choices, create markets, sell goods and conduct business where virtually every government initiative, from power grids to transport infrastructure, has failed. For most Africans, it is the single greatest invention since the wheel. It is the most potent driving force of the free market on the continent. And here I was talking to the leader of what would soon be the world's newest country about installing its first national communication system.

"I'll give it to you," I said.

It was a huge gamble. But the reward could be as massive as the risk. I would be getting in on the ground floor of a virgin economy

Back in Nairobi, I bought a steel shipping container, installed the necessary technology as well as air-conditioning to keep it humming in a steaming jungle, and did a few test runs. Eventually I was satisfied that we had the essentials of a basic communication nerve centre.

I hired a lorry, loaded the container, and told the Kenyan drivers to take it to South Sudan. There were no roads once they crossed the border, but these drivers were exceptionally skilful off-roaders. Somehow they got the equipment to John Garang's remote headquarters intact.

I then flew into New Site with an engineer to connect the bits and pieces. Our first challenge was the most daunting:

how to get the container off the back of the truck without the benefit of cranes or even a forklift.

There was only one way to do it. Shove it off, using my scant schoolboy knowledge of kinetic energy. I ordered all computers and other breakables to be removed, hooked a steel cable onto the container, then looped the cable around a stout tree. Workers placed car tyres on the ground behind the truck to act as cushions. Then we crossed our fingers as the driver revved the engine, slipped the clutch, and sped off.

It worked. With much screeching of metal and billowing dust, the anchor cable yanked the container off the moving truck. It landed hard and noisily but undamaged on the tyres.

We then re-installed the electronics, aligned the satellite dishes, connected the internet and just as I was about to switch it on, I invited John into the container, now his new communication centre.

"Take a seat," I said. "The first thing we need to do is to get you email."

He watched while I set up a Yahoo account in his name. We then banged off a message to his sister living in Australia.

When she replied a few minutes later, the astonished look on John's face was pure candid camera. This was a massive success, and the word soon spread in the village that the white man had brought magic. Next thing I knew there was a queue outside wanting to email relatives around the world.

The civil war had created a vast diaspora of Sudanese and for many, this was the first time they could speak — albeit electronically — to each other.

John now saw endless possibilities. A small shipping container with a couple of computers and a satellite aerial opened up a whole new world for his guerrilla movement. He could contact his legions of devoted followers, issue orders to his soldiers, and even raise funds. Oil-rich South Sudan is largely Christian, as opposed to the Muslim North, and there was much sympathy for its cause in America.

But the real prize for Dr John was to get a cellphone network. He called it a "happy box", and asked if I could do that for him.

"I want to be able to walk and talk," he said.

For this we had to set up a Global System for Mobile Communications (GSM) network. But we also needed an international code to dial, which was a problem as the country's official dial code was controlled by Garang's arch-enemy, the government in Khartoum. This presented an obvious security threat. The North could monitor all of Garang's conversations and as far as Dr John was concerned, that was out of the question.

There was another way. I went to see Dr John to explain the next step as this would entail entering the big league.

"What we can do is make up our own code for South Sudan and apply to the United Nations for approval. But that will cost a lot of money. How much can you put in?"

Garang emphatically shook his head. "We're not putting any in. We can't afford it."

This could destroy the deal before it got off the ground. I had already funded the start-up equipment, so decided I may as well follow the old adage — go big or go home. Cliché or not, it's a philosophy that has stood me in good stead for much of my life.

"I'll put some money in," I said. "But you need to as well."

John called a day later. "I've got a million U.S. dollars for you."

I had never expected him to come through. In fact, I think I am the first person to get cash out of a rebel movement, rather than the other way around. He said the money would come from a company, a global provider supporting American foreign policy objectives, and would be given to me in Nairobi.

I met their representative who was clutching a suitcase stuffed with dollars, as part of a U.S. initiative to support what they called "Christian oil". I could get all the equipment I needed, as long as it was made in America.

I then set up a company called Network of the World and started building a cellphone aerial and operations office in Rumbek, the second largest town in South Sudan.

We had to work fast as the Comprehensive Peace Agreement (CPA) between North and South was about to kick off. The key clause in the treaty as far as I was concerned was that any existing commercial contracts signed prior to the agreement would remain in force. As a result, it was incredibly important for South Sudan to have its own cellphone network up and running before John Garang signed the CPA.

Building masts in a shanty-town surrounded by tropical rainforests, hills and swamps is immensely challenging, and in this case even more so as we regularly had to sweep the roads for landmines.

Also, without any meaningful infrastructure, we had to build everything we needed from scratch. We even had to make our own bricks as the logistics of importing material into the area were so daunting as to be almost impossible. Consequently, I bought a German brick-making machine, which was basically a compressor with two large bins mounted on a trailer. All it needed was a bucket of sand, a cup of water and some cement, which was then compressed into a brick called a hydraform. Each brick was concave on top and convex beneath to ensure a snug fit and once dried in the sun, is harder than any other on the market. The beauty was we didn't have to log trees to fire-up brick-baking kilns.

I soon discovered that the best blocks were made by women, who had far nimbler fingers. This was vital with hydraform as the foundation has to be arrow-straight for the bricks to interlock. Otherwise, it topples over.

I got chatting to one of the women who told me she was a war widow. She was immensely grateful for the job as she could feed her two children. She said she was currently looked after by her brother-in-law, as in their culture, widows are inherited as wives by the dead husband's brother — commonly known as a levirate marriage. With this job, she could look after her family herself.

I asked if there were other women in her situation. She nodded. There were many.

I told her we had work for thirty.

"But who will look after their children?" she asked.

"The children will go to school here. I will get a teacher who will give lessons while the mothers work."

Productivity soared, and with the gang of war widows, we were soon producing twelve hundred bricks a day. Their children were taught under a tree outside. Within two weeks, the new network operations room was completed.

Now what to do with my brick makers? I didn't want to send them back to depending on the largesse of their brothers-in-law, so I contacted an Italian charity who agreed to fund the construction of a hospital. The women would make the bricks.

When that was completed, I presented them with a certificate of competency and a T-shirt proclaiming them to be master brick-makers. I also told them that as they were now skilled labourers, their daily wages were increasing from ten to fifteen dollars.

The next day nobody arrived at work. I asked Richard Herbert, my site manager and partner, what was going on.

"They say you have been stealing their money."

"What?"

I couldn't believe it. I had just given them a pay increase. I thought they would be thrilled. Instead, as far as they were concerned, the fact I was now paying them more "proved" I had been cheating them before. They couldn't grasp that the pay increase was because they were now skilled.

I called the workforce together.

"OK, you have two choices," I said. "Those who want to carry on working, now earning fifteen dollars a day, stand over there," I said, pointing to my right. "Those who don't, stand on the other side. I will pay you the five extra dollars for the days you have worked, but you will be out of a job. I will hire new people."

To my astonishment, all took the extra money rather than the increased salary. I paid them out on the spot, and closed the factory.

The next day they came back to work. Every one of them. I shook my head. "The factory is closed. There is no work."

Later that day, police arrived and arrested me and Richard Hebert. They locked us in the local jail, a filthy, run-down building that looked something like a "hang 'em high" cell in a B-grade cowboy movie.

I first met Richard at a luxury resort called Desert Rose Lodge on Mount Nyiru near Lake Turkana, where I was holidaying with my family. We got chatting and when he told me his background was communication technology, I told him I was about to set up a cellphone business in South Sudan. He shook his head and said, "You've got big balls, mate."

Soon afterwards, he agreed to come and work with me in South Sudan, and here we were behind bars in a fleapit swarming with mosquitoes, bizarrely accused of stealing money from war widows. I wonder if he regretted his decision. But like most Africans, white and black, Richard is as tough and stoic as they come.

It was late afternoon and I decided enough was enough. "No way I'm spending the night in this hellhole," I said to

Richard. "The food's disgusting and there're mosquitoes everywhere."

Slapping his arm to scatter the buzzing hordes, Richard agreed and called the guard over, telling him we were going to sleep in our camp.

The guard refused. "You have to stay here."

"Why?" I asked. Our camp was barely fifty yards away. "We can't escape. The runway is closed and there are no planes. So where can we go? We're definitely not sleeping here. Come and fetch us in the morning."

Fortunately, he saw the logic in that. It probably also gave him the night off. He unlocked the cell and as we were walking back to camp, we passed Rumbek's mayor.

I stopped in front of him. "You realise we have been put in jail?"

He didn't answer.

"We have just built you a hospital. We have brought computers and cellphones. We have got a teacher for the children of war widows. We're not here to steal anybody's money. If anything, the people who worked for us are stealing money from you by not paying tax."

That piqued his interest. "What's tax?" he asked.

"Everyone pays tax on money they earn. Otherwise how can you build roads and schools for your people?"

He mulled that over. In a town of almost zero formal employment, tax was not much of an issue. But thanks to what we were doing, Rumbek was gradually emerging from rudimentary subsistence to an embryonic economy.

"How much of this tax thing should they pay?"

"At least ten per cent."

He thought that was a brilliant idea.

The next morning, he arrived at the construction site and told the fired workers they had to pay a ten per cent tax on their previous earnings. Within the blink of an eye, the whole focus switched from me "stealing" their money to the mayor wanting to do likewise. Unsurprisingly, they did not share his enthusiasm for taxation. In fact, not to put too fine a point to it, they wanted to string him up from the nearest tree.

Eventually, after much shouting and haranguing, it was agreed that wages would have a five per cent tax deduction, and Richard and I were released from jail.

Perhaps I should have packed my bags and left then and there. The craziest situations in Kenya were havens of sanity compared to South Sudan. But one thing I have learnt as an entrepreneur is that what first seems to be a massive problem is more often than not a minor setback.

A few days later we turned on the network. The entire community arrived for the grand occasion, conveniently forgetting that not long beforehand Richard and I were behind bars being eaten alive by bugs. The village elder blessed the event, chanting in Arabic like a praise singer to chase away any demons lurking in the new building.

We gave the elder's son a phone and asked if he would like to call anyone. He said he had a brother who had fled to Canada during the war. No one in the family had spoken to him for more than a decade, but they knew his number in Montreal. I dialled it.

It was midnight across the Atlantic when the son answered. To say he was astonished to hear his brother's voice is a total understatement. They spoke animatedly for a while, and then the son handed the phone to his father.

It was one of the most heart-warming, emotional scenes I have witnessed. Tears streamed down the old man's face as he shouted into the mouthpiece, "This is your father in the bush."

He kept asking, in between sobs, yelling and whoops of joy, how could his son be in this tiny black box? For someone who has never heard a dial tone, let alone seen a phone, this was stranger than witchcraft. If ever I needed graphic proof of the power of communication, this was it.

Initially, the mobile network was set up so John Garang could communicate with his followers and soldiers. But as the story of the old man speaking to his son across an ocean many thousands of miles away spread, it became far, far bigger than a mere communication tool. The domino effect sprang into action. Fledgling markets, with shopkeepers now able to place orders and compare prices, sprouted in the town. As people learnt new skills, they started small businesses, selling perhaps one or two items. They began earning money, miniscule at first, but even those tiny amounts bought goods that jump-started other trade. They were even paying tax. I watched, fascinated, as a rookie economy as fragile as a bud tentatively took root before my eyes.

But for me, the greatest reward was watching a new generation of young entrepreneurs spring up. The cellphone network operated off prepaid cards costing a dollar, hawked mainly by teenagers in town. For every ten units sold, they got one free. My favourite was a superb natural salesman who sold sixty cards in a day. The next morning, he arrived with two friends and told us they were working for him so he needed more cards. At the end of the week he had bought himself a bicycle. A month later he had a motorbike and designer sunglasses. By the time we left, he had opened his own trading store.

However, the biggest impact was that with cellphones people could call neighbouring Uganda, a far wealthier country, and directly import goods ranging from food to clothes to fizzy drinks. Suddenly products many South

Sudanese had never seen started piling up on shop shelves. Not only that, on return trips Ugandan truckers took Sudanese merchandise back to sell in their country. To see first-hand the raw economic power of a mere phone, something we take for granted in developed nations, is almost beyond belief. From a dusty wasteland, Rumbek became a mini boomtown by Sudanese standards.

The network also brought some uniquely 'bush' problems. One angry customer carrying a gun accused us of selling him a broken phone. Waving the firearm in the air like a highwayman, he demanded the problem be rectified.

The nervous salesman hastily asked to see the phone, then surreptitiously clicked on the power button. The gunman walked away happy.

Another customer didn't have money, so wanted to barter a cow, the family's most prized asset. We gave him a phone.

We only had one return. A customer didn't like this new gadget as his wife kept calling him.

What started as a conversation in the bush with John Garang had now culminated in a network spread through all of South Sudan. Well, almost all, as we still needed to roll it out in the capital Juba. We would only be able to do that once the heavily armed North Sudanese army moved out of the city.

Most importantly, we had the network up and running before the Comprehensive Peace Agreement came into fruition. It would forever legally belong to the South Sudanese.

The historic accord between North and South was eventually signed on 9 January 2005, in the Nairobi football stadium in Kenya, amid huge optimism and expectations of peace. It was a massive celebratory event ending Africa's deadliest civil war and attended by leaders from around the world. Ironically, I was a seat away from the Deputy-President of South Africa, Jacob Zuma. He later became President of my former homeland, presiding over one of the most scandal-rocked reigns with accusations ranging from rape to multiple state capture and corruption claims. We didn't speak.

Six months later I got a dreadful phone call. John Garang was dead. Shockwaves reverberated around the stunned country.

Although still clouded in mystery, it seemed Garang had been flying home after a meeting with Ugandan President Yoweni Museveni, when his helicopter crashed near the Kenyan border.

The official reason was bad weather. Visibility was poor and the pilot had simply flown into the side of a mountain. All aboard perished. However, as the nation reeled in disbelief, rumours spread faster than an oilrig fire that the flight had either been sabotaged or shot down.

They say no one is irreplaceable, but Garang came as close to the definition of the word as anyone could. His mesmerising presence embodied the soul of the South's liberation movement. He was both the SPLM's political and military leader. He was its vision, its inspiration. No one else could fill his shoes.

But even more critical was the question on everyone's lips: would the Naivasha peace agreement hold firm? Would the devastating civil war, which claimed the lives of two million and displaced four million more, resume? Would the SPLM grab their guns and return to the bush?

We would soon find out. I flew to the movement's headquarters to facilitate communications and gave all its leaders phones. The last thing we needed was disinformation fuelling white-hot tensions already at tipping point.

First we had to arrange the funeral. The most fitting final resting place for Dr John was the capital, Juba, controlled by the North, but claimed by the South. This meant that the North would have to allow SPLM fighters *en masse* into the city, something unthinkable just a few days ago. But in such an emotionally charged situation, no one would dare challenge the body of the iconic guerrilla general being flown into the South's spiritual heartland.

I chartered a flight from Uganda to take SPLM leaders as well as Garang's friends and family to Juba. We arrived at the airport at about the same time as the plane carrying Dr John's body landed.

The open coffin was slowly driven into the city. I had the privilege of walking down the airport road behind it with his family and friends. An extraordinary sight greeted us. All along the road, soldiers from both North and South, men who had been at war for decades, stood shoulder to shoulder, saluting. From his coffin, Dr John Garang presided over the most magnificent act of humanity witnessed in the ravaged land he loved. More than anything else, his funeral freed the capital from Northern occupation.

We arrived at Juba's Catholic Church where the coffin was prominently placed for his legion of followers to pay homage. The church was packed to capacity and tens of thousands spilled onto the sidewalks and streets. Numerous strategically placed loudspeakers were set up to broadcast the funeral for those unable to get close.

Just before the service started, I phoned Bush House in London, headquarters of the BBC's famed World Service. "Please put me through to traffic," I requested.

The receptionist connected me to the duty news editor.

"This is Pete," I said. "I'm an ex-BBC cameraman and I'm in South Sudan. John Garang's widow is about to speak at his funeral. It's going to be massive."

"Will she speak in English?"

"Yes. Put me on live feed and I'll send it over."

I placed my Satphone next to a loudspeaker as Rebecca Garang stood. There was absolute silence. Even the perennial buzz of Africa, the cicada beetles, were still. The next few minutes would determine whether the civil war continued to rage. Or not.

Rebecca Garang held the microphone, aware that her country was poised on an abyss. She cleared her throat.

"I will not mourn the death of Dr John for one hour," she said, her voice strong and clear as it echoed around the church and roared, magnified by loudspeakers, into the streets. "I will not mourn his death for one minute. I will not mourn the death of our great leader for one second — but on one condition: that all of you respect the Comprehensive Peace Agreement for the whole of Sudan. A united Sudan.

"If Dr John sees a return to conflict, he will turn in his grave. Everything he lived for will have been a waste of time. So I call on all of you, and mostly the women in South Sudan, to honour the peace agreement."

It was amazingly powerful oratory, and thanks to the BBC World Service, broadcasted across the continent. All of Africa exhaled a gigantic breath of relief. The peace treaty would hold. If Rebecca Garang had spoken of a return to arms, if in her grief she had listened to the multiple claims that the helicopter crash was sabotage, the country would have gone up in smoke.

Thanks to our nascent telecom network in the bush, Rebecca's message of peace also echoed around the country.

The North Sudanese army left Juba soon after the funeral, and I was able to roll the cellphone network into the capital. The city was now the undisputed hub of South Sudan.

As the world's newest country was blessed — or perhaps cursed — with rich oil deposits, it attracted many investors. Among them were the Chinese, by far the biggest and most voracious stakeholders in Africa. The reason is simple: Africa's vast, untapped mineral wealth is vital for the expanding the Super Power's inexorable industrialisation. Obviously the country's oil wealth was key, but the Chinese also expressed interest in the cellphone network that I had largely financed and set up in partnership with the South Sudanese government.

As a result, the Minister of Telecommunications and I were invited to China as guests of telecom giants ZTE Corporation and Huawei Technologies. We flew to their factories in Shenzhen and were given in-depth briefings on some amazing high-tech equipment and systems of the future.

It was a fascinating trip. We were also shown around Beijing, taken to the Great Wall of China, and lavishly entertained wherever we went. This was going well, I thought. However, I did notice the Minister getting into a huddle every now and again with Chinese 'suits' whom I suspected of being government officials.

Back in Africa, the Minister seemed strangely withdrawn. Eventually I asked, "What's going on?"

His almost defensive answer wasn't what I was expecting.

"We have accepted a deal from the Chinese."

"What do you mean? What deal?"

"They're going to give us six-and-a-half million dollars' worth of telecom equipment."

"Wow, that's fantastic. They're giving it to us for free?"

"Not exactly. We've signed a promissory note granting them access to our oil."

I whistled. "With that cash injection, we'll grow our network quickly."

"No. It's now a government network. Not your network."

"But we're partners."

"Not anymore."

My head jerked up. I suddenly realised I was being fired. This was pretty sudden.

"Well ... then you will have to buy me out."

"We'll do that."

We signed a buy-out agreement, where I would be compensated for the work and investment I had put in, but the Minister said the new government could not afford to pay immediately. They would do so by the end of the year.

They never did.

The question I sometimes ask myself is what would have happened if John Garang had not died. I like to think he would have rewarded loyalty. I put in money, set everything up in extremely challenging circumstances, and provided computers, satellite dishes and cellphones when no other investors would go near the SPLM. I financed the entire start-up myself when the movement was in dire financial straits. And I got kicked in the teeth for it.

Dr John was an honourable man. He was our company's greatest ambassador. So who knows what would have happened. Just as I almost ended up owning my own airline in Iraq, if John Garang had survived, I might have been a telecom tycoon in South Sudan.

However, that is all in the realm of "what if". Instead, as JJ succinctly put it, the best business deal I did was leaving South Sudan. It was the day I stopped losing money.

Perhaps ... but it was an exhilarating adventure, starting up a network from nothing in a country ravaged by civil war.

Along the way I helped change the lives of many who now had jobs, skills, better life choices and a tentative foothold in the modern world.

I even had a unique story to tell, one I will cherish forever.

However, the Sudan saga was more than that. It was almost the final curtain for me.

Chapter Twenty-Two

On a wing and a prayer

I HAVE NO fear of flying — you can't in my line of work — but I don't have the best of luck with aeroplanes.

Two key incidents spring to mind; the Concorde that almost plunged into the Atlantic Ocean, and the American AWAC that was on the verge of shooting us down during Operation Restore Hope in Somalia.

But as I have frequently mentioned, I have a guardian angel who works overtime on land and air, and never more so than on a terrifying flight from Rumbek to Kenya.

We had nowhere decent to stay while building the cellphone network, and as Rumbek was destined to boom by Sudanese standards, I invested in a small boutique hotel called Safari Styles. It enjoyed the perfect location positioned alongside the runway with walking distance from the arrivals hut. However, we needed investors and I invited a potential partner to join me on a site visit.

It was only going to be a day trip, so at great expense we hired a turboprop King Air and two pilots from a Kenyan charter company, landing in Rumbek in the early morning. Scattered along the length of the runway were the mangled and charred remains of a jet that had crashed there previously, which didn't exactly set an upbeat tone for the day.

Then, as we jumped off onto the dirt runway, a group of enthusiastic Sudanese surged forward offering to carry our bags for a "mere" hundred dollars. We carried our own.

After inspecting the site and discussing what renovations were needed, we flew south to Yei where we had a lunchtime meeting, and then back to Rumbek.

As we were about to leave on the four-hour flight back to Nairobi, two Sudanese guys approached me and asked if they could hitch a lift. There were only four of us on the twelve-seater plane, so I told them to hop on board. They had never flown before, so this was to be a new experience for them. In more ways than one, as it turned out.

The sun set as we took off, and after about ninety minutes in the air we hit bad weather with thunder and lightning, necessitating a slight diversion. Other than that, everything was going smoothly.

Or so I thought, until I noticed some frenetic activity in the cockpit where the pilot and co-pilot were having an animated conversation.

The doors were open, so I entered the cabin. "Is everything OK?" I asked the pilot.

"Not really," he said. "We're still an hour from Nairobi and only have forty minutes' fuel left."

I couldn't believe it. "What?"

"We've either sprung a leak or they didn't fill the tanks properly in Sudan."

"What are we going to do?"

"We've been trying to radio Eldoret Airport to see if they'll open up the runway and turn on the lights. But no one is answering. So we're a bit worried and have declared an emergency."

A bit worried? I'll say.

Eldoret is an international airport close to the Ugandan border and within our depleted fuel range. But it seemed they had shut down for the night.

"Where are we now?" I asked. "Over Naivasha?"

The pilot nodded.

"A friend of mine, Ian Douglas Hamilton, has a farm near Lake Naivasha with a private airstrip. I'll call him on my cell and ask him to park cars on at each end of the runway, switch on the headlights and show us where to land."

The pilot laughed, but without mirth. "Pete, this a turbo jet that lands at high speed on tiny wheels. We can't come down on a dirt strip in the middle of nowhere in the dark. We'll cartwheel into the bush and that'll be the end of us."

"What are we going to do?"

The pilot shrugged fatalistically. "Go as high as possible to get the greatest gliding range when the fuel runs out. If you are religious, now is the time to start praying."

As he spoke a red light flashed on the dashboard with a loud buzzing alert. An instant later the port engine died.

The plane shuddered violently with the abrupt loss of power and started dropping rapidly. We were now over the Ngong Hills and still many miles from Nairobi.

The three of us in the cockpit watched the empty fuel gauge, praying the sole surviving engine would keep going.

It didn't, cutting out about eight minutes later. There was deathly silence in the cockpit. We were now just gliding on wings and losing altitude every second.

For some reason, the pilot turned on the landing lights. This was a critical mistake, as without a generator, the battery drained flat within a minute. The plane was plunged into darkness. Apart from no engines, we had no lights, no instruments, no automatic landing system, no brakes, and no radio.

To do something, I went back into the cabin and told our two Sudanese passengers to tie any suitcases or baggage that was loose. I had to use sign language as they spoke no English, and so was unable to explain our predicament. However, I managed to somehow make it clear that when we landed, I would be opening the emergency door and they must follow me out.

I then went and sat next to Johnny, only realising how nervous I was when I discovered we were holding hands. And we had only met that morning.

"Mate," I said, "we're going to be fine."

Johnny, who is a qualified pilot, shook his head. "This baby is going to hit the ground at two hundred miles an hour and the propellers outside the window are going to shear through the fuselage like a knife through butter. If we don't find a runway, we're done."

By now I could make out the distant lights of Nairobi in the darkness. The pilot was literally flying blind, aiming for where he thought the country's main airport, Jomo Kenyatta International, would be, without radio communication or navigation equipment. In fact, the only instrument working was a manual compass.

Suddenly the clouds broke and we saw the Nyayo National Stadium, Kenya's premier football ground that lies adjacent to the Nairobi-Mombasa Expressway. The pilot turned right to follow the four-lane motorway, as we might, by some sheer fluke, be able to land on it. It is usually choked with vehicles, so this was a serious case of wishful thinking.

As we turned, my cellphone signal came on as we were now close to the ground. It was nine-thirty, so I decided to phone JJ and say goodbye.

I had a lot to tell her. Primarily, I wanted to say how happy I was that I had married her. I wanted to say I would not have done anything differently. I had lived the most incredible life and done more than most people. A lot of that was thanks to her.

I wanted to say that my only regret was that she would have to carry on without me, and our three kids would not have a Dad.

I pressed speed-dial and was about to push the green icon to connect. For some reason, I paused. I was still alive. I was not giving up. Not yet.

I switched my phone off.

The plane was dropping rapidly, and although I fervently hoped this would not be it, I braced for the end. Strangely, I wasn't scared or annoyed that these might be my last minutes, as my life had been a good one. At least I wasn't going to burn alive as our fuel tanks were empty. Death would come as a massive smash into planet earth.

Then, miraculously, from the cockpit window we saw the airport runway lights glowing brightly ahead. Even more miraculously, they were on green and we were pointing in the right direction.

As a trainee pilot many years ago back in South Africa, I knew that if runway lights are green it indicates an aircraft is high enough to land. If they are red, the plane is too low and the pilot will crash before the runway. The green lights gave me an inkling of hope.

But not for long. A second later I heard the pilot say with some desperation that we were travelling at over two-hundred miles an hour — more than double the safe landing speed. However, he was loath to try and slow down as we needed the momentum to reach the runway. Otherwise, we would probably crash beforehand. It was a life-or-death Catch 22.

I heard the undercarriage drop, but as there was no power, we had no way of knowing if the wheels had locked into place. If not, we would belly-flop at high velocity with almost certainly fatal results.

Just before hitting the runway, the pilot finally tried to slow the plane using wing flaps — but again, there was no electrical power to do so.

As a result, we came in like a rocket. The mighty jolt as we hit the ground literally knocked the breath out of us. I was as winded as if I had been punched in the gut.

The plane zoomed uncontrollably down the tarmac like a runaway train. As the pilot was unable to feather the powerless propellers, it was tantamount to trying to stop an eighteen-wheeler truck with a handbrake.

Everything was a blur, although I could make out the emergency lights of ambulances and fire engines flashing crazily. Then one of the wheels skidded onto the grass, spinning the aircraft like a top and throwing us all into a heap.

Somehow, the plane stopped. Johnny and I yanked open the emergency door and ushered everyone out. We had survived.

Jokingly, I got down on my hands and knees like the Pope kissing the ground. I'm told air traffic control initially thought I was an Al Shabaab terrorist from Somalia bowing to Mecca.

We said goodbye to the somewhat bemused Sudanese. I'm not sure if they thought this was a normal landing, hitting the ground at breakneck speed and jumping out an emergency door. The only thing I'm reasonably sure of is they might have second thoughts about hitching a ride on a plane again.

Johnny was booked on a London flight that was leaving in a few hours so we sprinted across the runway to the international departures hall. It was a nine-hour trip to

Heathrow, and catching that plane had to be the most extreme "getting back onto a horse after falling off" therapy I have ever heard of.

The family were asleep when I arrived home. JJ woke as I came into the bedroom and I had just said I'd had a bit of a rough day when the phone rang. It was Johnny.

"Mate, I've been arrested."

"What for?"

"Illegally leaving the scene of a crash. You have to come back or they'll also arrest you."

I drove to the airport where we were questioned at length by aviation investigators. This resulted in Johnny missing his London flight.

The next day, to celebrate being alive, Johnny and I met for lunch at the Aero Club. It's based at Wilson Airport, so some pilots who had heard about us came over to ask what happened. They were stunned when we told them the story.

One shook his head incredulously. "To run out of fuel over the Ngong Hills; to have one engine last eight minutes longer than the other; to glide for sixteen minutes in pitch-blackness; to arrive not only at Jomo Kenyatta, but at the threshold of the runway with no navigation equipment — it's way, way beyond unbelievable. If you'd had a single extra knot of headwind, just one more passenger, or been a degree off course, you would never have made it."

The other flyers agreed. "Don't ever bother buying a lottery ticket. You've used up a lifetime of luck in a single night."

The key question nagging me was why had we run out of fuel. These things don't just happen, so I started asking around.

I then discovered our pilot had not checked the tanks while the plane was being refuelled in Rumbek. He had instead been too busy with one of his business partners in town. This was unforgiveable. On remote African airstrips, a rule of thumb is that the pilot *always* personally checks fuel levels with a dipstick.

Also, as avgas is triple the price in Sudan as it is in Kenya, pilots tend to put in the bare minimum. So in our case, the pilot had not only tried to get away with as little fuel as possible, he also hadn't checked.

Even worse, I discovered this was not the first time that he had run out of fuel.

There's no denying that he was an exceptional aviator and it was only his skills that got us down safely. But even so, his extreme irresponsibility had got us into this life-or-death situation in the first place. Consequently, I reported him to air crash investigators as next time he and his passengers may not be so lucky.

But this is Africa and I heard he was soon flying again, after perhaps a fine or slap on the wrist.

While my life didn't flash before my eyes, as the cliché goes, it certainly was a time for intense reflection. It also reinforced my belief in positive thinking and the power of choice. Although I was pretty certain I was going to die, something inside me refused to give up. When I said to Johnny Beveridge that I could feel in my bones we were going to survive, I chose to believe it — despite the fact that we were anxiously holding hands, something we still laugh about today.

But the best thing is that I didn't make that desperate last-ditch phone call to JJ. Instead, I was able to tell her personally about my "final" thoughts of our good life together.

Chapter Twenty-Three

Harvard — vision and vitality

WHILE WATCHING A crimson sun setting over Nairobi's skyline, a friend told me about a course at Harvard Business School specifically designed for what he called "visionary entrepreneurial leaders".

He was kind enough to remark I fitted that bill. As I have been described as a somewhat unorthodox venture capitalist more than once — Air Baghdad being a case in point — I listened to what he had to say.

It was called the Owner/President Management (OPM) course and my friend said it had been a life-changing experience both professionally and personally for his uncle, who had recently completed the three-year course.

"It's pretty isolated running your own business," he said, something I knew all too well. "The OPM not only inspires original ideas, you also tap into an incredibly rich network of like-minded people who face similar challenges. It's an absolute game-changer."

I liked the sound of that. But Harvard? One of the world's greatest universities? How would I fit in with those esteemed luminaries of academia? How would they view an application from someone like me?

Despite that, I always felt I had missed out by not having a tertiary education, so I guess I had a bit of an academic chip on my shoulder. Consequently, I went online and had a look at the OPM curriculum.

My friend was right. The course seemed not only impressive, but also extremely motivating. Basically, it was an executive MBA, but with the classic entrepreneur rather than corporate manager in mind.

To my surprise, I discovered I ticked all enrolment requirement boxes — owning or managing a business with at least ten years hands-on operating experience and an equity stake.

I was pretty sure Harvard would not admit me, but filled in the application form, wrote an overview of why I should be considered, then forgot about it.

To my pleasant surprise, eight months later Harvard wrote back saying I had been accepted.

The OPM is a three-year course, and graduates are accorded full alumni status and qualifications. Most studying is done remotely, but we had to commit to being at Harvard for three weeks each year for intensive lectures on business fundamentals and case studies.

I flew into Boston, awe-struck as a cab dropped me at the famed and fabulous campus, and walked into a hall where one hundred and fifty-six students from fifty-two countries sat. That diverse meritocracy is part of the course's attraction, providing a unique fusion of global outreach and outlook. In fact, JJ jokes that I only got in as I applied from Nairobi and Harvard probably thought someone from Kenya might be interesting.

Despite the large number of students, we were divided into what were called Living Groups of eleven people led by senior executives, resulting in intensely stimulating small group discussions and personal coaching outside the lecture halls.

Each day we received four of five case studies to evaluate. I have never been so absorbed or captivated in my life. I have also never worked so hard, starting well before dawn, researching and analysing the various dossiers.

The lectures were in an auditorium with professors tossing questions as sharp as javelins as they challenged us to the frontiers of our imaginations. We all wore name tags and I would be listening to some fascinating dissertation when suddenly a professor would whirl around, point at me and say, "Hey Pete, what do you make of that?"

Thinking furiously, I would give hopefully lucid reasons whether the business we were discussing would stand or fall. We had to fully commit and contribute to the debates — and we all did. If I hadn't researched or done rigorous background work beforehand, I would fall flat on my face. The energy, vitality and sheer exuberance buzzing like electricity was extraordinary.

A particular case study I clearly remember was that of a fledgling micro-fridge business. The product was a cross between a microwave oven and a bar fridge designed for university students. It cost ninety-nine dollars to manufacture — but only with a minimum factory order of one hundred thousand units. Consequently, the entrepreneur who invented the gadget had to mortgage his house and almost everything he owned to pay upfront production costs. However, a unit would sell for one hundred and ninety-nine dollars, so the reward could be as high as the risk.

That's all we were told. The professor then turned to us and asked, "What do you think? Is this a good business idea?"

I put up my hand. "I would not touch it with a bargepole," I said. "It's tantamount to being a second-hand car salesman only making money on the initial sale. There's no recurring revenue. No constant income stream. You need to make money when you're sleeping, and this business model doesn't do that."

The lecture went on for another hour. Then the professor looked at his watch and said, "I want to introduce you to Mike, the man who invented the micro-fridge."

At the back of the hall stood a guy wearing jeans and a white T-shirt. Clutching a mug of coffee, he walked to the lecture desk.

"Where's the guy who said he wouldn't touch my business with a bargepole?"

I put up my hand.

"What if I told you that after eighteen months I sold the company for seventy-eight million dollars?"

I was gobsmacked. How wrong could I be?

"OK, let me tell the whole story. For about two months I didn't sell a single unit. No one wanted to fork out almost two hundred bucks.

"Then one morning I bumped into a student and her mother walking from the car park. I was so desperate, I said to the mother, "Do you want to improve your daughter's quality of life? For under ten dollars a month?"

"She stopped, somewhat taken aback by my in-your-face approach. I showed her the micro-fridge, saying 'This will keep your daughter's fruit and vegetables fresh, and it also has a microwave that cooks healthy food. No fried junk. I'll even install it for no extra charge in her new room when she moves into another residence at the end of the year.'"

He paused and looked around the lecture hall. We listened silently, totally engrossed.

"I signed my first rent agreement that day," he said. "Although I hadn't made an actual sale, I was now getting money in each month. Money that was working as I slept. In fact, money that was guaranteed for three years, as that's the average time it takes to complete a degree."

I smiled. It suddenly all made sense.

He continued, "With that sale, I changed my business model from being a second-hand car salesman — as Pete put it — to a quality of life marketer. The mother bought the product because her daughter would have fresh fruit and healthy microwaved meals, not because she thought it was a bargain. The entry barrier was also now under ten dollars, not two hundred.

"My next move was to provide free microwave popcorn. But the students needed a microwave to cook it — which conveniently came with renting a micro-fridge. Sales went through the roof. I went from college to college, flooding the residence halls with units.

"After eighteen months, I met a guy emptying coins from student washing machines he owned. He asked how I collected my rental money. Direct debit-orders, I said looking at the sack of coins he was lugging around. He then asked how many units I had sold, how many colleges I operated in, and how many more potential customers were out there. I told him, and soon after his company made me an offer of seventy-eight million.

"Apart from changing my business model to making money around the clock, the key lesson of this particular case study is to find something that will improve someone's quality of life. My business only took off when I promoted that. If you do the same, your business is going to do well."

We listened, spellbound, at this almost fairy-tale account of business guts and glory. He had risked everything and triumphed. This was the calibre of people talking to us.

There were many others, including the social media geniuses who listed Facebook and Google. They shared ideas, visions and stories that I would never encounter elsewhere. I was having "eureka" moments every day, and the fascinating case studies we scrutinised with microscopic diligence vividly captured my imagination. This was no remote ivory tower of academia — Harvard articulated what had always been my professional beacon; that the confluence of ideas, risk, reward, and adventure was where I thrived. From selling packets of crisps as an eleven year-old to the meteoric success of NewsForce, and even the Sudanese cellphone debacle, it was what kept me going.

On one occasion an OPM Professor was working out a business approach with me when he suddenly said, "Look out of the window and tell me what you see."

It was a cold, miserable day.

"Grey," I replied.

"No. That's just weather. What you see is money. There is more money and influence in Boston than you will ever imagine. If you need money, I'll pick up the phone and we'll get it for you. If you need strategy, then listen to what I'm saying. Whatever you need, we can get for you. The powerhouse that is Boston and the network that is Harvard is beyond your wildest dreams."

It was true. For the next three years, these intensive stints at Harvard would be the most enjoyable and exciting of my life. I was plugging into an unbelievably rich network of people and a grid of astonishing energy.

The average day started at five a.m., studying for a couple of hours before breakfast, then gathering into working groups to discuss at least four case studies we had read the night before. After that we would get another dossier to study and discuss before breaking for tea. Then another before lunch, and two final case studies in the afternoon.

After classes, some of us would go to the gym, others for a run, or rowing up the Charles River to let off physical steam.

At night we behaved like raucous students, albeit with platinum credit cards at top restaurants drinking good wine. We invariably stayed out too late, but still rose at five the next morning to do it all again.

The three years passed quickly — far too quickly. On the last day of the course I was in the dining room reflecting on the incredible experience with fellow "OPMer" Harry Gross. "What are you going to miss most about Harvard?" I asked.

Harry was in his early seventies and the oldest guy on the course. He was probably also the wisest. He thought briefly, then replied, "I'm going to miss the friends and the people."

I nodded. "Me too. I can't imagine not having this to come back to next year."

We then had an idea. "Why don't we select some people, at least one from each continent, ask them to choose others and then get together annually for the next six years and travel to every corner of the world? There are a hundred and fifty-two people in the class, so if we pick the most diverse group — Christian, Muslim, Jew, Hindu, male, female, old, young — we'll have a fascinating time."

Harry said. "For this to work, we need to commit to three things; everyone has to pitch up each year, we have to learn from each other, and we have to give back, not just take."

In other words, the group ethos had to be bigger than our individual experiences.

Harry and I invited six class friends whom we thought would be the best fit. They each invited another two, and before we knew it, we had a group of eighteen people. We called ourselves the OPM 38 Adventure Group.

Our first trip was to Tanzania. We took our respective spouses or partners so it was quite a large gathering that arrived at the Dar es Salaam airport. Only then did it truly strike me what a phenomenally special group this was; eighteen Harvard graduates who all had the best interests of their classmates at heart.

In essence, the OPM 38 Adventure Group is a true "University of Life" gathering; an eclectic advisory board comprising people from every corner of the globe with an unimaginable wealth of divergent experiences, backgrounds, skills and knowledge. If any of us wanted advice or encouragement about absolutely any topic conceivable, expert guidance was instantly available. We were all entrepreneurs in various fields, and there was no challenge any of us faced that someone in the group had not faced before.

Topics ranged from visionary business trends, sport rivalries, humour and entertainment to differing political creeds — in fact, anything and everything. Each idea or opinion was treated with absolute respect. What many would call out of the box thinking was normal chat with this group. Our spouses, who came along not knowing what to expect, loved it.

The next year we convened in Delhi where the head of Tata Group addressed us on the intricacies of doing business in the teeming subcontinent. We also got involved with charity work supporting a retirement home.

The following year we went to Norway, and members' children over the age of fifteen were invited, which included Jessica, Tom and Rex. The added benefit was that the kids became friends, so they too plugged into an invaluable network of lifelong contacts around the world.

Then there was Australia, Mexico, Venice, Israel, and in 2019, Guatemala. On this occasion we supported a hospital that treated children with cleft palates. As one of our member's fourteen-year-old son wanted to be a doctor, we sponsored him to do charity work there during school holidays. It was an unforgettable experience for him.

The OPM 38 Adventure Group has proved so inspiring that instead of the original six-year time frame, we're going to keep it going for the next hundred. That may sound grandiose, but I have no doubt it will happen as all children of the eighteen founder members have expressed a desire to continue when their parents pass on. As a result, the benefit of this Harvard experience and the philosophy of what we have created — to learn, listen, share and give back — will continue for at least three generations.

    I still shake my head in wonder at such a magnificent legacy.

Chapter Twenty-Four

Back to the future

AFTER SEVEN YEARS in Kenya, JJ and I decided to call it quits and return to England. There were several reasons, but the overriding one was that we missed our children.

Jessica, Tom and Rex were at boarding schools in the U.K., and although they flew out to Nairobi for holidays, they were away for most of the year. This negated what I had pledged when I turned forty — to spend more time with my family.

Kenya had been a wonderful experience for all of us, and we were blessed that we had lived there and in our way made a contribution to the country. But as the kids got older, we knew they would not permanently settle in Africa. It had been great for them, but Kenya was more of a fun holiday than a way of life. It was now time to return to what we increasingly realised was home.

As much as I loved Africa, I had to admit that my stint at Harvard Business School had renewed my entrepreneurial vision in global terms. Nairobi was a springboard into Africa. But London was a springboard to the world.

We moved back into our house in Surrey, and it was great to be living as a fulltime family again, not just during holidays.

But from a business perspective, I suffered a severe culture shock. Africa had been a fine adventure, but the bottom line was I didn't have anything to come back to in England, apart from spending time with the kids. Seven years may seem a blink of an eye, but a lot can happen in that period. And in a fast-moving global hub like London, it does. I was the better part of a decade behind friends and business connections. I had stood still, while they had progressed.

I had to catch up fast. But it was substantially harder than anticipated. Bush phone networks and rural White Space internet options were not exactly in demand in the concrete megalopolis of London. I needed to reinvent myself and find something to do.

But what?

It's not easy to be an entrepreneur in London for the simple reason that there are far fewer fresh opportunities compared with emerging markets. In the big smoke, scores of great ideas and innovations have already been tried and tested, and if successful, firmly established. It is a far more mature market and doesn't lend itself to my type of venture capitalist creativity. Sure, I could find work as a media cameraman, but that would be regressing.

Such indecision was alien to me and turned toxic. I became disorientated, unsure of what to do next. Consequently, not much money was coming in, but costs of supporting three children at private schools and a Surrey home were going through the roof.

I needed to get my head right quickly and decided to keep London as a base but look elsewhere for opportunities. My focus was now primarily TV White Space projects, which we had successfully implemented before being thwarted by vested interests in Kenya. There's little doubt it's the most effective communication solution for emerging economies, and top of my list of likely candidates was Mexico. Coincidentally, I met a fellow-entrepreneur in London who also spoke of setting up internet opportunities in Mexico and we decided to do a joint exploratory visit. Despite its deadly drug cartel problem where narcos outgun both police and army, Mexico has vast potential. It's the third biggest country in the Americas with a burgeoning population of almost 126 million, urgently needing investment.

We did a presentation to the Mexican government hoping to get an internet licence, but nothing came of it. However, the trip was not in vain as I met a Polish investor, Dr Leszek Siwek, a successful entrepreneur with an impressive background in telecommunications data.

We got on well. In fact, so well that I loaned him my beach cottage in Kenya to spend a holiday with his family.

Soon afterwards we met up in London and he asked what I knew about renewable energy.

"Nothing, except that it's a good idea," I replied, wondering where this was going.

He said he had contacts with green energy interests in Poland, which lagged far behind the rest of Europe in reaching mandatory carbon emission targets. The main reason was the powerful Polish coal mining industry, which meant there were complex commercial interests at play that often trumped green issues.

Despite that, Leszek said there was no dispute that Poland was polluted and urgently needed alternative solutions to burning coal. The government had already tried wind farms, but there was significant public resistance to the growing number of ugly turbines littering the landscape.

"The future is solar," Leszek said. "Would you be interested in investing in a project?"

This was interesting as I had vowed that my next venture would be something I was passionate about. For me, this increasingly concerned the environment. There is no doubt today's lifestyle has a lethal impact on the ecosystem, and I have to own up to the fact that frequent flyers like me leave a big carbon footprint. I wanted to put something back, which was one of the key lessons I learnt at Harvard.

But it had to stack up financially. Keen as I was to get involved in eco-businesses, the projects had to be economically viable or — as I once said in the Business School lecture hall — I would not touch it with a bargepole. I needed to scrutinise Leszek's suggestion with my Harvard hat on and not throw money at something simply for "feel good" or naïve "save the world" reasons.

I also had to be far more cautious than I had in the past. Thanks to South Sudan cellphones and Mawingu, I no longer had millions of my own money to invest. In fact, the truth was I had not hit a homerun for some time.

But Leszek had planted an idea that would not go away. It buzzed incessantly in my mind. I eventually decided to fly to Poland and see first-hand what he was talking about.

It was a total revelation. I grasped right away that the proposed eco-project had interesting potential. Leszek had not been exaggerating when he said the country desperately needed green energy. Coal powered seventy-five per cent of the electricity grid, and it showed on both the landscape and in the skies. However, on the plus side, Poland is a big country. There was plenty of space, so there was no need to log forests or appropriate farmlands for eco-friendly infrastructures.

Of particular interest were the swathes of industrial wasteland surrounding factories in the smokestack manufacturing areas. This was where the true potential lay. Barren wasteland, or brownfields, could be converted into solar farms and power generated from the sun plugged directly into factory circuits due to close proximity. This could be a game changer.

Most importantly, we would not need government contracts or subsidies. That was my key stipulation when Leszek bounced the idea off me. I am never keen on getting into bed with bureaucrats, and my experience in South Sudan proved exactly that.

"I like it," I said to Leszek on our return. "I think this stacks up as a business opportunity."

We formed a company called Radiant Solar and recruited experts to advise on a bespoke business model for Polish factories. The final decision was mine and Leszek's, but the consensus was unanimous. This would work.

We were ready to rock 'n roll, but it seemed that our most essential requirement was patience. The biggest problem was the magnitude of red tape, not only in Poland but also from the European Union. It took many months to wade through mountains of paperwork and necessary permits, not to mention a serious financial struggle with trunk-loads of money flowing out. I exhausted my cash savings and had to go into debt to keep the company alive.

But I never despaired. My conviction that this would work was as solid as granite. Radiant Solar would be Poland's largest solar renewable plant, and, by example and technology, would make the planet a healthier place.

Eventually everything started fitting into place, and by 2019 we had identified ten potential sites, of which three — Chotkow, Serby and Swierzno — were secured.

Chotkow, near the German border in west Poland, is a 100-hectare site that will generate £3.1 million a year, while the 309-hectare Serby site, also in the west of the country, will generated £8.1m annually. At the time of writing, both these sites are at the "ready to build" stage. We are still waiting for the final environmental impact report for the third 92-hectare site at Swierzno, near the Baltic Sea, which will generate £4.5m.

However, early in 2020, an unforeseen crisis erupted — something none of us even remotely anticipated. It was called coronavirus, or Covid 19, and as everyone knows, it paralysed the entire planet.

Obviously we were not immune to this rampaging pandemic. We had to think on our feet —and having an extremely flexible business model with low overheads, including staff costs, enabled a swift reaction. Firstly, we halted all on-site construction work to prevent future — and expensive — work stoppages as the virus spread like a prairie fire. Then we used the period of forced isolation to upgrade administrative processes and update documentation to gear up for a running start when construction was scheduled to resume in March 2021.

I was in Australia during the height of the pandemic. JJ, Jessica, Rex and I found a haven on a remote working farm, which gave me plenty of time and space to breathe in the clean mountain air and think.

Throughout my life, I have tried to create opportunities in all circumstances, tragic or otherwise. And the current crazy times with the world hunkering down behind locked doors certainly provided much food for thought. So far, half a million people globally have perished, and few believe we can ever return to our old way of life. The key question is this: how do we build for the future in the swirling vortex of mass global uncertainty?

More specifically, do the fundamental sociocultural and socioeconomic ruptures triggered by the deadly pandemic present openings that were unimaginable — let alone unthinkable — just a few months ago? Can huge office blocks and shopping malls — the bricks and mortar of industry — survive after such tectonic shifts in how we work and shop?

It goes deeper. The virus has given an entire generation of city dwellers, more than half of the world's population, a glimpse of what traffic-free streets, cleaner air and quieter skies actually look like. Despite the crippling business carnage left in the virus's wake, billions now have a clear vision of how the planet could be with a determined shift towards green energy.

I have no doubt that green energy is going to be a blue-chip investment of the future. Even more so now that once-reliable assets such as commercial property begin to look somewhat shaky.

I am not alone in my thinking. With several European nations facing apocalyptic economic crises, post-pandemic governments are not just considering, but extolling, the benefits of a green recovery. Many are saying it is time to rebuild the world with clear eco-guidelines.

Radiant Solar will be at the forefront of this. I don't relish building on the rubble of tragedy, but the coronavirus has caused a paradigm shift and we have to think not only out of the box, but in totally new boxes.

Coincidentally, I was in the throes of developing another business when the virus exploded. It is a cellphone app that I believe could be a future global game changer. Among other features, it could make the rest of the world safer to visit again.

Something absolutely crucial in the new era of mass pandemic hysteria.

Chapter Twenty-Five
Bigger than ME

MANY OF MY IDEAS, successful or otherwise, evolve introspectively, sometimes over several years. The final result is often vastly different to the original concept.

My latest venture is a classic case in point.

It stemmed from a trip to Paris after meeting up with cameraman, film director and good friend Scott Hillier several years ago. I had worked with Scott at NewsForce. He is not only a gifted camera operator, he's also extremely resourceful in tight situations.

Scott is also a highly regarded movie producer and founder of the European Independent Film Festival. His documentary 'Twin Towers', which told the story of the Al-

Qaida attacks on September 11 through the eyes of several Harlem police officers, won an Academy Award in 2003.

While chatting, I noticed an unusual barcode on his camera case. I asked what it was. He pointed his iPhone at it and a URL link appeared stating that "This item belongs to Scott Hillier", giving his phone number and address. I thought "what a great idea", not only for theft prevention, but I have always believed personal digital identities are extremely useful tools. Not only will digital ID replace or be as accepted as physical ID, but, from a personal point of view, it allows people to electronically showcase themselves. Consequently, I mentally archived Scott's barcode as a future project.

Some months later I was commemorating Remembrance Day at the breathtakingly impressive Brookwood Military Cemetery in Surrey.

Brookwood is the largest of all Commonwealth War Graves sites with more than five thousand graves, and my eldest son Tom, an officer in the British Army, had recommended that I pay a visit. But most of the tombstones only record a name and date, which to me seemed a shame.

I suddenly remembered Scott's barcode. Every person buried in that revered ground had a unique story to tell. But how was anyone to know that with only a single line of flimsy information available? It wasn't quite the tomb of the unknown soldier, but pretty close.

If, instead, there had been a personal barcode, those paying their respects could unearth the entire personal history of each occupant — birthplace, hometown, loved ones, even their dreams and aspirations. This would bring to life, metaphorically, those who had made the ultimate sacrifice.

Apart from gravesites, there are also thousands of public benches in England dedicated to those departed. You find them in parks, riverbanks, bridle paths, sports grounds — they're all over the place. Yet almost without fail, the only information provided is an impersonal plaque with a name, such as "In memory of John Smith". It would be fascinating to know exactly why that particular bench was so special, something a smart-badge similar to what I had seen on Scott's camera case could reveal.

An idea took root and stuck in my mind. Why don't we "barcode" tombstones and community benches?

I contacted Scott with a proposal to start a business doing exactly that. He thought it was a great idea, but with one fault.

"Mate, barcodes are boring. Supermarkets use them. We need something fresh — we need to find a way of creating a smart symbol. That's far more powerful."

We called the new company "Vitas" (Latin for 'in memory of'), then scouted around trying to find someone able to smart-code the letter "V" that could be permanently embedded onto something like a stone memorial. We contacted top digital coders in America, Israel, U.K., France — but no one could do it.

Scott eventually came across a professor at the University of Madrid who was an Artificial Intelligence (AI) expert. He had a whole team working for him, and we hired them to crack the code. It took them six months to do so.

Simultaneously, Scott was in the south of France and had met a dynamic entrepreneur called Ronald Bruce. Ronald takes lateral thinking to stratospheric heights, and I flew out to meet him and Scott at a Paris restaurant. One of the first things Ronald suggested was that we shouldn't concentrate on dead people. Not only was the "living" market more … vibrant, but existing people were likelier to want digital signatures.

This reverted to my original idea that if someone had a digital symbol that belonged solely to them, rather than some bureaucracy, it would be a powerful business and personal device. This, we agreed, was far bigger than gravestones and park benches.

We changed the company's name to ME, as that's exactly what the company was about. A digital signature was intensely personal, and you don't get more personal than the word "me".

Scott succinctly summed up the thrust of where we were heading, telling a story of walking into a gathering of hotshot young film producers who studiously ignored him. If he had a smart ME code, they would instantly discover he was an Academy award-winning producer, not some random old fart. They would have been falling all over him.

It wasn't about Scott wanting respect — he has that in spades. It was about who he was. With our newly created AI code, we could forge a community of people able to exchange digital information in the quickest and most efficient way possible.

In its most basic form, a ME digital symbol contains a photograph, the most recent health test, up-to-the-minute temperature reading, and whatever other information the user wishes to share. With Covid flaring at the time, the health information alone was gold dust. It's instant and even in large crowds, such as football fans scanning their information on entering a stadium, people at risk can be easily identified.

We then decided we needed to ratchet the business up a notch, and I met up with Andy Reid who had recently sold his hugely successful telecoms company. By sheer coincidence, he was developing a new venture called "testedtrader.com" as he believed the Covid-crippled economy was going to kill millions more people than the actual virus. Unless we jump-started floundering businesses around the world, we faced a catastrophe of unimaginable proportions. But how to do that during the current pandemic horror show?

The first step, Andy decided, was to re-establish trust. To do this, people had to be confident they were in a safe working environment — hence the birth of testedtrader.com. Whether it was a plumber fixing a kitchen sink, or an estate agent selling a house, all crucial personal information about the person knocking at your front door had to be transparent at the click of a cellphone app.

It didn't take long for us to realise that with our ME code and Andy's business model, this was a potential marriage made in heaven. Every trader signing up to ME would have an AI badge, which customers could scan for full details of their skills, but equally importantly, their health in times of a crisis no one alive had experienced before.

We decided to launch ME using the Covid catastrophe as the single most crucial catalyst. The test-run was done in two hundred English pubs that had recently opened after a stringent three-month lockdown. The pubs would get a database of customers using ME apps, and if any patron had suspected Corona virus, everyone who had been on the premises could be instantly alerted. The bar owners were keen as they realised this was the ultimate track and trace system, but unlike ones introduced by government bureaucracies, data can be removed with a single swipe built into the app. This is no Big Brother system — on the contrary — as users had complete control of their own data and how it was shared.

The response was staggering. In that short period, forty thousand people scanned the ME code and signed up for the ME app. Extrapolating that, we should have three million users by August 2021.

The opportunities are endless. Dentists, whose businesses are as close up and personal as one can get from a virus perspective, can use the app as instant checks on patients' primary health. Schools, universities, airports, shops, hotels, restaurants, bars, gyms, travel, theme parks — industries that have lost billions — will be able to reopen, ensuring both workforce and customers are safe. I even spoke to the Queen's doctor who told me the app is ideal for Buckingham Palace staff, something particularly relevant after Prince Charles caught the virus.

Just as NewsForce championed satellite technology in transforming digital newsgathering, I believe ME will be fundamental in keeping businesses open. Using AI, the global economy will possibly never again have to shut down, no matter what brutal pandemics of the future throw at us.

For me, it goes further. ME is the culmination of my journey to date. I have had incredible opportunities and amazing luck in my life and I see ME as a natural progression of sharing information on a mind-blowingly large scale with a global community. If you, dear reader, want to speak directly to me, comment on this book, ask questions, berate me, tell me I'm wrong — or hopefully right — you can do so with the click of a ME app.

Also, as recounted in these pages, I am irredeemably indebted to magnificent people who have helped me on this roller-coaster ride. People such as Sister Bernard Ncube, who saved my life in a South African township. Or NBC bureau chief Heather Allen, who transformed my life by financing my first broadcast camera. When I tried to repay them, both instead asked that I rather pledge to do what I can to make a positive impact on others' lives.

My fervent wish is to honour that pledge.

Printed in Great Britain
by Amazon